Psychotrends

What Kind of People Are We Becoming?

SHERVERT H. FRAZIER, M.D.

SIMON & SCHUSTER
New York London Toronto Sydney Tokyo Singapore

Simon & Schuster
Rockefeller Center
1230 Avenue of the Americas
New York, New York 10020

Designed by Liney Li
Manufactured in the United States of America
1 3 5 7 9 10 8 6 4 2
Library of Congress Cataloging-in-Publication Data
Frazier, Shervert H.
Psychotrends: what kind of people are we becoming? / Shervert H. Frazier.
p. cm.
1. Social prediction—United States. 2. United States—Social conditions—1980– 3. Social psychology—United States. I. Title.
HN65.F72 1994
303.49—dc20 93–35897 CIP
ISBN 0-671-75159-X

The author gratefully acknowledges permission from the following sources to reprint material in their control: Adweek *for material from "A Death in the Family" by Debra Goldman,* Adweek, *October 7, 1991, p. 20. American Counseling Association for material from "Gender and Counseling in the Twenty-First Century: What Does the Future Hold?" by Murray Scher and Glen E. Good,* Journal of Counseling & Development, *vol. 68, p. 388 (4), March/April 1990, © 1990 ACA. No further reproduction authorized without written permission of the American Counseling Association.* American Health *for material from "Beyond Self," by Eileen Rockefeller Growald and Allan Luks,* American Health, *March 1988, pp. 51–53, © 1988 by Eileen Rockefeller Growald and Allan Luks. The American Psychological Association for material from "The Seville Statement on Violence" by Dr. David Adams,* The American Psychologist, *1990, vol. 45, pp. 1167–68; and "The American Psychological Association Task Force on Television and Society," 1988.* Daedalus *magazine for material from "The World and the United States in 2013,"* Daedalus, *Summer 1987, vol. 16, pp. 1–31. Editorial Research Reports for material from "Death Penalty Debate Centers on Retribution,"* Editorial Research Reports, *July 13, 1990, p. 398 (13). Forbes Inc. for material from "Dr. Pangloss, Meet Ingmar Bergman," by Joshua Levine,* Forbes, *March 30, 1992, © Forbes Inc., 1992.* Fortune *for material from "An Incredible Impact on Medicine,"* Fortune, *March 26, 1990, pp. 92–93, © 1990 Time Inc. Margaret H. Huyck for material from "Predicates of Personal Control Among Middle-Aged and Young-Old Men and Women in Middle America,"* International Journal of Aging and Development, *vol. 32 (4), pp. 261–65. International Management for material from "In Quest of Happiness," by Paul Thorne,* International Management, *July 1990, p. 64. Alfred A. Knopf, Inc., for material from* The Good Society *by Robert N. Bellah, et al., copyright © 1991 by Robert N. Bellah, Richard Madsen, William M. Sullivan, Ann Swidler, and Steven M. Tipton. Dr. Alfie Kohn for material from* The Brighter Side of Human Nature, *Basic Books, Inc. Ann Landers for material © 1985, Creators Syndicate.* New York *Magazine for material from "The Graying Yuppie" by Stan Pollan and M. Levine, © 1992 by K-III Magazine Corporation. All rights reserved. The New York Times Company for material from "Blacks Debating a Greater Stress on Self-Reliance Instead of Aid" by Lena Williams, June 15, 1986, copyright © 1986 by The New York Times Company; "Compassion and Comfort in Middle*
(continued on page 271)

ACKNOWLEDGMENTS

Heartfelt thanks to the many folks who contributed to this book, both professionally and with their moral support. I would like to thank the contributors who have made it their work to research, write about and conduct scientific inquiries into many fields discussed in this book. Their contributions are invaluable.

I would also like to thank the many librarians and assistants who helped in the voluminous research process for this book, especially those at the Boston Public Library, Concord Public Library, Coronado Public Library, Eau Gallie Public Library, Jacksonville Public Library, Melbourne Public Library, Bentley College Library, Harvard's Lamont Library, University of North Florida Library, University of Texas Academic Center and Perry Castaneda libraries and McLean Hospital Library.

Special thanks to Lyn Dietrich at McLean's for her professionalism and guidance, and to Carol Brown, Cathy Toon and David Mallon for their cooperation on this project.

I would like to acknowledge, with gratitude, the help of Deborah Maness, Mary Maness, Jill Head, Rick Runyon, Ale Statema, Alan Frazier and Gloria Frazier.

ACKNOWLEDGMENTS

Special thanks to Bob Bender, Johanna Li and Gypsy da Silva at Simon & Schuster and copy editor Carol Catt for their estimable efforts on behalf of this project.

Finally, thanks to David Rorvik and Stephen Frazier, who made this book possible.

To Gloria, my wife

With gratitude, for her immeasurable help
and indulgence throughout this three-year effort,
which so profoundly
touched our lives.

CONTENTS

INTRODUCTION

This book aims to provide a road map to the mind, both collective and individual, in the 1990s and early twenty-first century. It charts what are the most important trends that describe changes in attitudes and values, and helps predict how those changes may reshape many of our most important social institutions, including courtship, marriage, the family, our health-care and criminal justice systems. But beyond that, attempts to define trends in how we actually feel about ourselves and others.

This book helps answer such questions as: will we be less violent or more cruel and ruthless than ever before? Will we be more tolerant of minorities and cultural diversity or less tolerant? More selfish or more altruistic? More romantic or less romantic, capable of lesser or greater intimacy? More or less materialistic, more or less spiritual? Will we possess stronger or weaker senses of self and "community"? Will we have more or less reverence for life? Will we approach death with greater or lessening maturity? Will peace and cooperation win out over war, violence and aggression? Will communications between the sexes be enhanced or diminished, creating more rewarding or less rewarding relationships? Will we feel more "connected" or more lonely and isolated? Will "family" be as significant to us as it used to be? Will we be better or worsc parents? Will we be more or less tolerant of work? Will we experience more or less overall satisfaction in life?

INTRODUCTION

This detailed guide to the probable destinations of our collective consciousness in the next two decades will assist in helping to plan for the future and provide insights into living in the present, what to expect for yourself, your loved one, your society and your world—and how, if desired, to alter those expectations to accommodate changing realities before they overwhelm you.

Let it be conceded here and now that there is no genuine scientific methodology for projecting the future in any domain, let alone that most complex of all realms, the human psyche. Even to accurately assess where the individual and collective minds are "at" right now is a daunting task. Angus Campbell, Philip E. Converse and Willard L. Rodgers, in their estimable effort to define "the quality of American life" for the Russell Sage Foundation in the 1970s, noted that their predecessors had been obliged to fall back almost entirely on the "social indicators" in pursuit of the same goal. The social indicators tell us how much money people have in the bank, whether they are employed, what kind of housing they occupy, if and where they go to school, how much leisure time they have, whether they are victims of crime, whether they are married or divorced, have children or no children, what kind of health care they receive and so on.

The social indicators cannot be ignored. They are very important in charting trends. But we must not, as the Russell Sage researchers have cautioned, make of them "surrogates for the subjective experience of life." They add: "We are currently in a period of profound structural and institutional change in American society. Our social scientists have devoted much energy to documenting these changes but have given relatively little attention to their human meaning."

They cite, by way of a particularly instructive example, the 1954 Supreme Court ruling that "reversed a decision on racial segregation laid down by the Court fifty-eight years earlier." Why was racial segregation accepted as valid and moral in 1896 but not in 1954? What changes in attitudes and values—in the ways that people think and feel—made so momentous a transition in our social order not only possible but perhaps necessary?

Until relatively recently no one has attempted to study answers to such questions, in part because the psychological data needed to do so were either missing or inadequate or "permission" to analyze them was lacking. Only in very recent times have social scientists collectively validated inquiries into such psychological states as "happiness," "satisfaction," "pleasure" and "contentment," a development that is in itself as momentous as (and in as much need of explication as) that shift in Supreme Court consciousness.

INTRODUCTION

The shift that moves from the exclusive study of objective conditions to their interrelationships with psychological states is one that plunges us, as the Russell Sage scientists acknowledge, "into the subjective world of perceptions, expectations, feelings, and values and will involve us in excruciating problems of definition and measurement." Little wonder that they "regard this undertaking as an expedition into a land which is only partly known, an expedition in which we will proceed with a very rough map, devising new variables and inventing new measures as we go."

I owe a great debt to researchers like these, pioneers in charting changing psychological states. I have drawn upon the research of hundreds of scientists in this present effort to understand what sort of people we are and what sort of people we are likely to become. With computer assistance, I searched for those "new variables" and "new measures" wherever they could be found. Using a variety of databases, searching dozens of relevant fields, I have sifted from literally thousands of news articles, abstracts, scientific papers and surveys, and analyzed them both with respect to subject quantity and subject content. I employed programs that identify "key words" and concepts and used these, among other techniques, to help aggregate and "reduce" the data. For example, with such methods, all references in a database related to violence were reduced to 515 key articles, reports and surveys that underwent close scrutiny and then were further broken down to describe relevant trends and subtrends.

There was an arbitrary intent, at the outset, to divide the human experience into ten neat categories, but feelings, values, expectations and other emotions eventually aggregated into six categories that largely avoided the frequent overlap and redundancy of the ten. Those six categories, each embracing a spectrum of social indicators and emotional attitudes, relate to aggression, altruism, gender issues, family, evolutionary processes and overall life satisfaction. Each of these categories define a major section of this book.

To arrive at meaningful conclusions in each of these six realms of life experience, I tapped not only the insights of the researchers surveyed and cited but also those of many other professionals in sociology, psychology, sociobiology, neuroanatomy, economics, history, demographics and, of course, many of those in the field of psychiatry. Ultimately, I drew upon my own half century of clinical experience and study to make judgments about data that are sometimes highly *subjective* or tentative. And though I was always guided by the best available information, I did not hesitate to state some opinions or make suggestions about policies when it seemed helpful or appropriate to do so. In short, though this book is grounded in as much objective data as could be gathered and analyzed, it is, nonetheless, seasoned with a point of view that, if nothing else, I hope will help stimulate debate about the future of the mind and about *what sort of beings we want to become*.

ONE

Fury

More Violent/Less Violent?

THE TREND Americans will continue to be the most violent people on earth for some years to come but, within the next decade, will begin to reject as myth the *inevitability* of violence and, especially, of *increasing* violence. The consequences of this will be far-reaching and possibly epochal. A new consensus, gathering force in the scientific world today about the fundamental nature of human aggression will help fuel this shift in attitude. But what will most catalyze this change is the punitive and, finally, prohibitive cost, both emotional and financial, of a co-violent society, one that celebrates mayhem while simultaneously condemning it, a contradictory state that is able to flourish in an amoral milieu of "inevitability." Within the next ten years, as a matter of *necessity*, active, *preventive* solutions to violence, the seeds of which are already being planted, will take root, solutions that hold some real promise of supplanting the still governing but manifestly failing retributive *reaction* to crime and violence.

Overview

What's the World Coming To?

Crime headlines announce horror: kids shooting each other in the public schools, gang warfare, child abuse, serial killings, wife battering, dismemberment, cannibalism, animal sacrifice, cult murders, rape, hate crimes, bloody protests and ideological violence, police brutality, epidemics of suicide, muggings and other mayhem on once serene college campuses, drive-by shootings, random killings, terrorism, freeway violence, grade-schoolers committing homicides, erotomania ("fatal attractions"), drug-and-alcohol-related crime—and on and on.

Article after article, study after study, poll after poll make it clear that violence is *the* social issue of our time. Nothing concerns us more than our personal safety and security and the safety and security of our families and friends. Yet the best evidence suggests we are only *beginning* to take a mature, realistic view of violence, one that might point toward some genuine solutions. For the most part we presently mix pessimism and despair with resignation: we complain endlessly but do nothing, or very little, to change things. Our justification is that there's "no stopping violence"; its escalation is "inevitable." And then we go see the latest movie in which people, with ever-increasing regularity, get raped, mauled, mugged and minced, frequently to the cheers of those in attendance.

Many of us are still intensely titillated by violence; we deplore it at one level, embrace it at another, sending out confusing and, ultimately, destructive messages to the young. Our ambivalence toward violence is profound. We condemn crime, but as an intended antidote we prescribe a retributive process that so far has succeeded only in fostering *more* crime at ever-greater cost to society. Meanwhile we celebrate violence via the massive news coverage we give it, the films we watch, the television programs we view, the books we read.

We're still a relatively young nation, proud of our revolutionary roots, our (sentimentalized) cowboy/frontier origins, our "warrior culture," all of which are characterized by violence, something we seldom acknowledge.

Nor do we seem to be prepared to address the economic disparities that continue to create violent seismic tremors, largely along ethnic lines, throughout the country.

For a great many, this will clearly be the decade of the "wake-up call." The 1992 Los Angeles riots were an early indicator of that. But if that's bad news for some, it should be good news for society as a whole: the country will at last be convinced to apply new strategies to the problem.

Before examining hopeful signs that suggest a trend toward more successful management of crime and violence, let's acknowledge the magnitude of the present crisis. Perhaps our biggest problem is that so many of us believe we are *programmed* by natural selection to be violent, that aggression is an *innate* part of the human genome, an *inevitable* expression of the human condition.

Those who say this often cite our bloody heritage, the nearly 15,000 wars that punctuate recorded human history, not to mention all the undeclared massacres, pogroms, holocausts and other assorted atrocities that have attended human "progress." A general impression today is one of wildly escalating crime, an impression the headlines and news broadcasts consistently reinforce, especially in this country:

- The United States, we are authoritatively told, is the most violent nation on the planet.
- The United States is "number one" in the rate at which it imprisons people. More people are incarcerated, per capita, in this country than were ever incarcerated even in the most oppressive periods of the Soviet Union or South Africa. The rate of incarceration in the United States is, in fact, *four to twelve times greater* than it is in countries of Western Europe and up to *twenty times greater* than in some Asian countries.
- The murder rate in the United States, per capita, is ten times greater than that in Japan and Great Britain and at least seven times greater than that in Western Europe overall.
- The prison population doubled in the United States in the 1980s and is expected to continue increasing at a similar pace.
- More murders were committed in the United States in 1990 than ever before.
- Hate crimes—against African-Americans, Jews, gays, Hispanics, Asians and other minorities—are reportedly at an all-time high.
- There are an estimated 150 million *civilian* firearms in the United States, including at least 35 million handguns.
- Arrests of teenagers have increased *thirtyfold* since 1950.
- The average age of violent gang members continues to decline and is now 13½.
- Since 1968, the teen suicide rate has *doubled*. Suicide is the second leading cause of death among adolescents.
- Among 15–19-year-old minority youths, homicide is the leading cause of death.
- About 150,000 students now carry loaded guns to school daily, mainly for protection.
- A former Secretary of Health and Human Services lamented that "During every 100 hours on our streets we lose more young men

than were killed in 100 hours of ground war in the Persian Gulf."

- A criminologist declares that the 1990s will be "the bloodiest decade of juvenile violence we've ever seen." Another authority calls the present epidemic of youth crime "a slow riot."
- In total, children and adolescents today spend more of their lives watching television than they spend in school. In the course of this they witness an estimated 180,000 acts of extreme violence before graduating from high school.
- Hard-core abusers of cocaine and "crack" may actually number more than three times the current government estimates.
- Violent crime is up sharply on college campuses; 78 percent of the mayhem, which includes murder, rape and assault, is committed by the students themselves.
- The family is our most violent institution: at least 20 percent of all homicides involve family members killing other family members. Family violence produces one in every five emergency room admissions.
- Rape is reported to have increased 24 percent since 1981.
- Aggravated assault is up 59 percent since 1981.
- A violent act is committed against a woman in the home every 15 seconds, against a child even more frequently.

Is it possible to be even marginally optimistic in view of all this? Surprisingly, yes. The human mind *desires* "titillation" but it absolutely *requires* a core of security and peace. We're fast approaching that certain moment when the collective consciousness perceives a clear and present danger: that we have no more peace to squander. Nor the funds with which to squander it.

Additionally, science is now providing insights into human behavior that are beginning to create a more hopeful attitude in some of those charged with designing the policies that will govern our approach to crime and violence in the coming decades. Change is in the air.

The Seville Statement: Humans Are *Not* Inherently Violent

In 1986 a group of twenty eminent scholars from a dozen different countries, meeting at the 6th International Colloquium on Brain and Aggression at the University of Seville in Spain, drafted a document that effectively overturned decades of "received wisdom" and stereotypical thinking about the nature of human violence. The panel that drafted "The Seville Statement on Violence" comprised a group of leading authorities in the fields of psychology, psychiatry, ethology, neurophysiology, biological anthropology, genetics, sociology, psychobiology, political psychology, animal behavior and biochemistry.

The Seville Statement is a rare, truly seminal, report that has the power to profoundly influence politics, the sciences, economics, even philosophy and religion. The Seville Statement continues to gather steadily in power and influence and every year is endorsed by more scientific bodies and published in more prestigious scientific journals. It was adopted by UNESCO at its General Conference Session in Paris in late 1989 and was formally endorsed by the American Psychological Association, which published its full text in *American Psychologist* in late 1990.

The Seville Statement, based upon cumulative insights of some of the world's leading experts on violence, establishes that there is no scientific basis for the belief in the inevitability of human violence, aggression and war. The statement begins:

> Believing that it is our responsibility to address from our particular disciplines the most dangerous and destructive activities of our species, violence and war . . . we, the undersigned . . . challenge a number of alleged biological findings that have been used, even by some in our disciplines, to justify violence and war. Because the alleged findings have contributed to an atmosphere of pessimism in our time, we submit that the open, considered rejection of these misstatements can contribute significantly to . . . peace.

The statement is expressed in the form of five propositions supported by the research findings of the panel members:

1. "*It is scientifically incorrect* to say that we have inherited a tendency to make war from our animal ancestors." Warfare is *cultural*, not biological.
2. "*It is scientifically incorrect* to say that war or any other violent behavior is genetically programmed into our human nature." Except in cases of very rare pathology, genes do *not* predispose to violence.
3. "*It is scientifically incorrect* to say that in the course of human evolution there has been a selection for aggressive behavior more than for other kinds of behavior." In fact, natural selection puts very high value on the ability to cooperate and peacefully fulfill

social functions that support species survival and *discourages* the kind of hyperaggression that disrupts and threatens the social order. If our evolutionary legacy dictates anything in this context, it is not a predisposition to violence but, rather, a requirement to maintain that inner core of peace and order that I spoke of earlier—for it is in that core that we keep the keys to our survival.

4. "*It is scientifically incorrect* to say that humans have a 'violent brain.' " Unlike most other animals, humans have the ability to process and filter stimuli *before* acting upon them. Nothing in our neurophysiology *makes* us react violently to certain stimuli. We, and some of the other higher primates, have the ability to shape our responses through learning and socialization processes that we can select if we opt to do so.
5. "*It is scientifically incorrect* to say that war is caused by 'instinct' or any single motivation." On the contrary, war and many other forms of aggression are the product of very complex cognitive factors, including rational considerations; personal characteristics (such as obedience and idealism); social skills and so on.

In summary, the drafters of the Seville Statement conclude that

> biology does not condemn humanity to war [or other forms of violence], and . . . humanity can be freed from the bondage of biological pessimism and empowered with confidence to undertake the transformative tasks needed . . . in the years to come. Although these tasks are mainly institutional and collective, they also rest upon the consciousness of individual participants for whom pessimism and optimism are crucial factors. Just as 'wars begin in the minds of men,' peace also begins in our minds. . . .

Those who thought the Seville Statement was rhetorical pie-in-the-sky were no doubt among those most amazed by the sudden demise of the Cold War—a giant step toward resolving the global ideological violence that generations had come to believe was as intransigent as it was inevitable.

Are Things Really as Bad as They Seem?

As the truths of Seville are recognized they will oblige us to take responsibility for violence *and* empower us to respond to it more effectively. We are beginning to learn that violence, apart from being avoidable, has been exaggerated in ways that cause unnecessary harm.

When one examines crime statistics over long periods of time, rather than just comparing a couple of years as is commonly done in the media, a surprising fact emerges: there hasn't been much real change in overall crime rates in nearly twenty years. No trend was discernible between 1973 and 1981, and throughout most of the 1980s most crime rates *declined*. In general, crime was high in the United States for many decades and *continues* at approximately the same high rate per capita—*too* high for us to pay for much longer—but *not* escalating uncontrollably.

Of course, in tracking trends one notes all manner of "blips," which the media delight in mistaking for mountains. In the 1980s, for example, when the murder rate among African-Americans suddenly trended upward, this was "news" everywhere. Much less was said when the rate abruptly headed back down—and virtually no one ran to the presses or microphones to announce what might more legitimately be considered news: the fact that throughout the 1980s the murder rate among African-Americans was actually lower than it had been in the 1970s. There were significant declines in the assault and robbery rates among blacks; among whites the decline was much less marked.

The media have a fondness for headlines that announce that crime is "up 20 percent in just three years" and the like. And it's easy to create such headlines. In 1989, for example, one could send out this alarm: CRIME UP 15% OVER 1985 and be telling the truth. But *what* truth? For in 1989 you could also accurately have written this headline (which, however, never appeared anywhere to my knowledge): CRIME DOWN 6% SINCE 1980!

Even though 1990 was declared the most murderous year in history by media throughout the country, an examination of longer-term data indicates that while the murder rate was up 8 percent over 1989 and 9 percent over 1986 it was actually 4 percent lower than in 1981.

Rape appears to be escalating out of control, up 24 percent since 1981, but here—as with wife battering, child abuse, sexual abuse and hate crimes—*reporting* is up sharply due to society's belated willingness to take these crimes seriously. When women, children, blacks and other minorities could not find social refuge nor police, judges and juries willing to act upon their complaints, they seldom came forward. These crimes were always occurring and very likely at rates even greater than they are today, when society is less willing to tolerate them.

Bias in reporting methodologies has contributed enormously to the current distortion. FBI statistics, for example, have tended to paint a particularly alarming picture, showing crime rates in almost all categories moving steadily higher, year after year. By contrast, the Bureau of Justice Statistics indicate much more constant, but not generally escalating, rates. The difference can be explained by the fact that the Bureau of Justice Statistics are based upon public victimization surveys from throughout the nation, while FBI reports rely on crimes reported to the bureau by police departments. These police reports were very limited in the 1970s and have gradually improved over the years to more fully report on all crimes, giving the impression that crime itself (rather than the reporting of it) is moving steadily upward.

Fortunately, there appears to be the first glimmerings of a trend toward more responsible reporting on crime and violence. Government, social organizations and the media are all *beginning* to probe beneath the surface to expose more of the contradictions and complexities of the problem. We've frightened and titillated ourselves with the "more crime" story for decades. Now we want to know *why* crime persists.

Nowhere is the focus on crime more intense than in New York City, which has become a symbol, for the rest of the country, of the crime-and-violence-riddled future we all hope somehow to escape. Yet, even in New York, as various writers have recently pointed out, things are in many respects better or at least no worse than they have been at various times in the past about which we are now so nostalgic.

One writer noted that more than one hundred years ago police corruption was so bad in New York City that the legislature tried to oust the entire police force, only to witness a bloody battle outside city hall between the deposed officers and their intended replacements. Muggers were so prevalent in the 1850s that the citizenry took to toting pistols when venturing out at night. Central Park was so beset by crime in the 1870s that its creator recommended it be closed after sundown. Schools were so overcrowded and so riddled by violence in the 1860s that even the police officers who tried to intervene were shot down by teenagers.

But for whites, at least, New York City is today considerably safer than it was in the 1970s—at least in terms of the risk of being murdered. As the media are beginning to recognize, the flight of the white middle class from the city has as much to do with *heightened awareness* of crime, sometimes verging on hysteria, as it does with crime itself.

Today new waves of immigrants are rushing to New York. Consequently, some run-down sections of Queens and Brooklyn are already being revitalized. These newcomers, like so many of the immigrants who settled in New York before them, are imbued with a strong sense of family and community, qualities which have been in notably short supply in recent decades.

Immigration is also on the rise in several other cities where the flight of the middle class to the suburbs had, as in New York, been viewed as yet another sure sign of complete urban capitulation to crime and violence.

It isn't that crime today isn't so bad, after all. It's plenty bad. But our nearly catatonic fixation on violence, induced in part by the media's hypnotic focus on the subject, has long been a formidable obstacle to implementing useful reform. We have been left feeling helpless, victims of a "chain of violence" that particularly afflicts and damages our young. We have come to believe that the world is beset by crime and that ever more crime is to be *expected*.

In the next several years, however, we will change, not only because we are finally discovering we *can* change but also because we're beginning to realize we *must* change.

The Impossible Cost of *Not* Changing

If scientific research into the human mind supported the notion that we *are* inherently violent and that human aggression *is* inevitable then our present system of dealing with crime might make sense: react to crime with retribution; *punish* the offender with imprisonment in the hope that he or she will not repeat the offense when released; simultaneously use this punishment as a deterrent to others. At the very least, take the criminals out of circulation, and, in more extreme cases, execute them as the ultimate means of stopping them from committing other crimes and possibly to deter others who might be similarly inclined.

After all, if you can't prevent criminal behavior you have no choice but to react to it. But forget the possibility that this system actually does deter; as already noted, this country has been incarcerating people at an ever-quickening rate, handing out longer and more severe sentences every year to little positive effect. On the contrary, there appears to be a *counter* deterrent at work: the present system is characterized by an alarmingly high rate of recidivism. Already, as the prisons burst to overflowing, record numbers of unrehabilitated prisoners who have tasted society's retributive reaction to them are being released into the streets, their numbers up more than 16 percent in one year. Many will commit more crimes and go back to prison, further stressing a system that is about to bankrupt many states.

The present approach still has many defenders. It is currently popular to take a "hard-line," "tough" stance on crime. That means more prisons, longer sentences. In arguing for former President Bush's crime bill, then–Attorney General Dick Thornburgh declared, "We are not here to search for the roots of crime" but, "rather, to stop 'the carnage in our own mean streets.' " Translation: put more people in prison.

But economics has a way of deflating rhetoric. What's "tough" today will be viewed as tough tomorrow as well—tough on the *pocketbook*.

This may sound like a joke, but it isn't: Which costs more: to send someone to Penn State or to a state pen? Including all costs, it costs *seven times more* to send someone to a state pen (average sentence) than to put a student through Penn State.

Prisons are enormously expensive. Our prison population has doubled in the past ten years to more than 1 million. Costs in that decade for maintaining these prisoners nearly tripled and now stand at more than $25 billion annually. In many areas, it costs $25,000 a year to maintain a single prisoner. The average is now $20,296. And the cost of building new prisons is similarly going up sharply. In the state of New York, for example, it now costs more than $100,000 for *each* prison cell.

At present rates of incarceration—playing the "hard-line" strategy—we will need to double our prison space again by 2000. And then what? With continuing increases in the next decade we could easily spend—if we could raise the money—far more than one hundred billion dollars on prisons that arguably don't do the job. And that doesn't include the $50 billion to $100 billion per year we might require to maintain our prison population and the huge cost of replacing obsolete prisons on a continuing basis.

As one business writer, analyzing the impasse, recently put it, "What is clear . . . is that the trend toward greater incarceration is running into a fiscal stone wall." State governments are feeling the crushing weight of these costs—up 400 percent in some states in less than ten years. Prisons in at least forty states are already straining under the overload; simply stated, there's simply not enough money to keep them up and keep the prisoners inside.

"The response to the heinous crime of the month continues to be a vigorous, chest-pounding punitive response," says Alfred Blumstein, Dean of the School of Urban and Public Affairs at Carnegie-Mellon University, but "there is a growing awareness that we cannot keep this up forever."

In 1992 a bipartisan meeting of governors was convened to confront this issue. The emphasis was on trying to find alternatives to incarceration. "What we have been doing is not right," Governor L. Douglas Wilder of Virginia declared. "But it's very difficult for politicians, and I am one of them, to say we have been wrong and that we've got to revisit, revise and restructure the whole system."

According to *The New York Times*, "Criminal justice experts at the conference said the support among governors for alternatives to prison could reflect a shift in public policy away from prison terms toward a combination of punishment and rehabilitation in a community."

Joseph Lehman, Pennsylvania Corrections Commissioner, told *USA Today*, "we use prisons as the solution for everything. . . . It doesn't work. . . . My state had a 171% growth in the prison population in the 1980s, . . . You can't explain that by our 6% growth in the crime rate." He blames the prison boom in his state on politicians who play on the public's fear of crime.

Lehman is one of 450 criminologists who have joined together to form the Campaign for an Effective Crime Policy, a group that includes the heads of at least twenty state prison systems. The goal of the group, according to *USA Today,* is to "remove politics from the crime debate and criticize candidates who use crime for political gain. The group . . . wants less imprisonment and more education, drug treatment and sentencing alternatives."

There are many alternatives. And many, within the limited contexts in which they have been allowed to function, are working remarkably well. We'll look at those later in this chapter.

The next two decades will be a period of painful transition. But with even conservative authorities on violence now in agreement that imprisonment can effectively address only a very small part of the crime problem, movement toward innovative methods of intervention and prevention is inevitable. Ironically, the overwhelming failure of our present system will be used indirectly by some to *oppose* change. In the next decade our present situation will be exacerbated by the release into the community of tens of thousands of unrehabilitated, hardened, despairing men (and an increasing number of women) with few social or job skills. These "graduates of retribution" will be prime candidates for repeat offenses, fueling cries for still more retribution, making it more difficult for new approaches to gain footholds. But innovations will nonetheless gain in credibility as the decade advances, due to the impossible costs of continuing with the present system of incarceration.

Before proceeding to alternative approaches to dealing with crime and violence, let's examine several subtrends. These involve youth crime, family violence, rape, the influences of guns and drugs, suicide, murder, hate crimes, campus violence, female criminality and ideological violence. For background, it is important to keep in mind that from a psychological perspective, violent acts are part of a continuum that often begins with low self-esteem and a feeling of helplessness and fear, sometimes from abuse when young and sustained feelings of deprivation of love and affection. The ultimate action, which is violent, is therefore part of a process that begins much earlier than the action outcome. It is this common denominator, "violence as a process, not an event," that binds all of the following trends together.

Youth Crime Increasing

One category of crime that is definitely trending upward is violence perpetrated by our youth. Moreover, the average age of gang members (now 13½) will continue to decline. This phenomenon is not confined to large cities but is also evident in suburbia and in small towns and rural communities. And an increasing number of youthful offenders are emerging from economically advantaged families.

Shootings, according to government sources, are now three times more likely to kill minority youths than are diseases. Similarly, white youths are 11 percent more likely to be killed by guns than by illnesses of all kinds combined. Teenage arrests, as noted earlier, have increased thirtyfold since the 1950s. Homicide is the number one cause of death among minority youths aged 15–19. Psychologist Charles Patrick Ewing, author of the book *When Children Kill*, has persuasively predicted that this will be "the bloodiest decade of juvenile violence we've ever seen."

What's fueling this frightening epidemic, which has now spread from the streets into the schools where, in one recent twelve-month period, 150,000 crimes were committed? Drugs and alcohol are an integral part of the violence process. The immediate trend is for *diminished* drug use, but current usage is still dramatically higher than in most prior decades. Approximately 25 percent of all fourth-graders have tried marijuana; 50 percent of all high school seniors will get drunk at least once in any two-week period; about 50 percent of all youth crimes are committed while high on drugs or alcohol; 100,000 10- and 11-year-olds get drunk at least once a week; the average child sees alcohol consumed on TV an average of 75,000 times before reaching legal drinking age.

Reports that cocaine use is rapidly declining can be misleading. There has been some decline in use among adolescents recently but an increase in use among those 35 and older—which indicates the drug remains in demand and widely available. The number of cocaine-related emergency room visits increased again in 1991 after briefly trending downward. Use of *all* illicit drugs, including heroin and marijuana, is rising among Americans 35 and older, producing an atmosphere in which it will be easier for the young to obtain drugs.

What is clear is that decline—or no decline—in drug use, violence among teens continues to increase. The cocaine culture of the 1980s created a more violent attitude among adolescents that will continue to prevail for some years due to the development of cheaper "crack" cocaine.

Juvenile poverty and an explosion in the population of juveniles are other factors promoting the trend. This is the first time that the youth of our country will be less prosperous than their parents' generation. Attending this economic and psychological development is another first: declining access to health care among the young.

Broken families and fatherlessness are additional major factors. Where families have ceased to function, gangs have sprung up, providing surrogate families and a sense of belonging and security. In many cities gang membership has more than doubled in the past five years and will continue to grow rapidly over the next several years. Gang killings now account for 35 percent of all homicides in the United States.

The influence on the young of violence in films, television and other media remains controversial, though a trend that *perceives* an adverse media influence is coalescing. (See discussion of media violence later in this chapter.)

The greater availability of ever-more powerful guns is similarly perceived as a major factor in youth violence. (This issue is also discussed separately.)

A "maturity gap" is credibly hypothesized to account for the increase in violent crime among teenagers who do *not* come from disadvantaged homes. These teens are said to mature physically at earlier ages and be frustrated by the lack of opportunity to express this maturity in the adult world. The frustration can eventually be released in antisocial and violent behavior. The problem may be further aggravated, according to some findings, by heightened expectations promulgated by the media.

More Guns/More Murder

Does the availability of guns contribute to our very high homicide rate? Will more guns push the rate still higher? This is one of the most hotly debated issues today, creating a bitter polarity of opinions. An analysis of polls, research findings, lobbying efforts and news stories makes clear, however, that the public increasingly *believes* that proliferation of guns and the lack of meaningful controls over gun ownership contribute to increased homicide. This trend will certainly lead to greater—and more effective—gun control in the coming decade.

The central question is: do we have more murders today because people are more vicious—or because guns make it easier to kill? The evidence strongly suggests that an increased presence of guns has made unplanned, sudden confrontations far more deadly. The data suggest there is not a greater *intent* to kill, but the presence of a gun in a violent episode makes a killing more likely. Guns are now used in 28 percent of all crimes and in 64 percent of all homicides.

A number of investigators have effectively begun to separate fact from emotion in the "great gun debate." One of the most sophisticated analysts in this field is Franklin E. Zimring, professor of law and head of the Earl Warren Legal Institute at the University of California. He has also served as director of research for the Task Force on Firearms of the National Commission on the Causes and Prevention of Violence. Among his key findings, after two decades of research, are the following:

- The type of weapon used in an act of violence *does* matter. Some claim that if an assailant doesn't have a gun he or she will simply use another weapon, to the same effect. Zimring points out that this argument makes the unfounded assumption that those who kill *intend*, with absolute and uniform resolve, to kill. Zimring's analysis of many thousands of both fatal and nonfatal assaults involving guns and knives contradicts this assumption. Eighty percent of the time those wielding guns shoot their victims only once. Whether an attack results in death appears to be more the product of chance than of intent, since both lethal and nonlethal attacks almost equally involve wounds to vital body parts. Both types of assault are about equally the result of the same circumstances: sudden, unplanned arguments.

- Those unfortunate victims of gun attacks are *five times* more likely to die than those attacked by assailants with knives. Zimring's studies demonstrate that those using guns are no more intent upon killing than those using knives. The opposite may be true: knife wielders are more likely to inflict *multiple* wounds than gun users. Hence the overwhelmingly greater number of deaths caused by guns can only be attributed to the greater *power* of the guns themselves, to what Zimring and others call an "instrumentality effect."
- Some guns are deadlier than others. Handguns are used in more than three out of four gun-related homicides and robberies. And the bigger handguns that are becoming increasingly available are twice as deadly.
- When robberies result in death to the victim, guns are three times more likely than knives to be the cause of death.

Zimring has also identified and analyzed the different strategies that have been tried or proposed for "gun control." The least effective, in terms of saving lives, are laws that mete out stiffer penalties to those who use guns while committing crime and those that make it illegal for convicted felons to buy or possess guns. These are strategies that have little impact. Licensing guns, requiring gun registration and restricting sales of exotic weaponry (assault rifles and the like) are more effective measures that do not severely limit the legitimate use of guns.

A growing number of authorities believe that the real answer, however, is to sharply reduce the number of guns in circulation and severely restrict who can possess them. Zimring notes that in those Northeastern cities that have adopted laws restricting handguns there *is* a lower incidence of violent crime. Others have recently reanalyzed the situation in Washington, D.C., and have found that after that city implemented a tough handgun-control law both gun-related homicides and suicides dropped by a very significant 25 percent. Meanwhile, adjacent urban areas in Maryland and Virginia that were not affected by this law had unchanged rates of homicide and suicide. And for a nine-year period that was studied (the first nine years the law was in effect), there was no increase in non-gun-related suicides and homicides. More recently the murder rate in Washington, long one of the highest in the world, has risen again, but, say these analysts, the increase would have been far sharper—and come much sooner—without the laws that make the legal ownership of handguns difficult in that city.

Those who wish to obtain guns illegally, even where there are tough gun-control laws in effect, can certainly do so. But most murders are committed by those who do *not* plan or intend a murder but, instead, commit one in the "heat of the moment" when a gun is at hand.

Even if we assume that if you take one weapon away another will be substituted, an assumption not supported by fact, restricting guns could still save many lives. Sociologist Hans Zeisel of the University of Chicago, addressing this issue, using Houston and New York as examples, concludes:

> If the level of gun attacks in Houston were reduced from 42 percent to New York's level of 24 percent [New York has much stronger gun controls], 322 gun attacks would have been knife attacks. At present these 322 gun attacks resulted in 63 fatalities. . . . If they were knife attacks, roughly 12 fatalities would result—a reduction from 20 deaths per 100 attacks to 4 per 100.

The good news in all of this is that Americans are not becoming more violent by the hour, as some headlines seem to suggest. As Scott Armstrong, writing in the *Christian Science Monitor*, has observed: "Meaner streets don't necessarily signal a meaner society. Some recent studies have shown no significant increase in rapes and other serious assaults committed by teenagers, even though murders were up. . . . Experts . . . point out that several factors contributing to the surge in homicides—demographics and bigger guns—are not cultural."

Zimring, writing in *Scientific American*, concludes:

> At the heart of the debate over handgun restrictions is a disagreement about the character of life in the 21st century. Roughly half of Americans believe that strict handgun control is not worth the hardship of changing policy in the U.S. They assume that the weapons can remain a part of American life for the indefinite future. But just as many Americans see the removal of the current stockpile of handguns as a necessary down payment on the American future. They regard free availability of handguns as a severe threat to urban life. American policy on handgun control will ultimately depend on which of these attitudes prevails.

Growing awareness of the *independent* effect gun power and availability have on the incidence and severity of violent crime will tip the balance in favor of increasingly tougher gun-control strategies. As the evidence—in this case a literal "smoking gun"—becomes more visible, the public will finally respond.

FURY: More Violent/Less Violent?

Family Violence, Rape, Hate Crimes: Appearing to Increase

Domestic violence, rape and crimes directed at minority groups all appear to be increasing dramatically. As stated earlier, much of this increase is illusory, an artifact of heightened awareness and increased reporting of crimes in these categories. Indeed, the fact that today there *are* recognized categories covering these crimes is itself evidence of society's diminishing tolerance of them. Little more than two decades ago many acts that are criminal by law today (acts of discrimination and violence against black Americans, for example) were either ignored or were actually sanctioned, institutionalized components of our social, moral, legal fabric.

Similarly, until the 1970s, when homosexuals made themselves more effectively and politically "visible," aggression directed against that minority was tacitly, if not explicitly, overlooked, even condoned. For the most part, homosexuals were not even a part of the public consciousness until the 1970s, and "gay bashing," though there was undoubtedly plenty of it, was not even recognized as a legitimate complaint.

The reality of what is happening with respect to rape and family violence is equally obscured by the fact that, until quite recently, these crimes lingered in the "closet," were vastly underreported and, to some considerable extent, were publicly regarded as private transgressions to be dealt with *in* private. The political, social, economic mobilization of women, the formation of child-advocacy groups, as well as the gradually increasing awareness of these crimes have profoundly altered public attitudes in the past two decades. The momentum for greater societal responsiveness to these grievances continues to build.

The crime and violence complained of by women, children and minorities is real. But the situation is improving, not getting worse. As groups succeed in gaining recognition, a certain psychology that we call "crucible consciousness" grips them, as well as those with whom they come into conflict. It is in this crucible, this cauldron of great heat and severe testing, that the illusion of uncontrolled, runaway violence boils up into the public consciousness, distorting the progress that is actually taking place. The violence brought to bear against minorities *before* they make themselves visible and assert claims of equal protection under the law may not be quite so dramatic as some of the clashes we read about and see on television today, but it is surely more pervasive, more repressive and, ultimately, more deadly.

Crucible consciousness will not dissipate anytime soon, but the trend is clearly toward greater accommodation of minorities and toward a more pluralistic society. Perturbations in the next two decades will be many and often intense. But change *is* occurring—and the revolution of consciousness that attends this change is not, as some have claimed, a chimera of jurisprudence. It is not merely laws that are changing; it is also minds.

Opinion polls taken over the past two decades have demonstrated a steadily increasing tolerance for minorities. As recently as 1972, for example, fully 40 percent of the white population in the United States believed that black-white marriages should be illegal. Today that percentage has been cut in half. And, in that same space of time, the number of black-white marriages has nearly tripled. Changes in these deep, gut-level beliefs are particularly significant in terms of forecasting future attitudes.

The perception we have today of "runaway" hate crimes stems partially from the expectation that mind sets will change as fast as laws do, or even as fast as laws are proposed. There is some evidence that these unrealistic expectations are beginning to be checked—a fact that should gradually dampen the crucible effect.

Women, as a disadvantaged group, are the most highly evolved in this realization—and in taking a more measured, long-term view are being more effective in gaining rights they feel should be theirs. African-Americans, too, have moved in this direction—and there is evidence that gays and other minorities will follow suit.

The rapidly changing ethnic demographics of the country can be expected to have enormous impact on public attitudes. Inevitably, particularly during economic downturns, there will be notable scapegoating, tension and flare-ups of ethnic-related violence. But there are far more important effects related to the cultural diversification that results from significant immigration of the sort we've been experiencing for some time now. Out of that diversification, if history is any guide, will emerge greater accommodation. A number of sociologists have marveled over the relative ease with which this recent immigration is occurring. What particularly strikes many is how relatively violence free it has been.

A certain amount of *sanctioned* evil, in which aggression is directed against minorities by majorities, will no doubt persist. But there can be no doubt that, in the present era at least, that particularly odious form of violence is less tolerated than it ever has been. One chilling reminder of where we have been is a casual news report in the *San Francisco Bulletin* from a bit over a hundred years ago:

> Some citizens of this city, while hunting in Marin County yesterday, came upon a large group of miserable Digger Indians. They managed to dispatch 30 of the creatures before the others ran away.

While statistics related to hate crimes have only begun to be compiled—and without illuminating effect to date—those related to rape have been compiled for several years now. And, on the face of it, rape is up—sharply. There were more than 100,000 rapes in 1990, up 24 percent from what was reported in 1981. But, again, what do these statistics prove, since rape was so seldom reported in past decades? Many observers doubt that rape is increasing, certainly not at the rate the numbers suggest. As society continues to give greater credibility to those who report rape—and as it begins to more effectively prosecute *and* treat those who commit rape—the incidence of this crime, per capita, should begin to decrease over the next twenty years.

Organized Violence for Conflict Resolution: Not a Long-term Trend

Often these days it seems as if dozens of groups, with widely diverse political and social agendas, are abandoning the traditional channels of change and are resorting, instead, to violence in pursuit of their objectives. Antiabortion forces block access to clinics, and an extremist is alleged to have murdered a doctor at an abortion clinic; gay-rights activists tie up traffic and interrupt news broadcasts; environmentalists "spike" trees and harass military and whaling vessels on the high seas; animal-rights enthusiasts break into research facilities and "liberate" lab animals or spray paint on fur coats. And so on.

An analysis of such events indicates that this is not a long-term trend. It seems unlikely that the 1990s will come anywhere close to duplicating the 1960s, for example, in this kind of activity. In fact, worldwide, the most extreme expression of this type of violence—terrorism—has been in decline for nearly two decades. The 1993 terrorist bombing of the World Trade Center in New York City is a notable exception to this trend.

Backlash effects and generally poor results will continue to restrain the use of violence for conflict resolution. This is true of citizen vigilantism, as well. Citizen groups that spring up to "wage war" on drugs, for example, are often initially greeted with enthusiasm by communities, but the "honeymoon" is generally short lived, as these groups inevitably come into conflict with police, inflict harm on innocent individuals and raise the specter of mob rule.

More Female Criminals

Equal opportunity for crime and violence on the part of women? That, increasingly, appears to be the case. Recently, Ann Landers reported that "a veritable firestorm of opinions" was occasioned by one of her columns on whether men or women were the more violent. There is no doubt that men are convicted of far more crimes than women, but the trend is toward a definite increase in female-perpetrated crime. A ten-year analysis reveals a *138 percent increase* in female imprisonment, compared with a 94 percent increase in male imprisonment over the same period. Women are serving longer sentences now, too, reflecting the more serious nature of their crimes. And the FBI has reported a 25 percent increase, in a single year, in the number of women under age 18 charged with violent crimes.

So far this trend is more evident in urban areas and mostly involves juvenile females. Females under the age of 18 are just one step behind their male counterparts, according to many youth workers, in their willingness to turn to crime. For the first time, girls are forming armed gangs. The girls are using switchblade knives as "starter" weapons, just as boys did many years ago when male gangs first formed.

Youth workers and law enforcement officials across the country report that this trend began gathering force about five years ago and is continuing to gain in momentum. "We are seeing an incredible increase in the amount of violent activities that girls are involved in," Carol Lee Pepi, executive director of a major community outreach program, told the *Boston Globe*.

"It used to be that girls were picked up for shoplifting and such," she added, "but that's not the case anymore. Now, girls' involvement in violence is more pronounced. Gang activity has increased and it has gone from the point where young women are accompanying young men on activities to where they have formed some of their own gangs. It has brought us into a whole new reality."

"I've been with the Boston public schools since 1977 and have seen young girls change, and I can tell you that the equality has almost been complete," concurs John Sisco, chief of school police in Boston. "Girls are as quick to be prone to violence as boys."

What's behind this trend? Have females just suddenly become more vicious? Not likely. They have, for decades, been under the same pressures that have produced so much criminal activity among young males, especially in urban settings: broken families, physical and sexual abuse, relentless exposure to media violence, economic disadvantage, drug- and alcohol-related dysfunctions, poor health care, inadequate education—all part of the violence chain.

There is nothing in the female psyche that made it substantially easier for girls to quietly endure those pressures. But they were *expected* to do so. Aggressive behavior by females has long been culturally proscribed. But that proscription, along with many other constraints on female behavior, is now changing. We should not be as surprised as we are that females are proving themselves the equals of males in negative, as well as positive, accomplishments.

Real equality, however, has not quite been achieved in this context. Many of those studying this phenomenon note that the newly emerging female youth gangs exist only with the tacit permission of their male counterparts. The boys regard it as okay for girls to form gangs—but only so long as their lethality is considerably less than the boys' own. Hence the girls get knives, while the boys move on to increasingly powerful handguns and assault rifles.

The incidence in female violence, likely to continue to increase for some time, is not further evidence of increasing human viciousness but, ironically, is *partly* the product of diminishing repression of women and other minorities. This does not mean that society will or should be more tolerant of female violence. The same solutions that apply to male-perpetrated violence will apply equally to violence committed by females.

Campus Crime: Graduating

Media reports of crime waves on college campuses feed the feeling among many Americans that violence is running rampant and that there are no longer any safe havens, not even the once idyllic college campuses so many remember. The reporting of campus crime is still in its infancy, but to the extent that a trend can be discerned it supports the idea that colleges and universities are increasingly violent places. One survey, by the Center for the Study and Prevention of Campus Violence, indicates that 36 percent of college students have been the victims of one crime or another, mostly theft and vandalism. Some reports suggest that up to 80 percent of all campus crime is committed by students themselves.

In one recent yearlong period, a total of nearly 2,000 violent campus crimes were reported to the FBI, including rape, murder, aggravated assault and robbery. There were more than 100,000 additional reports to the FBI of arson, vehicle theft, larceny and burglary. Since most schools do not yet report these crimes to the FBI, these figures are regarded as the "tip of the iceberg."

In part, these statistics reflect the growing youth-crime problem. But they are also reflective of the changed nature of the campus. The typical campus of today is far more urban than it used to be—and it embraces a much broader cross section of the population, not just the economically advantaged. These campuses are, conceptually, much "closer to the street" than the campuses so many older people remember. And there is evidence that the urban campus actually *prevents* far more crime than it fosters, by getting the urban young into productive learning and training programs out of which many find gainful employment and become part of mainstream society.

Erotomania: More "Fatal Attractions"?

Erotomania is a delusional disorder in which one person fixates on another with fantasies of romantic, sometimes spiritual love. The object of this erotomanic fantasy is often a famous person (such as a movie star or popular singer) or an authority figure, such as a boss or professor. The deluded individual often believes that the object of affection or adulation is equally interested—even in the face of repeated rejections—and lavishes the target individual with unwanted calls, gifts, physical advances, letters and so on. Often the deluded person will stalk the other party and sometimes resort to violence in order to be "close to" that person. Sometimes the violence takes the form of "saving" the other person from imaginary harm. This may lead to abduction.

There are signs that this disorder is increasing. There is the suggestion that it is more common among college students, for example, who fixate on instructors and professors. Anxious, insecure individuals see a "quick fix" for all or most of their problems in a romantic liaison with a more powerful person. But the upswing in this delusional condition may also be explained, especially among younger people, by expectations of instantly available social liaisons and magical solutions to obtaining economic plenty.

Increasing Suicide Among Young and Old

Suicide is considered a form of violence but, in some instances, is actually a reaction to a violent and impersonal environment. There is no doubt that suicide is trending sharply upward among both young and old—and will most likely continue to do so for some time.

FURY: More Violent/Less Violent?

The rate of suicide among those under age 24 has *tripled* in the past three decades. Among teenagers 15–19, suicide is the second leading cause of death—right after accidents. More than one in seven junior high students now admit to having attempted suicide at one time or another. The suicide rate among male adolescents is particularly high—more than five times greater than among adolescent females, even though females actually make more attempts at suicide. (Males may not intend any more intensely than females to kill themselves, but they are more likely to have access to guns and to use them.) Suicide is two times greater, per capita, among whites than among blacks. And it is especially high among gay and lesbian youth.

A number of factors are contributing to the epidemic of suicide among the young. Not surprisingly, many of these are the same as those that are contributing to youth crime in general—drugs, alcohol, depression, isolation, availability of guns, broken families, economic difficulties, the chain of violence. Some have speculated that young black males find some measure of release, along with peer acceptance and support, in gangs and violent crime, while many young white males are emotionally more isolated and insecure and more often seek escape in suicide.

Ironically, some of the methods implemented to try to prevent suicide among the young may occasionally promote it. Up to 40 percent of the nation's teens are now exposed to suicide-prevention classes in school—yet the problem continues to grow. Some researchers are now reporting that these classes are ineffective and sometimes harmful because, by dwelling on the subject, they encourage suicidal thoughts and tendencies among those predisposed to self-destruction. The classes, their critics charge, lend *drama* to suicide that some find attractive.

One thing is certain: there are often "suicide clusters" that occur when a well-known student suddenly takes his or her life. That one suicide triggers several others in the same school or community. The enlightened and "healing" reaction to a student suicide was thought to entail encouraging classes to collectively grieve for the suicide victim and thus find release. Unfortunately, this kind of collective event *ritualizes* the suicidal act, endowing it with a certain reverence and esteem that seems to make suicide more attractive to others who may be contemplating it.

Suicide prevention should not be abandoned—but it should be modified. There is a trend toward that modification. The key seems to be to *de-emphasize* suicide as the cause of death and focus instead on the underlying pathology that led to the death. The term "suicide," as noted above, sometimes spreads an intriguing, even ennobling, mantle over what, more likely, is an ugly, perhaps squalid, set of circumstances, which may involve drugs; abandonment; physical, sexual or psychological abuse; abject loneliness; rejection; isolation and depression. By focusing on the real, *underlying* causes of death, some suicide-education programs are making it more difficult or, in any case, far less desirable for other adolescents to identify with the suicide victim. In addition, early diagnosis of depression is critical to the success of most prevention efforts.

Clearly, more study is needed to determine the most effective intervention. Adolescent suicide will not significantly diminish until society itself becomes markedly less violent, until drug and alcohol abuse are reduced, along with the availability of guns—and until we adequately address some of the more basic social and economic problems confronting them today.

While increasing rates of suicide have been a long-term trend among the young, the increase among those over age 65 is reemerging. In one recent six-year period there was a striking 25 percent increase. Ironically, medical advances are a most likely culprit. People are living longer but not necessarily better. Indeed, medical advances are keeping many alive, but the quality of some of these extended lives is so low that some would rather be out of their pain and suffering. Chronic illness, loss of spouse and isolation often lead to depression and suicide among the elderly.

Also important, however, is a gradually changing social attitude—one that may tacitly encourage the elderly to take their own lives. The trend suggests that many are less likely to argue with the aged parent/grandparent who says, "You'd be better off without me." These attitudes are influenced by economic adversity and population growth. There is a good chance that, with population stabilization and increased respect for elder citizens this trend could eventually be reversed. But for that we will have to look further than two decades ahead.

Media Violence: WARNING: The Following Program May Seriously Harm Your Mental and Physical Health

Media violence is something like smoking—and not only in that it sometimes seems to have an addictive component. The evidence that smoking is extraordinarily harmful to human health was persuasive well over a decade before there was sufficient resolve to reduce the incidence of smoking through tough labeling laws that mandated stern health warnings, through educational projects and statutory prohibition of smoking in an ever-expanding number of situations and places. Just as society finally began to heed the smoking evidence, so will it in the next two decades at least take seriously the evidence already in hand that demonstrates a causal link between media violence and the actual incidence of violence in our society.

Let's look first at television since it is the most studied medium in terms of its effects on behavior. Television is particularly pervasive: 90 percent of all American households have at least one television set. Children, as noted earlier, spend 11,000 hours in elementary and secondary school and, during that same period of their lives, watch an average of 15,000 hours of television, witnessing in the process some 180,000 acts of violence. Reflect for a moment on the massive amount of parental, community, legislative and research effort that goes into planning, monitoring and delivering those 11,000 hours of education. Then reflect on the negligible to nonexistent amount of oversight, planning and research that goes into gauging the effects on youth of those 15,000 hours of television.

If even a tiny fraction of TV's violent content was taught in our schools the outcry would be enormous. Yet in an ongoing trend, parents already distanced from their offspring by work and day care, complacently entrust their children to a TV "teacher" virtually without conscience, a "teacher" whose prime objective is to hold the viewer's attention, by whatever means proves most expedient, long enough to sell products.

As discussed earlier in this chapter, we now know violent behavior is *not* innate or biological; rather, it is *learned.* And social learning theory, which has been gaining steadily in force for three decades, makes it amply evident that we learn behavior by *observing* others. Thus television truly is a powerful, largely unsupervised *teacher.* But a teacher of *what*?

Should we be surprised to learn that research data that can no longer be ignored as flawed demonstrate what two investigators recently called "a consistent and causal relationship between viewing TV violence and aggressive behavior in children and adolescents"? George Comstock, Ph.D., and Victor C. Strasburger, M.D., writing in the *Journal of Adolescent Health Care,* have applied meta-analysis to nearly 300 experiments and studies involving approximately 130,000 subjects to find a "positive association between exposure to TV violence and aggressive and antisocial behavior."

Dozens of experiments have demonstrated that TV violence heightens emotional arousal, desensitizes the viewer to violence and disinhibits in ways that make violent behavior more likely. Still other experiments refute the idea that the dramatization of violence can have cathartic, purgative effects, providing a "safety valve" or constructive outlet for "violent inclinations." Apart from the fact that this theory, still popular with the merchants of violent programming, is based upon the discredited notion that humans have an innate store of pent-up violence, there is simply no good evidence to support it. When angry or violent subjects are exposed to angry or violent programming they demonstrate, in experimental tests of this theory, not diminished but *heightened* states of anger and aggression.

Since the early 1970s, the study of TV-influenced violence has become increasingly complex and sophisticated. By the end of the seventies there was little doubt in the minds of most objective researchers about the negative influences of TV violence. And in the 1980s the results of long-term studies demonstrated, to the satisfaction of many researchers, a direct cause-and-effect relationship between viewing TV violence and violent behavior itself. Defenders of TV violence had long claimed that such a relationship could not be proved; they argued, moreover, that those who were the most disposed to violence in the first place were the ones who were most likely to watch the most violent programming.

But, as Comstock and Strasburger note:

> The last 10 years has seen the evolution of the longitudinal study, field surveys conducted over at least a year's time, that not only establish correlations but produce a strong case for *causality* as well. Six such studies exist, and five unequivocally point to a strong connection between TV violence and aggressive behavior.

In one five year study of children ages 4 to 9, those who were exposed to the most violent TV programming were the most aggressive and antisocial at the end of the follow-up period, even when initial levels of aggression and antisocial behavior were carefully controlled for in the study design. These more violent youngsters were the most likely to regard the world as a "mean and scary" place.

Another study, using data that went back to 1963, revealed a strong relationship between viewing TV violence in the third grade of school and aggressive or violent behavior ten years later and again twenty-two years later. The authors of this study noted the "lifelong consequences" of early exposure to high levels of TV violence.

A particularly revealing study compared three communities in Canada, which the researchers called Notel, Unitel and Multitel. Notel was a town without television. Nearby Unitel had one station, and Multitel, also in the same geographic area, was able to pick up several channels. The towns were otherwise quite similar. This long-term study was able to find a direct correlation between the amount of television people were exposed to and the incidence of crime in their communities. Notel was a distinctly less violent place until it, too, finally got television and gradually "caught up" with Unitel and Multitel in its crime rate.

The American Psychological Association Task Force on Television and Society, after reviewing all of the research literature, has recently identified five highly negative consequences of violence in the media:

1. Media violence produces a "social script" that encourages violence. In short, it *teaches* violent behavior by dramatizing specific cues, circumstances, situations that the viewer begins to interpret as appropriate for violent action or reaction.
2. The preponderance of media violence is producing an overall shift in social attitude toward increasingly aggressive behavior.
3. Media preoccupation with violence is making the public more accepting of higher levels of violence and thus less effective in combating it.
4. Media portrayals of violence are desensitizing the public to violence.
5. Typical media portrayals of violence fail to show the consequences of that violence. Nor are the real roots of violence often, if ever, explored. Violent acts are thus trivialized.

Newton Minnow, while serving as chairman of the Federal Communications Commission during the administration of John F. Kennedy, called American television "a vast wasteland." Now, more than thirty years later, as a director of Communications Policy Studies at Northwestern University, Minnow says, "In 1961, I worried that my children would not benefit much from television; today I worry that my grandchildren will actually be harmed by it."

"Children come home from school, often to empty homes, and television is their major interchange with what is going on in the world," Marvin O. Kolb, M.D., said at a recent national meeting of the American Academy of Pediatrics. "To kids, everything looks real and with cumulative exposure, there is an increasing tendency to see violence as the norm."

"There is a distinct link between viewing violence and . . . overall violent behavior among children," states Dr. Deborah Prothrow-Stith, former Massachusetts Commissioner of Public Health and now an assistant dean at the Harvard School of Public Health. "We portray violence like we used to portray smoking, as the hip thing to do." In *Deadly Consequences*, her book about youth violence, Dr. Prothrow-Stith writes: "The violence . . . children see on television tells them that the violence in which they live is expected and normal—when in fact it is neither."

While there are signs that television programming is gradually becoming *less* violent for adults, the opposite trend prevails for children. George Gerbner, professor of communications at the University of Pennsylvania, recently reported that there are now twenty to twenty-five violent acts per hour of children's daytime programming compared with six per hour in evening adult fare. Another study reveals that television, in a recently surveyed twelve-month period, devoted 27 hours per week to violent war cartoons, up sharply from just 90 minutes per week in 1982.

Illinois psychiatrist Thomas Radecki, chairman of the National Coalition on Television Violence, notes that the other media are at fault, as well. One random survey of children 5 to 7 showed that 20 percent had seen the highly violent film *Nightmare on Elm Street*. Radecki's organization also reported that, prior to 1950, only 15 percent of all best-selling children's books had distinctly violent themes; now nearly 80 percent do, according to Coalition findings.

It's little wonder that so many children and adolescents suffer from what Dr. Gerbner has called "the mean-world syndrome." Children don't have the "real-world" perspective with which to make sense of the disproportionate coverage the media give to violence. And parents, increasingly, are not present to help provide that perspective or, having been "raised" by a TV surrogate parent themselves, lack any useful perspective on the issue.

A growing number of experts attribute escalating TV violence directed at the young to deregulation and a further weakening of the Federal Communications Commission under the Reagan and Bush administrations. Powerless as the FCC has become to regulate TV programming, it's perhaps understandable that one FCC chairman, in the 1980s, would say that "a television set is merely a toaster with pictures."

There are signs, however, of a trend toward more meaningful regulatory efforts. This trend is, in effect, a backlash against the government's "free-market" approach to television programming, an approach that is, more and more, viewed as a capitulation to those who would exploit the youth market at any cost to society.

FURY: More Violent/Less Violent?

In 1990 the PTA and organizations specifically concerned about the effects on children of TV violence joined forces to push the Children's Television Act through Congress. The bill mandates increased educational programming for children and, in effect, reduces the amount of time that can be reserved for violent programming. The bill has teeth: stations that don't comply can lose their licenses. The legislation also makes the youth market less attractive to those who would exploit it by limiting the allowable number of commercial minutes per hour to no more than 12 on weekdays and 10½ on weekends. The debate on media violence has escalated recently as Congress recognized the need for moderation in violent television programming.

Another hopeful sign is the emergence of evidence that it doesn't take violence to sell products. Contrary to what some programmers believe, or at any rate claim, Americans do not *crave* violence. In fact, Gerbner and other researchers are finding that people have to be *conditioned* over a period of time in order to be able to tolerate today's high levels of media violence. Most people have an actual reaction of *distaste*, often bordering on nausea, to initial exposures to violence. Continuing exposure gradually results in desensitization and tolerance. This phenomenon is reminiscent of these lines from Alexander Pope's *Essay on Man*:

> Vice is a monster of so frightful mien,
> As, to be hated, needs but to be seen;
> Yet seen too oft, familiar with her face,
> We first endure, then pity, then embrace.

The assumption that "violence sells" is being challenged by such research scientists as Christine Hall Hansen and Ronald D. Hansen, who have recently reported (in the journal *Communications Research*) that even though sex (provided it isn't too explicit) does help sell music videos, violence does not: "The hypothesis that violent imagery augments the appeal of the music and visual content of music videos . . . was not supported. In fact, data analyses supported the opposite conclusion—violence diminishes appeal." They discovered, in their experiments with several hundred students, that "increasing the level of violence decreased the appeal of both music and visual content." Adding sex to highly violent videos did not help.

Perhaps the marketers of these videos will begin to ask the same question with which these researchers conclude their findings: "Why is there violence in rock music videos at all?"

Television programmers, at least those who program for adults, have already discovered that it doesn't take violence to hold viewer attention and sell products. Media critics have been giving TV better marks over the past few years. During the same period, however, big-screen critics have been giving the movies increasingly lower marks. TV is seen as finally beginning to take advantage of its ability to more quickly and specifically focus on important social issues and to respond more effectively to the needs and desires of better-defined audiences.

As John J. O'Connor, writing in *The New York Times*, notes:

> Television is far more likely than any current movie to grapple with pressing realities, from domestic abuse to the homeless to AIDS. . . . As the opportunities for "serious" work in film are being pushed aside in the rush to blockbuster formulas, a growing number of name actors and directors are using television as an alternative outlet for their talent. . . . One thing would seem certain. A significant sea change has taken place in popular culture. It is now the typical Hollywood film that is becoming pointless and forgettable. And it is television that is showing distinct signs of being provocative and, on occasion, memorable. The old pecking order is very much on the verge of collapse.

Newton Minnow said: "A new generation now has the chance to put the vision back into television and to travel from the wasteland to the promised land."

But will the gradual changes in perception we've been discussing be enough to deliver us to that "promised land," or is the only ticket legislated regulation of television—and perhaps other media as well? There are signs that defenders of First Amendment rights are increasingly of the opinion that "violence is the real pornography," and the same sort of legal proscriptions that apply to pornography will be directed toward media portrayals of violence as well, and especially toward those that are judged to be devoid of "redeeming social value." Movement in that direction has begun and can be expected to intensify over the next two decades.

Are There Any Real Solutions to Crime and Violence?

There are many innovative programs being proposed today to deal with crime and violence, more than ever in the wake of the Los Angeles Riots of 1992 and with each new violent event. But can any of them work?

After all, in the 1960s, weren't there all kinds of grand proposals being considered that were supposed to solve a number of our social ills? And what good came of those? Very little, it's true—but not because they were all fatally flawed. The best of them showed some remarkable results, but they had barely gotten off the ground when funding for them dried up after reports in the late sixties and early seventies that youth violence was rising rapidly. It was time, the policymakers declared, to get "tough" again. And so, after only the briefest of pauses, it was back to prisons and more prisons. Some concerns about due process were set aside, and the juvenile perpetrators of violent crimes were, for all practical purposes, treated as if they were adult offenders. This process was further enhanced by reviews in some of the research literature that obligingly affirmed that rehabilitation was a failed concept.

Now, some twenty years later, we've come full circle. The dogma that "nothing works" is under increasing attack for its glaring failure to provide something that *does* work. Reassessment is rampant. Conservative and liberal criminologists alike are calling for innovation. Meanwhile, the scientific community is finding more and more evidence that experimental programs can work if given adequate time and support. Some of the same journals that carried the antirehabilitation reports are now publishing carefully documented repudiations of those reports.

Jeffrey Fagan of Rutgers University, supported by a United States Department of Justice grant, is among those who have reviewed the literature related to intervention and rehabilitation. Writing in the journal *Criminal Justice and Behavior*, he concludes,

> the nothing-works doctrine and the delinquency policies that flow from it are unfounded. . . . Ironically, the nothing-works critique itself is methodologically flawed. It was based on claims of ineffectiveness that were, in fact, problems in evaluation research. . . . When the strongest studies in these reviews are examined, the trends in treatment effectiveness appear consistently strong among those studies that used control groups and careful implementation analysis; more than half revealed positive treatment effects.

The programs that worked best, Fagan found,

> shared important characteristics: They were small, community-based projects with intensive supervision and reintegration efforts. In addition, they were developed and studied with a variety of correctional populations, in diverse areas of the country, and in varying social and economic contexts.

We have already discussed the problems of continuing with the present (more-prisons) approach. And as mentioned previously, theoretical obstacles to innovation are now being cleared away by more thoughtful studies and reappraisal of old studies and findings. After two decades of virtual stasis, the trend is moving from "nothing works" to "some things *do* work."

Lynn A. Curtis, president of the Eisenhower Foundation, states: "We need to implement what is already successful. We know what works. The reality is, we don't need any more demonstration projects." What works won't come cheap, he concedes, but what *isn't* working, he says, is costing us more.

Curtis joins a steadily growing number of influential individuals who are debating our present approach to dealing with crime. "Our national policy for at-risk youth," he told reporters, "is prison building. In many ways, our prison policy has become our national housing policy for the poor." And with prison cells now often costing $100,000 each, he notes, it's an enormously expensive policy.

"An indictment of a civilized nation," is how Charles Ogletree, professor of law at Harvard University, characterizes "the fact that we are spending $7 billion a year to incarcerate black males and less than 10 percent of that amount educating black males."

However reluctant as a society we may be to do so, we are now being forced to look for the *roots* of the crime problem in an effort to find genuine solutions. TEEN VIOLENCE RAMPANT IN U.S.; PANEL'S REPORT ON UNITED STATES YOUTHS GRIM; STUDY FINDS AMERICA'S CHILDREN IN TROUBLE, read the headlines. One group after another is reporting on the dire circumstances faced by many of America's young people. A panel convened by the National Association of State Boards of Education has documented the sharply declining material prospects of today's youth, its declining physical and mental health, its increasing involvement in crime, suicide, drug abuse, early pregnancy. Without "immediate action," the panel warns, we are at risk of a collapsing economy and unprecedented social unrest.

A recent study by the National Association of Social Workers notes that the deterioration of the traditional family is proceeding at a rate even more rapid than expected, resulting in, among other things, more runaway and "throwaway" children. In previous surveys, most children taking refuge in the shelters had come directly from home. In a later survey, however, 11 percent were living on the streets before going to shelters. And 38 percent had been living in foster facilities prior to running away. Additionally, the study finds that the reasons children run away are becoming more serious. Two thirds have been sexually and/or physically abused by one or both parents. One in three has an alcoholic parent. One in four has a drug-abusing parent.

In another study, the results of which were recently published in *Science,* Stanford University economics professor Victor Fuchs and Diane M. Reklis of the National Bureau of Economic Research, also cite the deterioration of family as one of the root causes of youth violence. But they also highlight a trend, one that began in the 1980s, toward diminished government spending on goods and services for children and youths. And the reduction is quite significant.

Today's youth are thus seen as twice vulnerable: they are being abandoned both by their families and by the state. In 1960 only 7 percent of all households lacked the presence of an adult male. Today nearly 20 percent of all children in the United States are in homes without an adult male.

An editorial in the *Boston Globe,* 29 April 1991, called for new commitment to youth:

> There was a time when families and extended families—neighbors and shopkeepers, churches and community groups—formed a natural network to provide counselling and guidance to youths, directed them to opportunity and help and steered them away from trouble and violence. But in urban America those days are gone. The broader society—through the agency of government—must now shoulder those tasks.

Government must play a vital role. But there is no need for *more* government, just better government more effectively allocating funds that are presently being wasted in ineffective service programs. At the same time, the *private* sector needs to play a greater role. Indeed, as we shall see, there is already a trend toward greater private-sector involvement.

Programs That Work: Prevention

Not long ago, plagued and prodded by the epidemic of youth violence, Boston's public school officials, its police and its city leaders convened a forum of young people from across the city and asked them what *they* thought would help. Typical of the responses was: "One way [to] prevent kids from getting involved in gangs is by giving us something to do. We need more adults taking an interest in us. We need to feel like we belong, like we're important."

Many adults are surprised by such statements. Even many well-educated, affluent parents have come to believe that their children don't want their advice or support, that they want more distance, not more closeness. But youth workers across the nation are increasingly reporting the same thing: that kids are literally crying out for more input from parents and other adults in their lives.

In Boston, the Winners' Circle program, which has been embraced by several of the city's schools, provides youths with an extended family that is an attractive alternative to gang life. The Winners' Circle concept helps remove barriers between young and old. In this program, students can meet regularly with their peers and representatives of the community, police officials, teachers, administrators and social workers to discuss and deal with problems they may be having at home, school or in the community. Student-service coordinators set up meetings in order to regularly monitor the mental and physical health of the students.

Though still in its infancy, the program is proving to be cost effective. The program has helped reduce drug traffic and is diminishing the need for special education—which is particularly expensive—by making sure that students get the most out of their regular classes.

Even relatively simple, adult-supervised recreation programs have proven to be very helpful in curbing violence, especially in high-crime areas. Savings in reduced vandalism, fire damage and police time more than make up for the costs of such programs.

In Los Angeles County, where there are an estimated 900 gangs with at least 100,000 members, a pilot program called the Community Reclamation Project is making gains in even the roughest neighborhoods by involving the business community, schools and law-enforcement agencies in providing *in-home* counseling to both parents and children and recreation and job-training opportunities for youth. Sometimes the most effective measure is to provide training and jobs for the *parents* of troubled youths rather than for the youths themselves. Working parents make better role models and tend to guide their children more effectively, perhaps because they command more respect.

In Portland, Oregon, a number of business leaders have joined with social workers and city leaders to meet with gang members and provide training and jobs through the private sector. This effort is resulting in less crime in targeted areas, which, in turn, makes for a better business climate in those areas.

In Columbus, Ohio, a program that began in one of the most crime-ridden housing projects in the nation was so successful in stemming violence and drug traffic that it was adopted by the state government. A key element of this program is to provide *male* educators, counselors and mentors for troubled youths, many of whom come from fatherless homes. The program, called New Directions, is a worthy model for many other inner cities.

Some other violence-prevention projects that have been notably successful include Positive, Inc., in Miami, Florida, Safe Streets in Los Angeles and the Boys and Girls Clubs of America.

Peaceful conflict resolution is now being taught in selected schools in more than 300 cities in 45 states—thanks in large part to a curriculum created by Dr. Deborah Prothrow-Stith, whose work was discussed earlier. The curriculum makes the ability to be able to resolve a disagreement without physical violence an achievement. The program encourages honest communication and emphasizes exercises to bolster self-esteem and the independence to resist destructive peer pressures. It also offers peer and adult arbitrators and, when needed, individual counseling.

One of the seemingly most radical youth-oriented innovations is actually one of the most effective and sensible: the abolishment of much of the class structure in schools. Instead of grouping children together in the standard classes that are governed by age, classes in these new schools are comprised of students who have *similar abilities and needs.* Classes are based upon various levels of ability in reading, spelling, math, etc. Children of various ages intermingle in these classes, working on whatever they require at levels they can most productively handle. The results are nothing short of spectacular.

Interestingly, parents do not think it at all odd for infants to progress at strikingly different rates, walking and talking at markedly different ages. But once children are in school, adults suddenly expect them all to conform, uniformly progressing through each stage of learning according solely to their ages. A not so wise—and potentially destructive—expectation if you think about it. It places a heavy burden on both teacher and student alike and can result in a need for additional, expensive, special education.

Schools that have experimented with the new system are finding that it has both social and academic advantages. Not only do children learn more efficiently but they also develop better socially and psychologically. The new system, because it is more attuned to the specific needs and abilities of each student, results in far less frustration and failure. Students are not stigmatized by being held back or channeled into slower paced courses as they often are now when lockstep expectations prove too much for them at a particular stage in their development. Discipline and dropout problems are diminished for the same reasons and because often destructive peer pressures are minimized in multiage classes.

The prototype of this promising new school system is Paint Branch Elementary in College Park, Maryland, a suburb of Washington, D.C. It has been operating for several years now, and student scores there have risen steadily since the program began, causing many other schools in the area and elsewhere, in Kentucky for example, to copy the Paint Branch approach. The ripple effect, in fact, is now international. Several countries are studying the system, and the Canadian province of British Columbia has decided to use the Paint Branch system in all of its elementary schools.

What makes the Paint Branch experience even more impressive is the fact that its students are mostly poor and minority. Yet they are performing at levels well in advance of students in even some of the most affluent, majority communities. By the time they are at the age of fourth graders in traditional schools, almost half of the students at Paint Branch are working at sixth- through eighth-grade levels. Reading skills are superior to those achieved in most other schools despite the fact that less than half the usual time is devoted to teaching them!

Contrast what is happening at Paint Branch with what is developing at many other schools, including many elementary schools. The general atmosphere, tainted by gunfire drills, metal detectors to turn back gun-toting students and breathalyzer tests, is scarcely conducive to learning or teaching. One can understand why parents, teachers and law-enforcement officials are ripe for innovation in our schools—a trend that bodes well for education and for the welfare of our young people.

Programs That Can Work: Intervention

The innovations discussed above are largely preventive in nature. What of those youths who are already in prison? Can they be returned, productively, to society and at reasonable cost?

Jeffrey Fagan, whose work was noted earlier, has designed a rigorously tested program that stands an excellent chance of becoming one of the effective interventive models. Its success in significantly cutting recidivism rates is especially impressive because the test subjects were selected from the most violent young offenders in the nation—those incarcerated for murder, assault, rape and armed robbery.

Emphasis is placed upon *graduated* reentry into society in what is called the Violent Juvenile Offender (VJO) Program. The program establishes a series of "security levels" through which the offender passes, gradually getting more freedom as he simultaneously achieves—and demonstrates—better community-living skills. The VJO provides intense supervision and reentry training.

A detailed cost analysis of the VJO reveals that it could result in substantial savings. It reallocates funds from what Fagan calls "the front end of the correctional process [secure care] to latter stages of correctional intervention—return to the community." An important benefit of this approach is enhanced public safety. The present system spends very little on preparing prisoners for a productive return to the community. Almost all of the money is spent on merely keeping prisoners locked up until their sentences are served; then they are dumped back into society with little meaningful supervision, and the recidivism rate is enormous. The public is exposed to offenders who offend again, endangering public safety.

The results of such programs as the VJO argue for getting on with rehabilitative intervention *as soon as possible.* There will always be the need for long-term incarceration of *some* offenders, but, for most, just "doing time" produces, if anything, only a negative return on investment.

Here's a sampling of some other interventive trends.

There are signs that prison populations may begin to get more effective treatment for drug problems. A start has been made in the federal prisons, where there are an estimated 27,000 inmates with serious drug-abuse problems. The General Accounting Office a few years ago criticized the United States Bureau of Prisons for not fully utilizing a congressionally funded intensive-treatment program. This criticism resulted in an easing of restrictions governing entry into the program and paved the way for an expansion of it in the future. The federal program is also having the effect of calling attention to the estimated 500,000 *state* prisoners with serious drug problems. Currently, less than 20 percent of those are receiving any kind of treatment preparatory to release.

Interventive treatment for rapists and other sex offenders promises to become big business in the coming two decades. Sex offenders now constitute a "growth industry," occupying 20 percent of all prison space, up from just a few percentage points of the total prison population two decades ago. This is a category of crime in which repeat offenses are particularly commonplace. Incarceration alone, as a "treatment" option, is a glaring failure. Since 1985, the average time served for rape has more than doubled. Nearly two out of three sex offenders, including rapists, repeat their crimes—*unless* they have interventive treatment. With such treatment, recent research indicates, that number can be reduced to one in three. Unfortunately, large numbers of sex offenders refuse treatment even though they are institutionalized.

Interventive treatment programs are rapidly evolving, both in the private and public sectors. Clinics to treat both sexual offenders and their victims may, within a decade, be almost as prevalent as drug and alcohol clinics are today. As James Parent, a Multnomah County (Oregon) parole officer, observes, "More and more people are finding sex offenders a lucrative business." Both Oregon and Washington state are already formulating licensing requirements to handle these rapidly emerging enterprises.

Treatment options, which continue to be refined, focus on efforts to get the offenders to acknowledge and understand the nature of their crimes and the consequences of their acts. Emotional reeducation efforts stress anger control. Some clinics utilize "aversion" therapy, associating harmful sexual behavior with unpleasant images and sensations. Some argue that the cost of these therapies—$2,000 to $5,000 per year per offender—is too high. But compared with putting the offender back in prison at another approximately $20,000 per year, the therapy appears cost effective. Other objections come from some civil rights leaders who consider aversion therapies inhumane.

Interventive measures are also becoming more effective in the realm of domestic violence. Shelters for "battered spouses," though still badly underfunded, are becoming more prevalent. Some are offering more sophisticated and intensive counseling than in the past. As national alarm over domestic violence grows, so will funding for prevention and intervention. Researchers working in this area have begun to recognize that previous efforts at treating those who commit domestic violence often failed because too much was expected too soon. A brief shot of therapy is not going to change an abusive male's behavior. Increasingly, the model for treatment will be the model used for substance abusers, incorporating measures that recognize the potential for relapse and including support groups and long-term maintenance therapy.

A Domestic Peace Corps: A National Program of Emotional Reeducation

There is an apparent confluence of opinion among many innovators that no matter how well certain programs might work, something *more* is needed. Many of these men and women speak in terms of bandaging one wound only to have the patient bleed to death from another. There is the feeling by some that our entire social fabric is unraveling and that isolated patchwork repairs, no matter how strong they may be, can't stitch it all back together again.

There's a trend to the belief that a comprehensive plan is needed. As our traditional center—the family—falls away, the resulting vacuum is filled with desperate efforts to find something to secure and sustain ourselves.

Barry Glick and Arnold P. Goldstein, writing in the *Journal of Counseling and Development*, worry that a program they have developed called Aggressive Replacement Training (ART) will not be as effective in the community as in an institutional setting. ART shows good results in changing the attitudes of assaultive youths "inside," but what will happen "outside"?

They recognize that violence is symptomatic of deeper societal ills—and that the problem of crime and violence cannot effectively be dealt with until we concomitantly deal with those underlying ills. These researchers, like many others, are suggesting, in effect, that significant sectors of the community at large, not just its overtly criminal elements, need to learn or relearn certain basics that used to be taught in families and close-knit communities.

ART is an intensive ten-week program of structured emotional learning and moral reasoning. It teaches how to constructively express a complaint, how to respond to the feelings of others (develop empathy), how to prepare for a stressful conversation, respond to anger, keep out of fights, help others, deal with accusations and group pressures, express affection and respond to failure. In each of these learning situations, the student is presented with hypothetical situations and dilemmas in which he or she is encouraged to develop reasoning ability and anger control. ART is a prototypical program of emotional reeducation of the sort that might effectively, many believe, be applied to entire communities.

Similarly, those on the leading edge of suicide treatment prevention and intervention are in agreement that the only real solution to the problem of suicide among children and adolescents is a comprehensive approach to juvenile mental and physical health. This is the view as well of the National Association of State Boards of Education and the American Medical Association.

Domestic violence has particularly devastating and long-lasting effects on the children who witness it or are the direct victims of it. Here, too, a number of influential groups are beginning to call for community-based intervention through new forms of the "extended family," such as the Winners' Circle program in Boston. Peter G. Jaffe and collaborators, writing in the *Canadian Journal of Psychiatry*, have reported that a secondary-school curriculum that teaches how to be aware of and respond to this form of violence can help prevent it. Teenagers, entering their first intimate relationships outside the family, they report, are particularly receptive to these new programs.

In Los Angeles, the demand is growing for more community and parental accountability for youthful offenders. Captain Ray Gott, a Los Angeles County sheriff, says, "Juvenile courts should really be family courts, with power to order parental training, drug or alcohol treatment and to hold parents accountable."

Those concerned about the effects of media violence seem particularly aware of the need for broader interventive measures. Comstock and Strasburger wrote:

> Clearly, the effect of exposure to TV violence is amenable to intervention and remedy. Effective interventions can focus either on increasing the undesirability of such behavior, or increasing knowledge and skepticism about the medium. The key ingredients, however, are making TV *less relevant* to the young viewer and making the young viewer *less susceptible* to TV. Education and training—by parents, schools, the PTA and pediatricians—are the only plausible solutions.

Harry M. Hoberman of the University of Minnesota, writing in the *Journal of Adolescent Health Care*, has similarly called for bolder, more comprehensive solutions to deal with the adverse effects of media violence and other youth problems:

> Ideally, a family based system for cultivating media literacy would be the primary means of remedying links between media experiences and their implications for children. However, significant changes in American society have occurred. Almost two thirds of mothers are in the work force; rarely is a parent home during the

> day to interact with children generally, and, particularly, in regard to the viewing of media. Moreover, those families most affected by these changes are those least likely to have the resources to provide their children with an environment that would most effectively mediate violent media portrayals. *Thus, given the realities of the current American family, a universal child-care system is both desirable and necessary*. [Emphasis added]. A central component of such a system should be the careful attempt to develop critical viewing skills in children of all ages; perhaps adolescents could even be involved as teachers of active viewing skills for younger children. To this end, a strong recommendation is made for a national commission to develop a model of a universal child-care system and to advocate for its establishment.

Hoberman suggests that all youth workers be educated in the effects of media violence. Such training, he says, should become a requirement for teacher certification. And "adolescents," he adds, "particularly those in parenting classes, should be educated as to the essential components of active, critical viewing."

In the quest for the most comprehensive and effective measures to help inoculate our society against violence, leaders like Lynn A. Curtis of the Eisenhower Foundation point to Head Start and the Job Corps as exemplary programs. Curtis asserts that Head Start is the single most effective crime-prevention program in operation today, followed by the Job Corps. These programs have survived since the 1960s because they work so well. The Job Corps provides occupational training for disadvantaged youths and has an excellent record of placing them in real jobs, undoubtedly diverting many from lives of crime. Head Start focuses on children ages 3 to 5 of low-income parents or parent. It is a program of educational, health and home counseling that better prepares children for school and helps parents get better training and a job. So far it has served more than 11 million youngsters. Many want to see the program expanded, not only to provide more services for its present target population but to extend many of the same services and innovations into elementary schools.

Many of the benefits of Head Start (which one study indirectly suggests could include as much as $6 saved by society for every $1 spent on such programs) are diluted by problems in the traditional school system, continued exposure to poverty, drugs, crime, broken families. In any case, the benefits of Head Start to the child, to whom the program is often available for only a year, cannot realistically be sustained indefinitely. At present, fewer than 20 percent of the nation's disadvantaged preschoolers get into the program at all because of funding limitations.

Economists studying the situation say it will take $5 billion to $10 billion per year to make Head Start available to every child who needs it. Extending many of the same services into elementary and perhaps even secondary schools would add to that cost considerably—but the evidence suggests the savings in crime averted, poor health prevented, domestic violence diminished, teen pregnancies reduced, drug-and-alcohol abuse lessened, productive employment increased and business enhanced would far more than cover these expenditures.

One hopeful sign is the interest that business and government are now taking in these programs. IBM and others, for example, have begun providing computer-based Head Start instruction to make the material more accessible, not only to children but to their parents, who often have to work throughout the day but can now avail themselves of the instruction at night or on weekends.

In addition, many state governments are now looking for—and beginning to find—ways of coming up with local funding for extended programs. In New York City, for example, most of the city's elementary schools have embraced a highly successful program called Growing Healthy that incorporates some of Head Start's best ideas. It is funded through a unique partnership of public and private interests, including Blue Cross/Blue Shield, several private foundations and a number of major corporations. It was set up jointly by the New York City Board of Education and the New York Academy of Medicine.

Inspired by the success of such innovations, however fragmented, social planners are talking of the need for what would amount to a national program to enhance and safeguard the mental and physical health of all Americans, a program of emotional reeducation, a "domestic Peace Corps" to salvage that inner core of tranquility and security that is a primary need and *break* the violence chain.

TWO

The Sexes

Better Relationships/ Worse Relationships?

THE TREND The Sexual Revolution, which went into high gear in the 1960s and 1970s, only to decelerate (but less than most thought) in the shadow of AIDS in the 1980s, will resume speed into the twenty-first century. The major trend continues to be away from reproductive sexuality toward psychological sexuality, i.e., the use of sex for physical pleasure and emotional intimacy, as well as for commercial or motivational ends. Periods of sexual excess, symptomatic of a cultural process that seeks to shrug off persistent inhibitions rooted in distinctly American tradition, will produce corresponding but temporary pauses in American society's progress toward greater sexual disinhibition. As the revolution matures over the next two decades, Americans will continue to become more sexually tolerant and diverse, and the politics of sex will continue to shift from sexism to "equal rights." The "gender gap" has become an issue in the political arena, and now science, medicine and psychology are joining forces with the new men's and women's movements in an unprecedented effort to create a genuine gender "détente" characterized by enhanced cross-gender communications. Those who decry the "death of romance" and the "emptiness" of nonprocreative sex will be preempted by those who welcome the overthrow of conventions that enforced gender stereotypes and stifled male-female communication.

Ironically, satisfying relationships will *appear* more difficult to come by in the next two decades than at any time in human history because the "language of love" will be more exacting, more precise than ever before. Women especially—but men in increasing numbers, too—will no longer readily tolerate the *illusion* of communication that has characterized, and made miserable, so many relationships in the past. Those who master cross-gender literacy are likely to enjoy the most satisfying relationships humans can achieve. Sexual détente will be further abetted by the aging—and concomitant androgynizing—of the population, diminishing many of the biological and psychological dys-synchronies that have impeded intimacy between the sexes.

Overview

The Sexual Revolution: An Interrupted Journey?

If you're confused by what you read and hear about sex these days, little wonder. Consider this sampling of magazine and newspaper headlines, all written in the "AIDS era": "Drop-in Casual Sex Tied to AIDS Peril: 33% of Unmarried Women in Federal Study Say Threat Has Curbed Behavior"; "College Women Surveyed About Sex: Students as Active as '75 Counterparts"; "The Rate of Teen-Agers Reporting Sexual Activity Has Increased"; "The End of Sex"; "The Spread of Sex and the Demise of Romance in the America of Our Times"; "A Nation in Love with Love"; "The 1950s Revisited: Romance Will Be Back in Favor, and So Will Flowers and Similar Gifts"; "Prosecute Porn? It's on the Decline"; "Smut Out of Rut, Defying Its Foes: Quality Up, and Hardcore, Like Kidvid, Accounts for 20% of Vidstore Income."

One thing is certain: interest in sex, judging by media attention, is at an all-time high. Sex gets more ink every year.

Has the Sexual Revolution been interrupted—sidetracked by herpes, AIDS and the "return to traditional values" we keep hearing about? In a word, no.

In a survey of sex researchers and their findings, Curt Suplee, writing in *The Washington Post* (SEX IN THE '90S), notes:

> No idea obsessed America's election-year psyche like the noisily touted "return to family values," with its implied promise of kinder, gentler sex lives in the years to come. Conjugal cocooning and dread of AIDS, we were told, were combining to create a

> daydream decade of sensible sex, marital stability and babies-on-board. . . . But . . . these may be the most misbegotten prognoses since the Great Herpes Panic of '82, when *Time*'s cover story predicted that the gregarious virus would bring "a grudging chastity back into fashion" and help "bring to a close an era of mindless promiscuity." Several billion random copulations later, the obituary seems somewhat premature. So do the latest Pollyanna forecasts.

The forces that originally fueled the Sexual Revolution are all still in place and, if anything, are intensifying: mobility, democratization, urbanization, women in the workplace, birth control, abortion and other reproductive interventions and media proliferation of sexual images, ideas and variation. Sexuality has moved for many citizens from a church- and state-regulated behavior to a medical- and self-regulated behavior. Population pressures and other economic factors continue to diminish the size of the American family. Marriage is in sharp decline, cohabitation is growing, traditional families are on the endangered list and the single-person household is a wave of the future (for details on all of these trends see the following chapter).

AIDS has generated a great deal of heat in the media but appears to have done little, so far, to turn down the heat in the bedroom. Some people speculated that when the federal government, through Health and Human Services Secretary Otis R. Bowen, announced at the end of the 1980s that "we don't have the fear of the breakout danger [of AIDS] into the heterosexual population that we once had" the party started anew. But, although "safe sex" became a watchword, there's evidence that the party never ended—except among homosexual males, many of whom dramatically altered their behavior in response to an epidemic that hit that group particularly hard.

It is true that in some surveys people *claimed* to have made drastic changes in behavior—but most telling are the statistics relating to marriage, divorce, cohabitation, teen sex, out-of-wedlock births, sexually transmitted diseases (STDs), contraception, adultery and sexual counseling. These are far more revealing of what we *do* than what we *say* we do. And these tell a tale of what has been called a "postmarital society" in continued pursuit of sexual individuality and freedom.

Arguably, there are, due to AIDS, fewer visible sexual "excesses" today than there were in the late 1960s and into the 1970s, but those excesses (sex clubs, bathhouses, "backrooms," "swinging singles," group sex, public sex acts, etc.) were never truly reflective of norms and were, in any case, greatly inflated in the media. Meanwhile, quietly and without fanfare, the public, even in the face of the AIDS threat, has continued to expand its interest in sex and in increased, rather than decreased, sexual expression.

Numerous studies reveal that women are "more sexual" now than at any time in the century. Whereas sex counselors used to deal with men's complaints about their wives' lack of "receptivity," it is now more often the women complaining about the men. And women, in this "postfeminist" era, are doing things they never used to believe were "proper." Fellatio, for example, was seldom practiced (or admitted to) when Kinsey conducted his famous sex research several decades ago. Since that time, according to studies at UCLA and elsewhere, this activity has gained acceptance among women, with some researchers reporting that nearly all young women now practice fellatio.

Some women—especially younger women—are committing adultery as often, or even more often, than their husbands. Women's images of themselves have changed dramatically in the past two decades due, in large part, to their movement into the workplace and roles previously filled exclusively by men. As Lilian Rubin, psychologist at the University of California Institute for the Study of Social Change and author of *Intimate Strangers*, puts it, "Women feel empowered sexually in a way they never did in the past."

A recent federal study revealed that at least half of all teenagers are having sexual intercourse and by the twelfth grade more than 70 percent have had sex. Another study, this one of a rural area, found that even by the eighth grade, 61 percent of the boys and 47 percent of the girls had had sexual intercourse. These percentages are up sharply from past decades. Attitudes among the young are changing profoundly, signaling the opening of a new chapter in the Sexual Revolution that some will find disturbing and others will view as a harbinger of healthier attitudes to come.

Some have attempted to attribute increased sexual activity among young people, in the presence of AIDS, to ignorance and declining educational standards. But sexual activity has remained high among well-educated college students, as well. Indeed, as the 1980s came to a close, studies showed that this activity was just as high as it was during the so-called promiscuous seventies. One thing that *has* changed is the increase in the regular use of condoms, up sharply since 1975.

In "Twenty Years of the Sexual Revolution, 1965–1985: An Update" (*Journal of Marriage and the Family*), researcher Ira Robinson and collaborators report, with respect to sexual behavior and attitudes, a "continuing liberalization for both males and females, with the larger shift for females." They note only one exception to this trend—a disapproving attitude toward promiscuity, particularly female promiscuity. This restatement of the sexual double standard needs further scrutiny, however, because, as some other, more recent studies have made evident, we are redefining, as a society, just what we mean by "promiscuity." In one of the studies of teen sexuality, for example, a similar disapproval was voiced. But, among these teenagers, "promiscuity" no longer had as much to do with numbers as with intention. If the intention was to have a relationship—even if it turned out to last only a weekend—then sex was not viewed as promiscuous. Additionally, it appears that certain activities, including oral sex, are no longer considered "heavy" enough to justify the "promiscuous" label, whatever their frequency.

Meanwhile, the "singles scene," far from fading away (the media just lost its fixation on this subject), continues to grow. James Bennet, writing in *The New Republic*, aptly characterizes this growing population of nonreproducers thus: "Single adults in America display a remarkable tendency to multiply without being fruitful." In a decade, their number grew from 47 million to 68 million, and there are now approximately 2,000 dating services catering to them.

Their libidos are the target of million-dollar advertising budgets and entrepreneurial pursuits that seek to put those sex drives "on line" in the information age. There are 800 lines, 900 lines, etc., that incorporate "voice mail," computerized personal ads, "live talk" all directed toward connecting singles (or those who pretend to be single). There are services specifically for Christian singles, college students, gays, lesbians, senior citizens, those looking for romance, those looking for quick sex, those interested in "domination" and a dizzying spectrum of fetishes. From singles bars to video dating to computer coupling to erotic FAXing, it's now "love at first byte," as one commentator put it.

One thing is certain: the computer is doing as much today to promote the Sexual Revolution as the automobile did at the dawn of that revolution. The automobile, which was once called "the portable bedroom," now gets a powerful assist from the electronic matchmaker and the extensive use of sex in mass marketing.

The evidence that "sex sells" continues to accumulate and to be exploited by advertisers and marketers of all kinds. Sexually oriented programming continues to proliferate in the media, and the sales of erotica and pornography (and computer-generated porn), recently declared in permanent decline, are actually going up. Sexual fantasy is another growth industry, one that will soon be boosted by such technological innovations as "virtual reality," which will generate increasingly sophisticated computer-driven and simulated experiences, including experiences some are calling "cybersex" and "virtual sex."

Political ideologies, buttressed by economic adversities, can *temporarily* retard the Sexual Revolution, as can sexually transmitted diseases. But ultimately the forces propelling this revolution are unstoppable. And ironically, AIDS itself is probably doing more to promote than impede this movement. It has forced the nation to confront a number of sexual issues with greater frankness than ever before. While some conservatives and many religious groups have argued for "abstinence" as the only "moral" response to AIDS, others have lobbied for wider dissemination of sexual information, beginning in grade schools. A number of school districts are now making condoms available to students, a development that would have been unthinkable before the outbreak of AIDS.

A recent Roper poll reveals that 81 percent of those questioned agree that "it might take some pretty explicitly sexual material to fully inform teenagers" about AIDS risk. Some 64 percent say they believe condoms should be distributed in high schools. Nearly half endorse the distribution of condoms in *junior* high school.

Despite all these "gains"—or "losses," depending upon your outlook—the revolution is far from over. The openness that it has fostered is healthy, but Americans are still ignorant about many aspects of human sexuality. A majority of us still can't pass a simple test of sexual knowledge. The test, prepared by the Kinsey Institute and the Roper Organization, asked such questions as: "A women or teen-age girl can get pregnant during her menstrual flow (her 'period'). True, False, Don't Know?" (The correct answer is True.) Only 45 percent of those taking the test got even passing marks.

Sexual literacy in America is still relatively primitive. Sexual research is needed to help us deal with teen sexuality and pregnancies, AIDS and other sexually transmitted diseases (STDs) and a number of emotional issues related to sexuality. It has been more than forty years since the epochal Kinsey studies were conducted, and, until recently, there has been no in-depth follow-up study.

Research into sexuality, despite its controversial political nature, is critical to an understanding of the dimensions of the issue, especially in the AIDS era. More will be said about this in the last section of this chapter. Suffice it to say for now that there is still plenty of room for the

Sexual Revolution to proceed—and its greatest benefits have yet to be realized.

The Revolution versus Romance

The idea that the Sexual Revolution is at odds with romance (not to mention "tradition") is one that is widely held, even by some of those who endorse many of the revolution's apparent objectives. Back in the early 1980s, consummate social commentator George Leonard wrote a book called *The End of Sex*, in which he stated:

> I want to keep the best of the Sexual Revolution. The new freedom to talk openly about erotic matters is a blessed thing. A few straightforward words can sometimes clear up misunderstandings that would have produced a lifetime of guilt and shame in the devastating silence of times past.

Leonard goes on to applaud the Sexual Revolution for providing an atmosphere in which diversity ("homosexuality, bisexuality, or any other nonexploitive, nonproselytizing erotic preference") could begin to flourish, in which the women's movement could begin its transformative effort to achieve social justice and equality—but then focuses on some "wrong turns" in the Sexual Revolution. Those wrong turns, he says, were made "wherever we have split 'sex' from love, creation and the rest of life, wherever we have trivialized and depersonalized the act of love itself."

A bit more recently, writing in *Saturday Review*, Frank Gannon decried "the demise of romance" in the wake of the Sexual Revolution. He fondly recalls the 1950s as the "dynamically romantic time . . . the days of heavy petting in the back seats of sexy cars to the beat of seminal rock 'n' roll." He laments the developments of the sixties, seventies and eighties. He seems distinctly unhappy that "over the last twenty-five years virtually every barrier has fallen, concerning what can be written, printed or filmed about sex" and that there has sprung up "a cottage industry of sexual advice and explication." He contends that the "rise of feminism also struck a blow to the already reeling romance."

But by way of chilling examples of what all this freedom has wrought, Gannon can only conclude that "today's sexual cutting edge is S&M; today's sexual frontier is androgyny." That was 1985. Since then neither sadomasochism nor androgyny (in the sense Gannon uses the term) has made any inroads into mainstream America. The mid-1980s database is replete with verbiage on androgyny and "gender blending"—mostly occasioned by the success of such pop stars as Michael Jackson, David Bowie, Boy George, Grace Jones, etc.—replete with warnings that by the 1990s boys might no longer clearly be boys, nor girls clearly girls. In this case the media exaggerated transitory phenomena.

There is nothing in our findings to indicate that romance and the Sexual Revolution are inimical—unless one's defense of "romance" disguises an agenda of "traditional" male dominance and the courtly illusion of intimacy and communication between the sexes.

The trend now, as we shall see, is away from illusion and toward—in transition, at least—a sometimes painful reality in which the sexes are finally making an honest effort to *understand* one another. *This* is today's sexual "cutting edge."

The Revolution and Relationships

To some, it may seem that the sexes are farther apart today than they ever have been. The real gender gap, they say, is a communications gap so cavernous that only the most intrepid or foolhardy dare try to bridge it. Many look back at the Anita Hill affair and say that was the open declaration of war between the sexes.

"Where are the men who really like being with women?" asks psychiatrist Robert E. Gould. "There's a sad but simple reason why they seem so scarce," he writes in *Working Woman*: "Most men really don't like women."

At the same time, according to Gary Langer, writing for the Associated Press, "U.S. women increasingly believe most men are mean, manipulative, oversexed, self-centered and lazy." These conclusions are based upon the results of a 1990 Roper Organization poll.

And then there are those provocative Ann Landers surveys to consider. When Landers asked her women readers, "Would you be content to be held close and treated tenderly and forget about 'the act'?" she got nearly 100,000 responses, 72 percent of them opting for intimacy over intercourse, while bitterly complaining about the inadequacies of their relationships with men. Landers astutely concluded that the problem is not that women are "anti-sex" but that they find the ways in which men communicate—or, rather, fail to communicate—with them the real source of dissatisfaction.

This conclusion was further reinforced by the response to another

Landers question to her readers: "Has your sex life gone downhill after marriage?" A staggering 140,000 people answered, 82 percent in the affirmative. "Those who are unfulfilled," Landers summed up, "are describing something beyond the bedroom scene. They are talking about the state of their marriage." Again, too little real communication.

Landers, of course, makes no pretense about conducting scientific social research, but surveys that elicit responses more than one hundred times greater than the samples analyzed by professional pollsters cannot be ignored. Moreover, Landers' results coincide with the findings of many controlled surveys, all of which point to serious problems in communications between the sexes. The mistake many make in interpreting these studies, however, is that there has been a *recent* breakdown in those communications, hence all this new discontent. This conclusion usually goes unchallenged, but there is nothing in the data we have seen from the past several decades to indicate that sexual and gender-related communications were ever better than they are today. On the contrary, a more thoughtful analysis makes it very clear they have always been *worse*.

What has changed—and this is all-important—is our *consciousness* about this issue. Problems in communication between the sexes have been *masked* for decades by a rigid social code that strictly *prescribes* certain behavior while, with equal inclemency, *proscribes* other behavior. Communication between the sexes has long been preprogrammed by this code to produce an exchange that has been as superficial as it is oppressive. As this long-submerged process begins to be exposed by its own inadequacies in a rapidly changing world where attendant and supporting codes are fast eroding, we suddenly discover that we have a "problem." But, of course, that problem was there for a long time, and the discovery does not mean a decline in communications between the sexes, but rather provides us with the potential for better relations in the long run.

Thus what we call a "breakdown" in communications might more aptly be called a *breakthrough*.

Some fascinating research in this context is that of Seymour Parker, professor of anthropology at the University of Utah. Parker demonstrated that men who are the most "mannerly" with women, those who adhere most strictly to the "code" discussed above, are those who most firmly believe, consciously or unconsciously, that women are "both physically and psychologically weaker (i.e., less capable) than men." What has long passed for male "respect" toward women in our society is, arguably, *disrespect*.

Parker's study of 190 undergraduate students (reported upon in *American Anthropologist*) found that what many men regard as "decent," "proper" and "considerate" responses to women actually mask their conviction, exposed in a carefully designed questionnaire, that women are inferior. "One opens the door for a woman because she is weaker than a man, and one treats a woman circumspectly because she is not quite as rational or reliable as a man." This, of course, is not what men *say*; it may not even be what they always consciously *think*; but it is what they have *learned* to believe.

Parker concludes:

> The findings of this study have some implications for the issue of social change. It is clear that etiquette between the sexes has been changing steadily in recent years. The sample of respondents was divided in a way as to lump together, in one group, all those who tend to reject the ritual of gender manners. In what ways are individuals in this low manners group different from the others? Results . . . show that they see relatively little difference between masculinity and femininity, and also are least discomfited by behavior that deviates from traditional sex role prescriptions. It may be that these are "androgynous" people who are able (i.e., flexible enough) to draw on both "masculine" and "feminine" behavior as needed. Their predilections about etiquette appear to be related to their cognitions and affects. Furthermore, although they constitute a minority, it is in this group that one finds the largest percentage of respondents who are aware of the symbolism of this public ritual and are most likely to reject it as sexist and as dissonant with their cognitions. *They are the likely agents of social change.* [Emphasis added.] The major protagonists in any arena of social conflict may be those individuals who are not only influenced by ubiquitous social sanctions, but who are also motivated by internalized symbolic meanings.

Psychiatrist Gould, who says men don't like women, similarly focuses upon the *learned* code of communication that begins in early childhood. Boys learn from an early age, he says, that they are the stronger, the more daring, the less susceptible to emotion and dependence upon others. Boys who deviate from these teachings are, typically, dismissed as "sissies" or "wimps." All feminine-identified traits must be repressed, not uncommonly, Gould points out, "by developing a hypermasculine or macho stance," by holding "girls continually in contempt because their feminine traits are, by definition, contemptible ones" in our society. Boys, he adds, quickly go on to discover "that masculinity equals power equals first-class citizenship, while femininity equals second-class." And, he goes on to say:

> Even parents who try to raise their children in a nonsexist way are overwhelmed by the contradictory messages around them from television, movies, commercials and other adults. Yes, men learn to translate sexual attraction into "love" of a romantic kind but "liking" based on shared experiences and respect for "female" ways of thinking and behaving is not taught to little boys. And the process of re-education in the adult male is formidable.

Yet even this pessimistic viewpoint yields to the conviction that what has been learned can be unlearned—especially if *women* force the issue, which is precisely what is happening now. Women's views of *themselves* are changing and that, more than anything else, is working to eliminate many of the stereotypes that supported the image of women as weak and inferior. Women, far from letting men continue to dictate to them, are making it clear they want more *real* respect from men and will accept nothing less. The authors of that Roper poll that finds women fed up with the sexual status quo conclude that "women's growing dissatisfaction with men is undoubtedly derived from their own rising expectations. The more independent women of today expect more from men." They want a genuine dialogue; they want men to recognize that they speak with a distinct and equal voice, not one that is merely ancillary to the male voice.

The Sexual Revolution made possible a serious inquiry into the ways in which men and women are alike and the ways in which each is unique. This revolutionary development promises to narrow the gender gap as nothing else can, for only by understanding the differences that make communication so complex do we stand any chance of mastering those complexities.

Murray Scher and Glenn E. Good, writing in the *Journal of Counseling and Development*, give voice to ideas that are rapidly gaining in currency:

> Gender roles are not divinely ordained: They are not unchangeable. They are simply cultural artifacts that have become established during the long history of people, as well as the short history of our society. We have been raised to believe that we cannot

> change them nor should we. What we are now coming to believe, however, is that gender roles can be different and that the possibilities are endless, and alluring, if we are willing to take the necessary risks.

This realization, by itself, is liberating—and it is a realization that is beginning to create fundamental change. Scher and Good continue:

> To some extent there already is a change in the way women see themselves, and a change is beginning in the way men see themselves. Most young people do not see themselves as bound and tied by rules and expectations as their parents and grandparents were. Many of the distinctions between genders will blur, insofar as qualities and behaviors that were once seen as solely gender related will become the property of both genders. Increased emotionality, or at least the expression of it, for example, will be more widely accepted. Women will demonstrate their anger more, and men will demonstrate their hurt more. . . . The 1960s taught us that all societal rules could be broken, and that we might be wounded by that initially but we would recover. Into the 1990s and the next century, we will see a further overturning of societal prescriptions and proscriptions. This, too, may be somewhat traumatic but will ultimately be freeing and salutary.

Finally, the aging of the population may, in itself, become a powerful "gender-blender," making the sexes respond more alike and thus better able to communicate productively with one another. We'll expand on this idea in the next section.

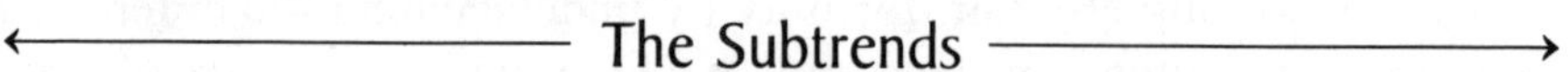

The Subtrends

There are a number of subtrends that support the idea that we are moving steadily away from reproductive sexuality toward a psychological sexuality that, increasingly, satisfies personal rather than societal needs. A number of these subtrends are dealt with in the following chapter, related to the present and future status of the family: decreasing popularity of marriage, increasing popularity of nonmarital cohabitation, later marriage, smaller families, more childless couples, more singles, more gay/lesbian and other "alternative" family forms. The subtrends dealt with here focus on sex and gender and the science, psychology and politics of relationships, irrespective of family forms.

Better Communications Between the Sexes

Some are convinced that men and women actually speak different languages—and, to some extent, they are right. There *are* differences in the way the sexes communicate, and, for the first time, we're beginning to make a serious scientific inquiry into those differences, the illumination of which should lead to *better* communication between men and women in coming decades. The sexual Pidgin English of the past is no longer acceptable to many. The flood of "he said/she said" books, articles, seminars, research studies of recent years reflects a pervasive desire to progress from bonehead communications to English 101. The Sexual Revolution has taken us from the backseat of the car to the front row of the classroom.

Females, for much of early human history, have been viewed as merely inferior—or defective—males, so much so that their anatomical distinctions were long regarded as imperfect manifestations of male physiology—and the vagina was not even assigned a proper anatomical name until 1700! If women behaved differently from men it was only because they were like but *less* than men—no need to investigate further. All mysteries were, ultimately, *male* mysteries.

Today, suggestive of how far we've come, both sexes often regard the other as a mystery—and one another's brains as different and distinct as their genitalia. The scientists see these differences, too, but are divided over their probable origins. It's a debate over "nature versus nurture": are biological or cultural factors responsible for the different ways in which the two sexes "process" the world? Is the female's apparent superiority in verbal skills and the male's apparent superiority in spatial ability inherent or learned? Are the genders' differing styles of communication genetically encoded or the product of being reared differently?

These questions—and their answers—are crucial in the effort to bridge the linguistic and psychological gender gap. Not unexpectedly, the sociological and biological scientists are at war with each other over these issues, but some answers are beginning to emerge. It appears likely that *both* nature and nurture account for the differences being studied. This means that some, but not all of the different ways in which men and women think, behave and communicate are attributable to cultural variables, which, if neutralized, would narrow the gap.

Constance Holden, writing in *Science*, observes:

> Evidence to support a narrowing comes largely from the past decade's meta-analyses—studies of studies that crunch disparately gathered data into cumulative results. One such analysis, on "gender differences in verbal ability," published in the *Psychological Bulletin* . . . by [Janet] Hyde [of the University of Wisconsin] and psychologist Marcia Linn of the University of California at Berkeley, proposed that, in fact, overall sex differences had almost disappeared. . . .
>
> In a companion meta-analysis on math performance . . . Hyde and psychologists Elizabeth Fennema and Susan Lamon of the University of Wisconsin again found declines in the average effect size: In this case, it was presumed male advantages that were diminishing.

Others have, similarly, reported a narrowing gap in abilities long believed innately gender related. The argument is made with some force that as males and females achieve greater equality in educational, economic and social opportunity, their abilities to perform jobs and communicate in various contexts also become more equal.

Others dispute these findings and point to another body of research that suggests, with equal strength, that once all the cultural "artifacts" that currently separate the sexes are cleared away there will still be a biologically based linguistic and behavioral gender gap—and a good thing that is, too, they contend (in a restatement of *vive la différence*), for without distinct male and female "voices" the human animal would be a diminished species. Once we can hear those voices, without all the cultural "static," they add, we can commence graduate studies in cross-gender communications.

No differences have been found in overall intelligence between males and females—nor, after decades of looking, is it likely that such differences will ever be found. But experts in neurobiology and biobehavioral medicine *are* finding sex-linked differences in brain structure, mediated by both prenatal and postnatal hormonal influences, and these biochemical and physiological variations are being linked to sex-specific differences in the way we view one another and the world.

The search for gender-linked variations in brain structure commenced in the 1960s with the work of anatomists Greggory Raisman and Pauline Field at Oxford University. Their results, with male and female rats, astounded their peers, very few of whom believed there were any significant anatomical differences between male and female brains. The Oxford scientists discovered that the two parts of the hypothalamus, a major brain structure, are more closely connected in female rats than in male rats. Their landmark report, published in *Science*, set multitudes of other researchers in motion, and, today we know that there are notable structural differences in human male and female brains, as well.

Ann Gibbons, writing in *Science*, refers to "the rapidly expanding body of evidence showing that the brain is a sexual organ. . . . Men's brains are on average larger than women's by 15 percent—about twice the difference in average body size between men and women." This should not be interpreted as a sign of male superiority. The best evidence suggests something quite different—that the human brain, like the human body in general, as it turns out, is *female* at base, that we all start out, at conception and in the early phases of prenatal development, as essentially female. Only in the presence of masculinizing hormones do the female brain and genitalia undergo modifications that permit the emergence of the male—just the opposite of what was believed to be the case by male-dominated societies for centuries. So much for Adam's rib. The male brain is heavier because it's the basic female model with an "adapter kit" added on.

The areas of the brain that appear particularly sensitive to male hormones include the hypothalamus, the corpus callosum and the hippocampus. Structural differences in these—and other areas of the brain—are only beginning to be correlated to cognitive, emotional and behavioral variations. Some of these early findings are already hinting at anatomical explanation of why males and females have differing verbal and mathematical skills. And some researchers are already extrapolating from these early anatomic insights explanations for all manner of male-female differences. Some, for example, are claiming that men are less able to express emotion because there are fewer synaptic connections between the right and left sides of their brains: input flowing into the nonverbal side of the male brain may not get expressed, nor may its emotional content be acknowledged.

Others are claiming that certain areas in the brain that are known to be larger or better developed in the female than in the male account for greater female sensory discrimination: women see better in the dark, hear better than men, are more sensitive to different tones of voice and so on. Indeed, structural brain differences make women so sensitive in some contexts that "women are probably 'hearing' much more than what the man himself thinks he is 'saying,' " according to geneticist Anne Moir and writer David Jessel, authors of the book *Brain Sex: The*

Real Difference Between Men and Women. This, in part at least, accounts for many of the "he said/she said" arguments that so often characterize relations between the sexes, they believe.

Deborah Tannen, linguistics expert and author of the book *You Just Don't Understand—Women and Men in Conversation,* spently nearly two decades recording and analyzing conversations between the sexes and reports that women and men have distinctly different conversational and communications styles (which many now believe are in significant part mediated by neurobiological disparities). Interviewed by *People*, Dr. Tannen said:

> Men use language to preserve their independence and maintain their position in a group. . . . Women use language to create connections and intimacy. . . . What men mean by communications is, "When we have an important topic to discuss—like what car we should buy—we can talk about it." For women, communicating means establishing intimacy by sharing their concerns, their daily experiences and their fleeting thoughts. Many men perceive this as a lot of talk about nothing. . . . When women share their daily troubles, men feel that they have to solve the problem. They misunderstand the depth of concern because they wouldn't raise a problem for discussion unless it were very serious. This makes men feel burdened, and it upsets women because when their mates offer solutions, it cuts short the discussion and creates a feeling of inequality.

A number of researchers note that men and women have very different ways of dealing with conflict between each other. To many women, an argument means "the relationship is over." And the man's response to this is likely to be: "Are you crazy? Let's have dinner." Dr. Tannen explains:

> For men, taking oppositional stances is a basic way of doing things: in many cases it's even a way to become friends. For example, boys that are friendly playfully put each other down. Men see a refusal to argue as the worst sign of not caring. But women don't see a positive side to it.

Women may often see conflict where men do not. Carol Gilligan, a Harvard psychologist, pointed out, for example, that if a grade-school boy gets hurt in a sports competition he's simply removed from the arena and the game goes on. But if a girl gets hurt, all the team players rally round her in sympathy and the game is ended. To go on is viewed by the girls as disrespectful and uncaring.

Just as there are cultural and biological differences in the conversational and behavioral "styles" of men and women, so are there similar differences in their styles of loving, perhaps the "bottom line" in cross-gender communications. Ethel S. Person, writing in *Atlantic Monthly*, notes that men and women have different passionate quests—"the passionate quest being that which constitutes the central psychological theme of a person's life." She continues:

> For women, the passionate quest has usually been interpersonal, and has generally involved romantic love; for men, it has more often been heroic, the pursuit of achievement or power. One might say that men tend to favor power over love and that women tend to achieve power through love. . . .
>
> By and large, women escape into love, whereas men fear being made vulnerable by love. Women establish their feminine identity through loving, whereas men must be sure of their masculine identification before they can fall in love. Consequently, women often distort love in the direction of submission, men in the direction of dominance. . . .

Understanding the nature and origin of these differences is a necessary first step in bridging them. Most of these differences are believed to have evolutionary roots, that is, they exist, at least in part, due to their survival value. Sexual fantasies, for example, differ dramatically between the sexes and are often a point of contention between them. Men are much more oriented toward explicit sexual fantasies. Researchers Donald Symons and Bruce Ellis, writing in the *Journal of Sex Research*, reported that male undergraduates had sexual fantasies 50 percent more often than female undergraduates. The male fantasies were far more sexually focused, involved many more imagined sex partners and showed little concern for mood or setting. Females focused more on nonsexual intimacy, where mood and setting were very important.

Symons and Ellis suggest that these differences are not due to cultural components and learned behavior but, rather, are the result of evolutionary forces that promoted the perpetuation of the species. Natural selection favored sexually aggressive males who mated quickly and frequently, which in turn requires the biological capacity for "fast and frequent sexual arousal." The same process favored females who were not subject to easy or frequent arousal but, instead, focused on the care and feeding of their offspring under the protection of one (strong and aggressive) male.

Clearly, the trend today is toward an illumination of the differences that have so often placed obstacles between the sexes. The new effort by a (still) male-dominated society to understand the female psyche is encouraging. Anastasia Toufexis, writing in a special issue of *Time* ("Women: The Road Ahead"), put it this way:

> Times, happily, change. Today the interior lives of women are being intensely scrutinized by a band of educators and ethicists, linguists and psychologists. Far from being deficient, their studies show, women are as fully developed psychologically as men, and their ethical judgments are equally valid. The reality is that women experience life differently from men; consequently, they think differently. In the words of Harvard psychologist Carol Gilligan, a central figure in this dynamic research movement, they have "a different voice."

When these "different voices" are clearly heard, the sexes will not merge blissfully, speaking and communicating in perfect harmony. But they will certainly understand one another far better than they do at present.

Greater Equality Between the Sexes

Despite talk in the late 1980s and early 1990s of the decline of feminism and declarations that women, as a social and political force, are waning, equality between the sexes is closer to becoming a reality than ever before. Women command a greater presence in the workforce and wield greater political power than they have ever done. They are assuming positions in both public and private sectors that their mothers and grandmothers believed were unattainable (and their fathers and grandfathers thought were inappropriate) for women. Feminism, far from dead, is trending in vital new directions. Nonetheless, much remains to be achieved before women attain complete equality—but movement in that direction will continue at a pace that will surprise many over the next two decades. Women, in the next few years, may consolidate more gains than they made in the past twenty years.

The cold war between the sexes is fast thawing, thanks in large part to the new female activism, some of the results of which were reflected in the last national election. Women ran for office in unprecedented numbers and won in unprecedented numbers—with the support of men, as well as other women.

Women voters, who have long outnumbered male voters, are, collectively, a sleeping giant, a giant whose slumber many say was abruptly interrupted during the Clarence Thomas-Anita Hill hearings in late 1991. The spectacle of a political "boys' club" raking the dignified Hill over the coals of sexual harassment galvanized the entire nation for days. Viewing those excruciating hearings, says political consultant Celinda Lake of Washington, D.C., "We [women] recognized collectively how silly we had been . . . How did we expect all these men to react—and why . . . haven't we done something about it before now?"

Psychologist Dorothy W. Cantor, author of *Women in Power: The Secrets of Leadership*, told the L.A. Times–Washington Post News Service, "Suddenly the reality of males governing us was in our living rooms. And the money started coming in [to women's political organizations] in record amounts." Some of these organizations more than doubled their memberships within a few months of the hearings.

The Hill-Thomas hearings, moreover, heightened the public's consciousness with respect to sexual harassment, bringing that issue into the headlines. Predictions that Hill's treatment at the hands of the all-male Senate panel would intimidate other women were unfounded, and, in fact, more women than ever before have since been emboldened to file complaints of sexual harassment. As a result, both sexes can expect to receive more sexual respect in the workplace in coming years. More frequent reporting may give the mistaken impression that harassment is increasing, but, like rape, it is actually declining as society shows a diminishing tolerance for such behavior. Still, given the pervasiveness of this social ill it will be some time before it is entirely vanquished.

On another front, even though women still have a long way to go to match men in terms of equal pay for equal work, as well as in equal opportunity, there is a definite *research* trend that shows women can match men in the skills needed to succeed in business. This growing body of data will make it more difficult for businesses to check the rise of women into the upper echelons of management and will gradually help change the corporate consciousness that still heavily favors male employees.

Here are a couple of samples from the research literature.

J. Tsalikis and M. Ortiz-Buonafina (*Journal of Business Ethics*) report that women in top management positions "have [compared with their male counterparts] similar ethical beliefs, and they process ethical information similarly." Will this help women? Yes, in the sense that some business owners have feared that women might be *too* ethical and thus put them at a competitive disadvantage.

Belle Rose Ragins, writing in the *Journal of Management*, reports on a study, the results of which reject the idea that perceived power among business managers is gender typed. This study showed that "male and female managers received equivalent ratings when perceived as using the same forms of power." Again, good news for women. Ragins concludes: "This study indicates that subordinates respond favorably to managers who are perceived as having power, irrespective of the manager's gender or the sex-role stereotypes and behavioral expectations held by the subordinate." In other words, women in positions of power command as much respect and cooperation as men in equivalent positions.

There are a growing number of studies showing that women organize, conceptualize and communicate at least as well as men in top managerial positions, but women have yet to fully crack the so-called "glass ceiling" that keeps most of them from going all the way to the top. But as women grow in political power—and their effectiveness in business continues to be documented—the glass ceiling will become increasingly fragile. What Samuel Cohn of Texas A & M University called "occupational sex-typing" will be seen for what it is—discriminatory. Indeed, a great deal of sex-typing has already been discredited by knowledge and diminished by law.

As for feminism, many a conservative wrote its obituary in the 1980s, only to find it risen from the dead in the 1990s. Actually, its demise was always imaginary. As the *Boston Globe*'s syndicated columnist Ellen Goodman observes, the movement lives on, changed but with a new vitality, among a broad spectrum of women:

> They are young mothers, daughters of feminism, who expected to stay on the fast track and left it for motherhood because their firms and companies expect 70-hour weeks. They are women in their 20s who grew up assuming independence and find their freedom limited by fear of male violence in the dorms and on the streets.
>
> They are women who find it impossible to believe that "they" might take abortion rights away. Women who look in vain for a skirt among the suits at a Senate hearing or an international conference. . . .
>
> They are women who have made it into the inner circle of men

> only to become conscious of how hard it is to make a difference. They are women who struggled with their own self-image only to watch their daughters immersed in a magazine of messages about female flaws and products for improvement.
>
> They are women as well who are discouraged by the realization that "they don't get it," angered by an image on MTV, turned off by a blonde joke and exhausted by the sheer tenacity of the way things are. And they are also the men who share the lives and perspectives of these women.

"Movements" make headway only in a context of dissatisfaction. And, clearly, there is still plenty for women to be dissatisfied about, particularly in the wake of a decade that tried to stifle meaningful change. As Goodman concludes, "A constituency for a second generation of change exists now in the expectations gap."

The "new feminism," as some call it, is less doctrinaire than the old, less extreme in the sense that it no longer has to be "outrageous" in order to call attention to itself. The gender consciousness that was, perhaps necessarily, overemphasized in the past is increasingly perceived as gender restrictive. The movement today is less introspective, more goal oriented and pragmatic. Demands for "liberation" are superseded—and subsumed—by a well-organized quest for power. Women no longer want to burn bras, they want to manufacture and market them.

Perhaps we need only look at what's happened to humor in this country to see how far feminism has come. A decade ago only about 2 percent of the nation's comics were female. Today that number is estimated at close to 20 percent. And when female comics first appeared on the national scene, their humor was usually self-deprecatory; then it focused almost entirely on "women's issues"; today it has progressed to the point that it covers the world—it's gone beyond gender specifics. Some who study this phenomenon believe that women comics are now even more daring and innovative than most of their male counterparts and are better able to deal with many subjects that were long considered taboo.

The New Masculinity: Toward a More Sensitive Male?

A couple of decades ago men laughed at images of women burning their bras. Today women—and not a few men—are laughing at images of sagging weekend male "warriors" in loincloths, beating drums, toting spears, dancing in circles around fires in search of their "inner Wildman." *Esquire* devoted an issue to this subject, sending a reporter to participate in a "New Warrior Training Adventure Weekend," at which dentists, accountants, lawyers and so on assumed names such as "Harley 'Mountain Goat' Fauntleroy" and were schooled in the new male bonding, in "trusting instinct" and in venting rage. Encouraged to reveal himself, one "warrior," typical of many others, shouted, "I want my balls back, Mother!"

To say that the men's movement today is confused is to understate mercifully. Many men say they want to be more "sensitive" but also "less emasculated," "more open," yet "less vulnerable." While the early flux of this movement is often so extreme that it cannot but evoke guffaws, there is, nonetheless, something in it that commands some respect—for, in contrast with earlier generations of males, this one is making a real effort to examine and redefine itself. The movement, in a word, is *real*.

Innumerable studies and surveys find men dissatisfied with themselves and their roles in society. Part of this, undoubtedly, is the result of the displacement men are experiencing in a culture where *women* are so successfully transforming themselves. Men are shocked to find that they have been defining themselves to a far greater degree than they imagined in terms of their relations with women, relations that are now shifting, and not usually on male terms.

There is evidence, too, that men are dissatisfied because their own fathers were so unsuccessful in their emotional lives and were thus unable to impart to their sons a sense of love, belonging and security that an increasing number of men say they sorely miss.

Additionally, more and more men say they want to spend more time with their own children, but as the economics of the times make that more difficult this contributes to still more frustration. An increasing number of men, however, *are* showing a willingness to postpone career advancements in order to better fulfill their roles as fathers. (See the following chapter for more on this trend.)

The real trend has nothing to do with beating drums or becoming a "warrior." It relates to the human desire for "connection," and this, in the long run, can only bode well for communications between humans in general and for communications between the sexes in particular. This has to be accounted as an evolutionary advance made possible by a society that can finally afford the time and energy required for such self-examination. Many psychologists believe that men, in the next two decades, will be less "emotionally closed" than at any time in American history.

More (and Better) Senior Sex (On the Aging and Androgynizing of Society)

People used to talk about "sex after 40" as if it were some kind of novelty. Now it's "sex after 60" and it's considered not only commonplace but healthy. That there's a Sexual Revolution among seniors is attested to by a number of studies. In the mid-1980s, many commentators characterized as "shocking" and "astonishing" the findings of a national survey that revealed that better than 65 percent of women and 80 percent of men in their 70s remain sexually active (having intercourse at least once a week), that 43 percent of women aged 50 and older practice fellatio, that 56 percent of men aged 50 and older practice cunnilingus and so on. A more recent survey confirms those findings.

Some fear that expectations among the aged may outrun physiological ability and that exaggerated hopes, in some cases, will lead to new frustrations—or that improved health into old age will put pressure on seniors to remain sexually active beyond any "decent" desire to do so. But most seem to welcome the trend toward extended sexuality. The *desire* for sex in later decades of life is heightened, studies suggest, by society's growing awareness and acceptance of sexual activity in later life. Medical science no longer tells women, for example, that "it's all over" at menopause. Indeed, there's good evidence to suggest that, even without hormonal replacement, women can overcome some of the adverse effects of menopause through *regular* sexual activity.

In fact, some psychological and physiological changes related to aging may actually promote better sexual response in women. Dava Sobel, writing in *Health*, states:

> Relieved of worry about pregnancy, many women find sex more pleasurable. At 60, a woman's orgasms may be more frequent than earlier in life, says Dr. Helen Singer Kaplan, director of the Human Sexuality Program at the New York Hospital–Cornell Medical Center, because female orgasm is, in part, "a learning process."
>
> The male and female physiological changes that occur with age provide a fertile ground for a more leisurely enjoyment of sex, especially the "second language of sex," as named by Dr. Robert N. Butler, author of *Sex After Sixty*. . . . "When people are young," Butler says, "sex tends to be urgent and explosive. It's

> concerned largely with physical pleasure and, in many cases, the conception of children. This 'first language of sex' is biological and instinctive—and wonderfully exciting. But sex is not just a matter of athletics and production. Some people recognize this early on and simultaneously develop a second language of sex, which is emotional and communicative as well as physical."

This thinking meshes with that of a number of other researchers. Alice S. Rossi, professor of sociology at the Demographic Research Institute of the University of Massachusetts, writing in *Daedalus*, observes that "as a 'new' nation, American society has been both more youthful and more masculine than other Western countries." That is changing now as the population here becomes older and more predominantly female. There are forces at work, discussed earlier, that are enhancing equality and communication between the sexes in the first half of life. Now, Rossi contends, the aging and androgynizing of the population will bring the sexes, in the second half of life, even closer together over the next several decades.

Rossi reviewed a large body of data to show that women and men, followed in long-term studies of personality from adolescence onward, undergo predictable changes, with women becoming "more analytic and assertive" and men "more giving and expressive" with the passage of time. With aging, the two sexes develop "supplementary qualities that are conventionally defined as appropriate to the opposite sex." This androgynizing process (quite different from the superficial "gender blending" we spoke of earlier) was observed in four distinct cultures, prompting Rossi to conclude that:

> the evidence suggests that the changes reflect a decline in sex and gender differences that take place following the peak reproductive phase of the human life span. Hence, estrogen decline in women and testosterone decline in men from early middle age on seem likely to play a contributing role in the personality changes taking place as men and women age. Even sexual responses differ in the human male from mid-life on, for men become more like women in their sexual behavior as they age, with a focus on sheer sensual touching and enriched fantasies; as Ruth Weg put it, older men engage in touch for its own sake rather than merely as a way station to intercourse. . . .
>
> Political and economic pressures are now blurring traditional gender roles in the first half of life. . . . If the tendency of the human organism in the second half of life is toward more androg-

ynous qualities in both sexes, then these recent political and economic changes in gender roles in early adulthood may make for a smoother passage through the transitional years of middle age. In an era marked by so much technological and political change, and by personal lives that are often fragmented by disparate and conflicting roles, with periods of loneliness, heartache, and isolation, there is comfort in the idea that more androgynous qualities may become stable characteristics of men and women throughout their lives.

More (and Possibly Safer) Teen and Young Adult Sex

As noted in the introduction to this chapter, the Sexual Revolution continues unabated among the nation's teens and college students. Even in the AIDS era, college students are as sexually active as ever, and sexual activity among teens has actually increased significantly in recent years: nearly 40 percent have had sex by the ninth grade, 70 percent by the twelfth grade. This is a trend that is unlikely to be reversed. Fortunately, according to a recent survey, 78 percent of sexually active teens report using some form of contraception. Nearly 50 percent of all male teens say they use condoms, a considerable improvement over past years. Federal goals are for 90 percent of all teen males to use condoms by the year 2000.

One long-term study of sexual attitudes among college students finds a twenty-year trend toward a more "liberal" sexual outlook continuing. There has, for example, been a very sharp drop in the number of students who believe premarital sexual intercourse is immoral. The drop, over a twenty-year period among the population studied, was from 33 percent to 16 percent among males and from 70 percent to 17 percent among females!

Attitudes among younger teens also continue to change in the same direction. Among girls, the stigma that once attached to "going all the way" has diminished but promiscuity is still frowned upon, though, as noted earlier, the definition of "promiscuity" is changing. That there is still something of a sexual "double standard," however, prompted one teenage girl to write a letter to Ann Landers, wondering when equality would ever be achieved in this regard. Ann responded:

> Deeply ingrained concepts die hard. The kind of thinking you describe has been part of our culture for hundreds of years. My guess is that the equality between the sexes that you would like to

see will probably take shape in about two decades—not soon enough for you to enjoy but your daughters will.

The best evidence indicates Ann is right on the money with that prognostication. But this is not to say that in another ten or twenty years society will be applauding teen promiscuity, whatever the gender of it, but, rather, that the same attitudes that prevail at any given time toward promiscuity will increasingly apply with equal force to *both* males and females. It's interesting to note, in this regard, that in the last couple of years some researchers have reported for the first time that some promiscuous male teens are being described as "tramps" by both their male and female peers. The times are definitely changing.

Greater Diversity of Sexual Expression

As sex shifts from its "traditional" reproductive role to one that is psychological, it increasingly serves the needs of the individual. In this context, forms of sexual expression that were previously proscribed are now tolerated and are, in some cases, increasingly viewed as no more nor less healthy than long-accepted forms of sexual behavior. Homosexuality, for example, has attained a level of acceptance unprecedented in our national history.

Among factors influencing public opinion in this regard are recent findings that most sexual preferences are *not* learned but, rather, have their roots in genetics. The old idea that people *choose* to be homosexual (or bisexual or heterosexual) is being challenged by such findings.

See the following chapter for more details on the emergence of diverse family forms, including those involving fictive kinship groups, unrelated singles, gay and lesbian couples and so on.

More Contraception/Less Abortion

Though abortion will remain legal under varying conditions in most, if not all, states, its use will continue to decline over the next two decades as more—and better—contraceptives become available.

After a period of more than two decades in which drug companies shied away from contraceptive research—due to such factors as litigation over intrauterine devices and opposition from religious and conservative groups—interest in this field is again growing. AIDS, a changed political climate and renewed fears about the "population explosion" are all contributing to this change.

Additionally, scientific advances now point the way to safer, more effective, more convenient contraceptives. A male contraceptive that will be relatively side-effect free is finally within reach and should be achieved within the next decade, certainly the next two decades. Even more revolutionary in concept and probable impact is a vaccine, already tested in animals, that some predict will be available within ten years, a vaccine that safely stops ovum maturation and thus makes conception impossible.

Religion and Sex: A More Forgiving Attitude

Just a couple decades ago mainstream religion was monolithic in its condemnation of sex outside of marriage. Today the situation is quite different as major denominations across the land struggle with issues they previously wouldn't have touched, issues related to adultery, premarital sex, homosexuality and so on.

A Special Committee on Human Sexuality, convened by the General Assembly of the Presbyterian Church (USA), for example, surprised many when it issued a report highly critical of the traditional "patriarchal structure of sexual relations," a structure the committee believes contributes, because of its repressiveness, to the proliferation of pornography and sexual violence. The report called for a new ethic of sexuality, one that eschews the exploitation of women and the exclusion of homosexuals, unmarried heterosexuals and others, one that replaces old concerns about "who sleeps with whom" with new concerns about whether those in sexual relationships are motivated by genuine mutual desire and are "full of joyful caring."

The committee's recommendations were rejected by the General Assembly, but the fact that such a committee was established at all represents a sharp departure from the past; that it produced a report so critical of traditional religious thinking on sexuality is even more indicative of the forces of change. Nor was it a one-time fluke. The same sort of thing has been happening in most other major denominations. It is safe to say that major changes are coming. Mainstream religion is beginning to perceive that the Sexual Revolution must be acknowledged and, to a significant degree, accommodated with new policies if these denominations are to remain in touch with present-day realities.

Expanding Sexual Entertainment and Commerce (From Video to Virtual Reality)

The use of sex to sell products, as well as to entertain, is increasing and can be expected to do so. The concept that "sex sells" is so well established that we need not belabor the point here. The explicitness of sexual advertising, however, may be curbed somewhat by recent research findings that highly explicit sexual content is so diverting that the viewer or reader tends to overlook the product entirely.

Sexual stereotyping will be less prevalent in advertising in years to come. All this means, however, is that women will not be singled out as "sex objects"; they'll have plenty of male company, as is already the case. The female "bimbo" is now joined by the male "himbo" in ever-increasing numbers. Sexist advertising is still prevalent (e.g., male-oriented beer commercials) but should diminish as women gain in social and political power.

There's no doubt that films and television programming have become more sexually permissive in the last two decades and are likely to continue in that direction for some time to come. Where society may call "Halt" or at least "Slow down," however, is in the realm of media depictions of sexual violence (see chapter 1). With the advent of "tabloid TV," Americans can expect to be exposed to ever-more sexually oriented programming, and a recent content-analysis of soap operas shows that they have upped the sexual ante considerably in the past ten years, an ongoing trend.

Meanwhile, reports of declining sales of pornography in the 1980s are now being replaced by reports of sales gains in the 1990s. Al Stewart, writing in *Variety*, put it this way:

> Adult video took a pummeling in the late 1980s, and plenty of people, from preachers to feminists, would like to see it kayoed. Instead, it's on the rebound, and an increasing number of vids are being discreetly tucked under the arms of customers leaving the video store.
>
> Quality is improving. Prices are stabilizing. The vids are aimed more toward couples than singles. Stores that carry hardcore say it accounts for about 20 percent of their bottom line. . . .
>
> Last year the industry rallied back from a two-year slump. Some $395-million worth of hardcore adult vids were sold last year at the wholesale level.

Many believe that the recession and low quality, more than any contrary social current, accounted for the downward blip in sales of porn in the late eighties. The sales trend, which had been upward for many years, now appears to be back on that track. Concurrently, there are reports of increased sales of camcorders, accounted for in part by couples wanting to make their own erotic videos.

On another entertainment front, *Time* reports, "Computer games have shattered the sex barrier":

> Are the kids in bed? The curtains closed? It's time to turn on the computer and start playing some of the hottest electronic games around—games so hot that they threaten to melt your microprocessor. Welcome to the world of high-tech titillation, where characters perform feats of onscreen electronic eroticism that leave little—or nothing—to the imagination.

Those who thought the decline of *Playboy* magazine meant the public was losing interest in the erotic simply haven't been keeping up with the media. Among the new video games are such programs as Sexxcapades and MacPlaymate.

But all of this will surely pale alongside the brave (or brazen) new world of "cybersex" and virtual reality, the first erotic emanations of which may well be experienced by Americans in the coming two decades. Virtual reality aims to be just that—to provide artificial, electronically induced experiences that are virtually indistinguishable from the real thing. It will doubtless be decades before VR (TV's successor) attains that level of technological virtue, but even its first, stumbling steps will likely prove irresistible to the public.

Video and computer scientists from around the world are already convening at national symposiums to discuss the latest VR developments. There the latest cybernetic "feedback" devices—gloves, harnesses, goggles and the like—are earnestly discussed, and big business is at hand, paying close heed. VR is expected to have a lot of important applications, putting architects and engineers, for example, in three-dimensional contact with the realities they hope to construct, but the entertainment potential of these innovations, many believe, will eventually dominate the field.

Howard Rheingold, author of *Virtual Reality*, is one of many who have speculated on cybernetic sex. He notes that the term "teledildonics" was coined by computer expert Theodor Nelson "to describe a machine that would enable people to experience sex-at-a-distance." No such machine yet exists, but, adds Rheingold, "VR sex seems inevitable, given the history of human proclivities." He envisions virtual sex thus:

> Picture yourself a couple decades hence, dressing for a hot night in the virtual village. Before you climb into a suitable padded chamber and put on your 3-D glasses, you slip into a lightweight (eventually, one would hope, diaphanous) bodysuit, something like a body stocking, but with the kind of intimate snugness of a condom. Embedded in the inner surface of the suit . . . is . . . a mesh of tiny tactile detectors coupled to vibrators of varying degrees of hardness, hundreds of them per square inch, that can receive and transmit a realistic sense of tactile presence. . . .
>
> Now, imagine plugging your whole sound-sight-touch telepresence system into the telephone network. You see a lifelike but totally artificial visual representation of your own body, and of your partner's. Depending on what numbers you dial and which passwords you know and what you are willing to pay . . . you will find one partner, a dozen, a thousand, in various cyberspaces. . . . You can whisper in your partner's ear, feel your partner's breath on your neck. . . . You can run your cheek over (virtual) satin, and feel the difference when you encounter (virtual) flesh. Or you can gently squeeze . . .

You get the (virtual) picture. The Sexual Revolution, far from over, is in for some new, high-tech curves.

Solutions/Recommendations

A Need for More—and Better—Sex Education (to Include Gender Sensitivity/Communications)

Even though more than 90 percent of parents want the schools to provide their children with comprehensive sex education, only 10 percent are getting that education, according to Debra Haffner, executive director of the Sex Information and Education Council of the United States (SIECUS). At present, only seventeen states and the District of Columbia mandate some form of sex education in their schools. Many of these programs, experts say, are markedly deficient and haphazardly administered, a state of affairs that would be deplorable under any circumstances but which is inexcusable in this AIDS era.

The situation was made more controversial in recent years by countervailing demands from the political and religious right that sex education be limited to calls for total sexual abstinence among teens. A vocal minority prevailed in numerous locales, making the only acceptable sex-education texts those that prescribe abstinence, denouncing all premarital sex and any form of sexuality that deviates in any way from married heterosexuality.

Fear and exaggerations are commonly used by the proabstinence lobby, undermining the credibility of authority in the same way that it was undermined by early government efforts to curb marijuana use. Young people see through these exaggerations very quickly and go on, unfortunately, to ignore not only the fictional or inflated risks but also the *real* ones.

These same conservative forces also were instrumental in getting a national sex survey of teens canceled, a survey that was badly needed to help formulate more effective strategies for combating AIDS, teen pregnancies and alcohol/drug abuse. The Bush administration's Secretary of Health and Human Services canceled the survey, even though top medical officials within that department said the survey was vital to the nation's health. Earlier, Bush administration officials, again bowing to pressures from the extreme right, called off a survey of adult sexuality called for by the National Institutes of Health.

While forces opposing these studies, on grounds that they will somehow incite people to lust, promiscuity and homosexuality, have prevailed, teenagers have escalated sexual activity to unprecedented levels, and the United States today has the highest teenage pregnancy rate of any developed country in the world. The irresponsible policies of the proabstinence—"just say no"—groups help expose today's youth to a deadly vacuum of ignorance. Out of it comes more teen disease, teen pregnancy, shattered lives and—the ultimate irony—more, not less, abortion.

A study comparing the United States with five European countries reveals that teen sexual activity is about the same in all of them. But teen pregnancy and teen abortion are *far* more prevalent in the United States than in those European countries. Why? Because the European countries have vastly superior sex education, are more open and mature in their sexuality and make contraception readily available to the young.

The political climate is changing here. Some of those who have resisted public-health-oriented sex education and contraceptive services for the young have recently been swept from power, and others, favoring comprehensive teen programs, have taken their places. Joycelyn Elders, Surgeon General in the Clinton Administration, is a strong supporter of sex education and condom distribution. In the next few years, the studies that are so badly needed to help assess sexual behavior and devise tactics for safer behavior *will* be conducted.

Some progress is being made now. As noted earlier in this chapter, more and more schools are distributing condoms—not only because of AIDS and teen pregnancy epidemics but also because of the alarming rise in sexually transmitted diseases (STDs) in general. There are now more than 3 million cases of STDs among teens annually—and the incidence of syphilis among teens aged 15–19 leapt by 50 percent in the last decade.

We must formulate a national policy of *compulsory, comprehensive* sex education. SIECUS has already researched and designed such programs for kindergarten through senior high. These programs can provide a useful model for a national program. They deal with both the physical and the psychological/emotional aspects of sexuality. They do *not* promote sexual activity but, rather, deal with what is there; they provide positive counseling for both heterosexual and homosexual teens. They are sensitive to gender issues and can provide a starting place to promote better communications between the sexes, beginning at an early age when healthier attitudes and behavior are more easily learned.

As psychiatrist Gould noted, the real battle for sexual equality and harmony will be fought, not so much in the workplace as on the playground and in the schools, where so many of our lifelong attitudes are instilled.

Time to Call Halt to Sexual Violence in the Media

While there is no credible evidence that erotic—and even explicitly erotic—media portrayals in and of themselves result in antisocial behavior, there is mounting data supporting the idea that sexual *violence* in the media can have potentially harmful effects. We need to redefine "pornography" to focus on those sexual portrayals that are clearly exploitative, nonconsensual and violent.

Researchers at many different centers have documented the desensitizing—and, ultimately, brutalizing—effects of sexual violence in the media. Researchers at the University of Wisconsin, for example, carried out a number of well-designed studies, some of which are ongoing, in which male subjects are exposed to a variety of films, some of which are erotic but not violent and some of which contain abundant sexual violence.

It's the films with the violence that prove troublesome. When men first view them they are usually disturbed by them, as measured by a number of tests. With continued viewing, however, the men's levels of depression and anxiety rapidly recede, until they return to pre-viewing levels. Moreover, films the men had initially considered offensive soon become acceptable, then enjoyable and even humorous.

More ominously, men who were thus desensitized, by prolonged exposure to these films and videos, responded very differently to a reenactment of a rape trial than did men who had not been exposed to the same programming. The rape victim in the reenactment was judged far more guilty, worthless and undeserving of justice by the men who saw the films than by the men who did not.

The need for media regulation is especially acute in this context. It appears likely that a strong movement in this direction will occur in the next several years, as more data help document the social costs of media violence and as more women assume leadership roles in the Sexual Revolution.

THREE

Family

More Traditional/ Less Traditional?

THE TREND Despite recent pronouncements that the traditional family is making a comeback, the evidence suggests that over the next two decades the nuclear family will share the same future as nuclear arms: there will be fewer of them, but those that remain will be better cared for. There will be fewer traditional families of a husband, wife and children. There will be more new families, which are already appearing: families of the *mind*, not of the genes. The *psychological* family will supplant the biological family. Far from having calamitous effects the existence of these new families will enhance freedom and satisfy practical and emotional needs that are now going unfulfilled. This will not, or course, be accomplished without considerable transitional flux, the shock waves of which may intensify before they diminish.

Overview

The Family Is Dead/ Long Live the Family

After sifting through myriad studies, surveys and opinions related to the American family, its past, present and possible future, it was amazing—and a bit amusing—to find what appears to be one of the most succinct summations of an enormously complex situation in the trade journal *Adweek*. Perhaps no one should be surprised that the ad people came the closest to getting the "story" right with respect to what is happening to the American family. After all, their livelihoods depend upon accurately measuring the social pulse. Debra Goldman's article begins:

> The 1990 Census reads like an obituary for the American family. The nuclear family—Mom, Dad and the kids—melted down to only one household in four. They are now outnumbered by couples (married or not) without children, and they are about to be overtaken by single folks of all varieties.
>
> For all these indicators of the dwindling of the typical family, there have never been so many pious reaffirmations of the values of the institution itself. For marketers, "family" is the hot button. Pundits are predicting that the '90s will be the decade of retreat to the hearth as Americans try to recreate the snugness of home sweet home. This approach is selling phone lines, perfumes, packaged goods.
>
> But don't be mistaken. The growing emotional relevance of family life is not a sign that the family is coming back; it's a sign that it's disappearing.

Goldman invokes "the hobby syndrome" by way of explaining this apparent contradiction. She credits Jagdish Sheth, marketing professor at the University of Southern California, with this summation of the "syndrome": "When an activity or institution ceases to have a practical or economic utility, it returns as a hobby." Sheth contends that it is part of human nature to "try to preserve the emotional content of an activity after it no longer performs its practical function."

Sheth cites as an example the hunter, whose function was once vital to the survival of the species. It's been a while since cave days, but hunting persists, albeit in an entirely different context and on a very limited scale. As Goldman notes, "despite the millennia between the spear-toters and the hipboot-wearers, a lot of the psychic satisfactions of hunting live on: the Male Bonding Thing, the Man Against Nature Thing." Similarly, though Mom's three daily homemade meals are now for the most part only a dim memory in most households and entirely unheard of in others, cooking, Goldman observes, endures, not for the purposes of sustenance but, rather, as "a vehicle of self-expression."

Likewise, she adds, "today, as family farms are carved into exurb real estate tracts, gardening has become the rage among white-collar weekenders who would gag at the smell of fresh cow manure."

The tone may be a bit flip, but Goldman makes perceptive observations:

> The family is now in that twilight state between outmoded necessity and necessary pleasure. Yes, the institution is "back," as the trend meisters say, but it's back as a hobby, an avocation, a set of psychic requirements rather than material obligations. The ties that bind are emotional, not economic . . . it's important not to confuse the desire for the family with the facts. . . . Sell to the emotional yearning, but don't mistake it for the reality.

For many, of course, the traditional family is still a reality. But Goldman's point is an important one: we must not confuse our nostalgia for the nuclear family with any real intention to make it once again the central feature of American life. The trend is in quite another direction.

There are those who will take issue with that contention. After all, some recent surveys (a Roper poll conducted for *Good Housekeeping* magazine, for example) show that, for the first time in a decade, a majority of women reject as their ideal the mixing of family and career. And, contrary to what the census was predicting just a few years ago, the birthrate in the United States has been trending upward for the first time since the 1950s, producing a boomlet that some say will blossom into a full-fledged 1990s baby boom.

In California, where many trends are born, children are a growth industry. The long-term trend toward smaller families is being reversed there, according to the Center for Continuing Study of the California Economy. The center is predicting that "California should become a comparatively more child-oriented market in the next decade." Families, it forecasts, will constitute 70 percent of all households; the proportion of married couples with children will increase sharply.

The clincher, according to those who are predicting the imminent resurgence of the nuclear family, is the fact that, for the first time in three decades, the number of women entering the workforce has leveled off. Add that, some argue, to the fact that women are having more babies, and the happy handwriting is on the wall.

Others write with warm reassurance about the "boom" in books, seminars and other programs related to pregnancy, childbirth and parenting. Attendance at such seminars is said to be at an all-time high. And family reunions, in the last couple of decades about as popular as taxes, are now "in" again.

AIDS, others assert, sent singles into a spin. Promiscuity is out, they say; monogamy is in; everyone wants to couple.

And how about this? Divorce—that great American institution that afflicts better than half of all marriages—is leveling off and even declining a bit after decades of increase.

So how can one possibly discern a trend that says the traditional family, far from making a comeback, is destined to become an enclave, if not a relic in twenty-first century society?

The facts, separated from nostalgia and wishful thinking, speak persuasively. The overwhelming trend, throughout this century, has been toward lower fertility rates in the industrialized world. This trend was interrupted by the baby boom that came after World War II and by a few minor boomlets along the way, but the overall trend is clear and dramatic—and there is no reason to believe it is being reversed now.

The current baby boomlet is due partially to the result of "last-minute" births to women of the baby boom generation. Aware that their "biological clocks" are ticking and their opportunities to give birth will soon be foreclosed by menopause, a last "wave" of these women is now opting for reproduction. Hence, for a few years the birthrate in the United States will continue higher than it has been and then will decline again.

In any case, more babies do not necessarily mean more families, at least not more traditional families. If there has been a real baby boom in recent decades, it has been (and continues to be) among *unwed* mothers. Only about 5 percent of all babies were born to unmarried women in 1960. Now that figure is 25 percent—one in every four! And more and more of these women are choosing not to marry after giving birth.

And women leaving the workplace? It's true that women's attitudes toward work have changed over the past decade. Many women believed work outside the home would be more rewarding than it is—and that their husbands would help out far more than they have in the home. But because women are expressing greater disillusionment with their workplace experiences does not mean they will be heading back in hordes to assume the role of housewife and mother for the simple reason that even if they wanted to do this—and more in-depth research shows that they do *not*, at least not on a long-term basis—they *could not.* Our economy has undergone major transformations since the days of

Ozzie and Harriet, and it is now an economic necessity that a majority of women, including a majority of those of childbearing age, work. Family income has remained flat or has actually declined over the last twenty years, *even* with both husband and wife working. The need for women to continue to work is going to grow more, not less, intense in the next two decades.

Right now the number of women entering the job market appears to be stalled, neither declining nor increasing. This is not because women are abandoning the job market but because, according to labor analysts, the market is already glutted with women. The rate at which women were entering the market simply couldn't be sustained in the current economy. Right now, approximately 75 percent of all women aged 20 to 44 are in the workplace. And the number of working women with children is at an all-time high and has *continued* to increase even during the recent recession; this unquestionably reflects the economic pressures of child rearing. Additionally, 53 percent of all women who left work after having a child returned to work within a year of giving birth in 1990; in 1980, only 38 percent of women in those circumstances did the same.

What of the dip in the divorce rate? Here, too, things are not what they seem. It isn't that people are divorcing less but that they are "cohabiting" (living together without marriage) more; fewer marriages mean fewer divorces. This can scarcely be accounted good news for traditionalists.

And that situation in California, where it appears the nuclear family is again popular? Well, as Cheryl Russell, writing in *American Demographics*, observed recently:

> A closer look at these trends shows that traditions are not returning to California, but immigrating there. The state's rapidly growing Hispanic and Asian populations are more likely to live in traditional families than are the state's non-Hispanic whites. Married couples with children comprise fully 45 percent of California's Hispanic households and 39 percent of its Asian households. In contrast, only 24 percent of the state's non-Hispanic white households are couples with kids. With over 40 percent of the state's population projected to be Hispanic or Asian by 2000, the lifestyles of these groups are reversing the trends.

Even this California trend is destined to be a footnote in the prevailing text. Numerous studies make clear that, with the passage of time, immigrant populations, driven by the same forces, desires and social expectations that have shaped the rest of the country, become inexorably less traditional in family structure.

It would seem, then, that friends of the traditional family have little to cheer about these days. For purists, the nuclear family is not just a Mom-Dad-and-two-kid unit but one in which Mom stays home and tends to the children and the household chores while Dad brings in all the income. In 1960, 61 percent of American households fit this description. Today only 26 percent do. How quickly and dramatically things change. The dad of 1960 aged 20–34 was a wage earner who actually stood a decent chance of being able to support a family of four. His counterpart today is far more likely to be living below the poverty level and, in many cases, is single, unemployed or underemployed and is back home living with *his* mom and dad.

Demographers now believe that the number of families consisting of married couples with children will dwindle by yet another 12 percent by the year 2000. Meanwhile, single-parent households will continue to increase (up 41 percent over the past decade). And household size will continue to decline (2.63 people in 1990 versus 3.14 in 1970). More unwed pregnant women will opt to remain single (about 75 percent today compared to 45 percent in the early 1960s). The number of households maintained by women, with no males present, has increased 300 percent since 1950 and will continue to rise into the twenty-first century.

People are continuing to delay marriage, which, in turn, depresses the fertility rate. Age at first marriage is pushing up into the mid- to high-20s-range. And the overall marriage rate (measured per 100 women aged 15 and up) has plummeted from about 10 in the 1950s to 5.6 in recent years—the lowest it has been since the Great Depression. These trends developed and persisted despite a vastly expanded youth population occasioned by the baby boom.

Particularly alarming to some is the fact that an ever-increasing number of people are choosing *never* to marry. And, throughout the developed world, the *one-person* household is now the fastest growing household category. To the traditionalists, this trend seems particularly insidious. More than 25 percent of all households in the United States now consist of just one person. This percentage is about double what it was in 1960.

There can be no doubt: the nuclear family has been vastly diminished, and it will continue to decline for some years but at a more gradual pace. Indeed, there is a good chance that it will enjoy more stability in the next two decades than it did in the last two. Many of the very forces that were said to be weakening the traditional family may now make it stronger, though not more *prevalent.* Developing social changes have made traditional marriage more elective today, so that those who choose it may, increasingly, some psychologists believe, represent a subpopulation better suited to the institution and thus more likely to make a go of it.

Moreover, as the concept of "family" expands to include nontraditional groupings, even the traditionalists may benefit. With respect to children, the objectives of all family forms are much the same. Thus the "family lobby" will be strengthened by the addition of new and often unexpected allies.

From Biology to Psychology: The New Family of the Mind

As we try to understand new forms of family, we need to realize that the "traditional" family is not particularly traditional. Neither is it necessarily the healthiest form of family. The nuclear family has existed for only a brief moment in human history. Even if we limit ourselves to American history the nuclear family is of fairly recent origin. Before the Industrial Revolution in the nineteenth century, American families were quite different from the idealized version of today, and it can be argued that, in some respects, they were more productive of good social and individual mental health.

In the preindustrial era, families were more like business ventures, with husband and wife working together on farms or in other enterprises, their children helping them and learning the family trades in the process. Parenting was far more of a genuine co-venture than it is today, and children perceived themselves to be far more needed by the family than they do now.

With the dawn of the industrial age, husbands moved away from the family center into factories, offices and other jobs outside the home, leaving wives to be the sole caretakers of the children, who eventually came to be more and more deprived of functional significance within the family context.

The shortcomings of this family form are dramatically reflected in today's high rate of marital dissolution, youth crime and suicide. Many of the ills that are attributed to the breakup of the nuclear family are, in fact, just as arguably *caused* by that "traditional" form, a mutation of family that, among other things, offers children less parental guidance than the preindustrial family, while creating sociopolitical schisms along gender lines.

Heretical as all this may sound to some, note that even the mainstream press has begun commenting on the unusual (not to say unnatural) qualities of the nuclear family. Here's *Newsweek*'s summation:

> The historical irony here is that the traditional family is something of an anomaly. . . . Most scholars now consider the "breadwinner-homemaker" model unusual, applicable in limited circumstances for a limited time. It was a distinctly white middle-class phenomenon, for example; it never applied widely among blacks or new immigrants, who could rarely afford to have only a single earner in the family.

Moreover, most people don't realize that no sooner had the nuclear family form peaked around the turn of the last century than erosion set in, which has continued, with one notable interruption, ever since. For the past hundred years, reality has chipped away at this social icon, with increasing divorce and the movement of more women into the labor force. The end of World War II temporarily set the country up to go into a baby-making mode and, in an early evocation of the "hobby syndrome," made the nuclear family a fad again. But only until the 1960s, when the prevalent trends of the century once more asserted themselves.

The "desanctification" of the nuclear family proceeds along many fronts, creating a more receptive atmosphere for the emergence of new family forms. Historian Stephanie Coontz, author of *The Social Origins of Private Life: A History of American Families*, has argued with particular effectiveness that our policymakers (who, as *Newsweek* observes, grew up with the mythic TV families of "The Adventures of Ozzie and Harriet," "Father Knows Best" and "Leave It to Beaver") considerably overestimate the value of the nuclear family. Writing in *The Wall Street Journal*, Coontz contends that the decline of the traditional family is *not* at the root of our social and economic problems:

> Take the issue of female-headed families, which usually dominates discussion of the fact that one in five U.S. children—almost one in two black children—is poor. To be sure, female-headed families are much more likely to be poor than two-parent families of the same race, both because women earn less than men and because it is increasingly difficult for one wage earner of either sex to support

a family. But how much childhood poverty is caused by family dissolution or could be cured by reviving "traditional" family structures and values? Surprisingly little.

Coontz's contentions are supported by a number of recent research findings. One long-term University of Michigan study of 5,000 families, for example, has revealed that breakup of traditional family structure accounts for less than 15 percent of what Coontz calls "childhood transitions into long-term poverty" whereas various economic changes account for better than 50 percent of all such transitions. Other researchers have reported that since 1979 poverty is increasing faster in those families where both husband and wife are present than in those headed by a single parent. Today more than 40 percent of America's impoverished children live in households with both parents present.

Additional supporting points made by Coontz and others:

- Without working women breaking with "tradition," 60 percent of all U.S. households would suffer a significant decline in real income.
- Many of the problems of African-Americans cannot be attributed to the high rate of marital dissolution and "nontraditional" (female-headed) households in that population. These family conditions are the consequence rather than the cause of poor economic status.
- A variety of studies show that "traditional family values" can actually undermine family life. Men who have "breadwinner" values, for example, are the most likely to abandon their families when they lose their jobs or suffer pay cuts. Similarly, abusive behavior is most frequently reported in those families that most fully subscribe to the traditional gender roles: male dominance, female passivity. And teenage girls who have the most traditional ideas about women's roles in society are the most likely to become pregnant out of wedlock, while the social mavericks are the least likely. Related to this, perhaps, is the additional finding that female high-school dropouts (often those who quit school to marry) are far more likely to divorce than are career women; these dropouts, in fact, have the highest divorce rate among women.

So there is a trend toward the realization that the "traditional" family is neither particularly traditional nor especially healthy that supersedes any intermittent nostalgia for the nuclear family. Yet our needs for nurturance, security and connectedness continue and, if anything, grow more acute as our illusions about the traditional family dissipate.

Our longing for more satisfying sources of nurturance has led us to virtually redefine the family, in terms of behavior, language and law. For example, New York's highest court has ruled that two unrelated people who had lived together in a rent-controlled apartment for ten years legally constituted a family and thus could not be denied protection from eviction, a protection that had previously been reserved exclusively for those related by blood, marriage or adoption. Such protection, the Court of Appeals declared in its 4–2 decision, "should not rest on fictitious legal distinctions or genetic history, but instead should find its foundation in the reality of family life."

What some found particularly shocking about this ruling was that the "couple" involved was not merely unmarried and unrelated but consisted of two gay men.

"It is the totality of the relationship as evidenced by the dedication, caring and self-sacrifice of the parties which should, in the final analysis, control," the court ruled.

The court thus swept aside a number of conventions, replacing them with factors it considers more relevant in determining whether a relationship should receive the same benefits of the law given to those in traditional marriages and families: "level of emotional and financial commitment" and "exclusivity and longevity" of the relationship.

Dr. Pat Voydanoff, chairwoman of the family section of the American Sociological Society, commenting on this case in *The New York Times*, said, "In the past, a family was seen as an economic unit, important for economic exchange, such as inheritances. More recently, families have been perceived as a psychological unit."

Thus, in another court decision, four unrelated elderly people who banded together for mutual support and psychological nurturance were declared to be "a functionally equivalent family" that could not be denied housing in an area that had been zoned "single family."

Increasingly, the family imprimatur is being given to:

- Single parents, irrespective of whether currently married or ever married, and their children
- Unmarried couples of the opposite sex who live together with or without children
- Gay and lesbian couples who live together, with or without children (many have children by prior heterosexual marriages or unions)

- Nontraditional groupings of relatives who live together, e.g., grandparents rearing grandchildren, stepfamilies, foster families, divorced mothers living with adult sons, widowed or unmarried sisters living together, etc.
- Even long-term roommates, unrelated elderly people, communal groups with or without sexual involvement and/or children

The "extended" family becomes more extended all the time to encompass a spectrum of psychological and sometimes financial needs that have previously gone unfulfilled or underfulfilled.

Asked to pick the best definition of "family," nearly 75 percent of some 1,200 adults randomly selected by the Massachusetts Mutual Life Insurance Co., chose this one: "A group of people who love and care for each other." Only one quarter of the sample picked the traditional definition: "A group of people related by blood, marriage or adoption."

Laws are perhaps not changing as rapidly as attitudes, but an effort is being made to keep the law "current." Several major cities have now passed "domestic partnership" laws that extend many of the same legal benefits enjoyed by married couples to unmarried couples, including those who are gay and lesbian. These benefits vary from city to city but include such things as health and other insurance benefits, sick and bereavement leave, housing protection and survivor benefits.

The California Legislature's Joint Select Task Force on the Changing Family has recommended that laws be structured to identify families by *function* rather than by marriage and genetics. Other states, notably Washington, Maryland, Wisconsin and the District of Columbia, are working on comprehensive plans to reconceptualize the family.

While the state is beginning to get the message, the church has lagged behind. The more liberal denominations, not unexpectedly, have been among the first to redefine "profamily." The Rev. Scott W. Alexander of the Unitarian Universalist Association in Massachusetts, for example, called his denomination "profamily" and declared that it supports "all kinds and configurations of families . . . whether they are Ozzie and Harriet families, . . . or Harriet and the kids families, or Ozzie and the kids families."

But there has been some significant change even in more conservative religious circles. Catholic Cardinal Roger Mahony of Los Angeles has asserted that "we must be conscious of the need to be inclusive and to recognize and address the gifts and needs of all forms of family: the divorced and separated, single, single parent, as well as married couples with or without children."

Attention—and controversy—has tended to focus in the media on homosexual unions, but as Thomas F. Coleman, adjunct professor of law at the University of Southern California Law Center, observes:

> Although same-sex couples are properly protected by these legal changes, the primary beneficiaries will be the millions of parents and children who live in foster families and step-families and the millions of unmarried heterosexual men and women who live together as domestic partners. . . . America would be better off if our leaders would accept what the public already knows. Family diversity has arrived and is here to stay. The challenge we face is not how we can turn back the clock, but rather how we can forge solutions to our problems that do not pit one type of family against another.

The dramatic changes that are occurring now in the concept of family will intensify over the next two decades. The politics of family will be entirely transformed in that period. "Strange bedfellows" will seem a barely adequate description for a radically changed—and already emerging—profamily coalition. The process will not be without interruptions and setbacks. Some lower-court rulings may be overturned by a conservative U.S. Supreme Court, the traditional family will be revived in the headlines from time to time, but the economic and psychological forces that for decades have been shaping these changes toward a more diverse family will continue to do so.

The Subtrends

Some of the subtrends related to family, such as child abuse and domestic violence in general, are covered in other chapters. Trends related to the *quality* of relationships are discussed in the chapter on the sexes and relationships.

Deceptively Declining Divorce Rate

The "good news" here is largely illusory. Our prodigious national divorce rate, which more than doubled in one recent ten-year period, now shows signs of stabilization or even decline. Still, 50 percent of all marriages will break up in the next several years. And the leveling of the divorce rate is not due to stronger marriage but to *less* marriage. More people are skipping marriage altogether and are cohabitating instead.

The slight dip in the divorce rate in recent years has caused some prognosticators to predict that younger people, particularly those who have experienced the psychological pain of growing up in broken homes, are increasingly committed to making marriage stick. Hence, they say, the 1990s and beyond will see the country trending back toward the 1950s, when divorce was far less prevalent—to the days, in fact, when divorce was considered "pathological" (in contrast to the 1970s, when it began to be viewed as "liberating").

Others, more persuasively, predict the opposite, that the present lull precedes a storm in which the divorce rate will soar to 60 percent or higher. Underlying this prediction is the fact that the children of divorced parents have always proved more likely—not less likely—to divorce in later life. There is an enormous pool of these "children of divorce" entering adulthood now.

Certainly it is true that these young people want to avoid the pain of divorce—but the best evidence suggests that the "divorce boomers" will do this, not by making their marriages persist at all costs but, rather, by avoiding marriage altogether.

We have gone from viewing divorce as pathological to seeing it as liberating to, today, regarding it as highly stressful. In reality, this change of perspective has more to do with our altered perceptions about marriage than with divorce itself. As sociologist Alice S. Rossi has noted, "When divorce rates first began to rise steeply, they were not interpreted as reflecting disenchantment with marriage per se, but only as disillusionment with specific marital partners, since divorce was typically followed within a few years by remarriage." Developments since then have produced a new interpretation because the rate of remarriage among divorced individuals has been declining. Marriage is increasingly viewed as inimical to the quest for individual freedom that is behind so many of the changes in family life and structure.

The trend, which is reflected in the way mental-health practitioners and researchers now view both marriage and divorce, is toward healthier relationships and less concern over "holding the marriage together." Arlene Skolnick, University of California, Berkeley, research psychologist and author of *Embattled Paradise: The American Family in an Age of Uncertainty*, was asked by a *USA Today* reporter why she isn't more concerned about today's high divorce rate. She answered:

> There are serious problems. But we should devote the energy spent lamenting divorce to thinking about what can be done to improve adjustment of adults and kids. . . . Some divorce is inevitable—longevity means people have to live together so much longer. And there's a new high value on companionship and freedom, it's not just an economic arrangement anymore. We forget the misery of children in unhappy marriages, when people stayed together "for the kids."

The most ambitious long-term studies on the psychological effects of children of divorce are now yielding results that are bound to have far-reaching consequences. These studies make clear for the first time that the damage to children that has been attributed to divorce actually occurs before divorce takes place. This predivorce developmental trauma has now been convincingly documented in a massive British study of 17,000 families and in an ongoing study involving 110 American families. The academic problems of many children, for example, have long been blamed on divorce, but these new studies prove that this damage begins and intensifies with the conflict *preceding* divorce.

Moreover, these studies show that prolonging troubled marriages merely prolongs and aggravates the damage. If there is any message in these studies concerning the *timing* of divorce, it would appear to be this: children between the ages of 8 and 16 are likely to suffer the most from marital dissolution. Boys seem to be more acutely affected by marital strife and divorce at the time they occur but recover more quickly after divorce. Girls appear to exhibit longer-term adverse effects. They tend to marry and have children of their own at younger than average ages and are considerably more prone to divorce. They are also more likely to be unwed mothers than girls in intact families. But, again, these are not the effects of divorce per se but of marital strife.

The politics of divorce is undergoing rapid change. The conservatives' claim to be the defenders of the sanctity of marriage rings with decreasing clarity in view of those studies, mentioned earlier, showing that the "breadwinner" mentality predisposes some men to abusive behavior and family abandonment, particularly in time of economic stress. (Jews are the most "permissive" when it comes to separation and divorce, but they experience very low rates of marital dissolution themselves; in contrast, Baptists, who are among the staunchest opponents of separation and divorce, have very high rates of marital breakup).

There will be other sociopolitical shifts in family trends. The relative poverty of single women with children is due not only to low-paying jobs for women but also to the fact that so few men pay court-decreed child support. Since the United States differs from most other industrialized countries in that it seldom attaches the wages of men who refuse to pay child support, the effect of divorce is often to make the female partner poorer and the male partner more financially secure. This will change in the next two decades, as men are made to pay a much higher price for divorce. At the same time, the concept of "no-fault" divorce will become increasingly discredited as social scientists and policymakers acknowledge the full extent to which this idea has contributed to the feminization of poverty.

Expect interesting fallout as our understanding of both the politics and the psychology of divorce continue to mature in the next two decades. The Scandinavian model that serves so well and in so many social contexts as a bellwether is instructive here. Despite a very high rate of marital breakup, Sweden has far fewer social problems than the United States. Rutgers University sociologist David Popenoe, writing about this in the *Journal of Marriage and the Family*, makes these observations:

> If the non-marital cohabitation dissolution rate is added to Sweden's already high and growing divorce rate (and keeping in mind that non-marital cohabitation is increasingly replacing marriage), it is reasonable to posit that Sweden has the highest rate of family breakup in the industrialized world. . . . Family dissolution is one of the few classically defined social problems that is getting worse in Sweden. Other social problems that have long been thought by outsiders to be "traditionally Swedish," such as alcoholism and suicide, have been diminishing in recent years. Moreover, these problems have never been as serious in Sweden as they have been in many other countries.

If the breakup of the family is the cause of most social ills, as so many still claim in this country, then how do we account for Sweden, with its declining suicide and alcoholism rates and a crime rate the United States can only dream of?

The answers will help tell us where we are headed in the next couple of decades. There is convincing evidence that men and women are more genuinely equal in Sweden than anywhere else in the world. Female day-care workers in Sweden are paid as much as male industrial workers. And about 75 percent of all women ages 16–64 are in the Swedish labor force (compared with 60 percent in the United

States). The "housewife" is an endangered species in Sweden; 85 percent of all Swedish mothers of children under age 7 are in the workforce.

All of this is relevant because when a Swedish woman splits up with the father of her children she is not as disadvantaged as her American counterpart—not only because of her equal pay but also because social programs in Sweden (which, even though recently trimmed, are still the most generous in the world) further insulate the child caretaker from the economic chaos that causes so much trauma to children of divorce in this country.

The Swedish experience coincides with findings from some of the long-term studies of divorce that are now underway—to the effect that the *economic* consequences of family strife and dissolution are among the most crucial factors in producing psychological trauma among adolescents. These findings can be expected to change the nature of divorce law and child-support enforcement, as well as produce increased support for other child-care programs in this country.

Other new findings concerning divorce and family breakup may have unexpected results. It has been known for some time that couples who have children before marriage are considerably more likely than others to divorce once they are married; but now it is also known that premarital *conception* does not, by itself, predispose to a greater incidence of divorce. This might provide a unique argument for abortion—in the *interest* and *protection* of marriage.

Similarly, it is known that children, at least for a time, help hold marriages together and that childlessness in a marriage increases the chance of divorce; but there is a recent finding that is not widely known: couples who have one or more sons are more likely than those who have a daughter or daughters to stay together in marriage. Researchers attribute this to increased paternal involvement in child rearing when a son is present. This may become a new argument for sex-selection technologies that let parents "choose" the sex of their offspring.

It is quite possible that increasingly sophisticated research into the variables of divorce may enable couples and marriage counselors to create more lasting unions. But the major reason why there will be fewer divorces in the future is because there will be fewer marriages.

Cohabitation Increasing

The rate of cohabitation—living together without legal marriage—has been growing since 1970 and will accelerate in the next two decades.

There were under half a million cohabitating couples in 1970; today there are more than 2.5 million.

Actually, Americans have been slower than many Western Europeans in joining the cohabitation trend. The popularity of marriage waned earlier not only in Scandinavian countries but also in Holland, England and France. But with married-couple households now trending toward only two out of four in the United States (down from three of four in the early 1960s), cohabitation is certain to increase in the next two decades. Including those couples who consider themselves married by "common law," the percentage of consensual unions in the United States has risen from about 1 percent in 1970 to more than 5 percent today. The margin for rapid growth in the years immediately ahead is suggested by Sweden's current 25 percent, up from just 1 percent in 1960! Canada's proportion of cohabiting couples has risen to 8 percent, France's to 13 percent in the same time frame. And among young people under age 24 the rates are considerably higher, up to 68 percent in Sweden.

Much has been made of the fact that the rate of breakup among cohabiting couples is much higher than among married couples. This holds true even when married and unmarried couples with children are compared. The statistical bases of these comparisons, however, are flawed by the fact that, among other things, the divorce rates among married couples do not take into account separations without divorces. And so the differences are not as great as claimed. Without the alternative of cohabitation, it is certain that the divorce rates would be far higher than they are.

The trend for the postindustrial world is very clear: less marriage, more cohabitation, easier and—if Sweden is any indication—less-stressful separation. Those who divorce will be less likely to remarry, more likely to cohabit. And in the United States, cohabitation will increasingly gather about it both the cultural acceptance and the legal protection now afforded marriage.

More Single-Parent Families and *Planned* Single Parenthood

The United States has one of the highest proportions of children growing up in single-parent families. Single-parent households are generated both by divorce and separation and by births out-of-wedlock. More than one in five births in the United States is outside of marriage—and three quarters of those births are to women who are not in consensual unions. More than a third of out-of-wedlock births are to teenagers. In Sweden, fully half of all births occur outside of marriage, but the associated problems are less acute than in the United States because, in Sweden, fewer teens are involved and more of the unmarried mothers have cohabiting males (and state-supported programs) to help them.

In the United States, the problem is particularly severe among African-Americans; more than 50 percent of all black children now grow up in single-parent households. Among white children, at age 17, 40 percent are in homes with only one biological parent; for African-Americans of the same age the corresponding figure is 80 percent. The rate at which black single-parent families are forming, however, has been slowing for several years.

What is significant about the single-parent trend is the finding, confirmed in a number of recent surveys and studies, that many single women with children now *prefer* to remain single. The rush to the altar of unwed mothers, so much a part of American life in earlier decades, is now, if anything, a slow and grudging shuffle. The stigma of single parenthood is largely a thing of the past—and the economic realities, unsatisfactory though they are, sometimes favor single parenthood. In any case, women have more choices today than they had even ten years ago; they are choosing the psychological freedom of single parenthood over the financial security (increasingly illusory, in any event) of marriage. In the early 1960s, more than half of all unwed expectant mothers hurried to the altar before giving birth; today only about 25 percent do, and the number continues to decline. Among African-American women and younger women of all races, the percentages are smaller still.

Nor is it just the poor and disadvantaged who are opting for single parenthood. Today a majority of unwed pregnant women from higher income brackets are also resisting marriage. Indeed, there is a minitrend toward *planned* single parenthood that promises to become more pronounced in the near future. With artificial insemination and other "test-tube" reproductive opportunities, the desire to use these innovations is gradually defining a new social frontier, as well. As sociologist Rossi observes:

> A trend worth watching in the years ahead is the incidence of artificial reproduction. So far, insemination by anonymous donors has been relied upon largely by married couples with fertility problems, but there is scattered evidence that some proportion of current users of these services are women who want a child but do not wish to marry. One California clinic reports that one-third of its

clients are composed of such women. Our impression is that many well-educated women who have devoted their twenties to becoming established in their careers find themselves groping for a solution to the dilemma of wanting a child before their reproductive prime runs out, but having no suitable spouse on the horizon.

The real trend here is one that dissociates childbearing and child rearing from marriage, just as there has long been a trend dissociating sex from marriage. But this requires some qualification: the dissociation is from *traditional* marriage, for there is evidence that gay couples and even unmarried heterosexual pairs who are friends but not lovers are using these new reproductive technologies for joint ventures in child rearing.

Organizations have begun to form in support of planned single parenthood, such as Single Mothers by Choice in New York City. Psychotherapists report that more and more of the women who consult them are coming forward with their desire to have a child without a mate. One Boston-area therapist reportedly has more than 1,000 such women in her practice. Many therapists view this trend positively; they argue that children thus carefully planned for and so keenly desired will be especially well loved and cared for. Again, a permutation of family promises to help fulfill deep-seated psychological needs with increasing frequency in the near future.

More Couples Childless By Choice

In the topsy-turvy 1990s, with more single people wanting children, it shouldn't surprise us that more married couples *don't* want children. What the trend really comes down to is increased freedom of choice. One reason for increasing childlessness among couples has to do with the aging of the population, but many of the reasons are more purely psychological. Individual choice can express itself more clearly as social pressures to conform in this context recede. The old idea that "there must be something wrong with them" if a couple does not reproduce is fast waning.

Even so, demographers have been surprised by the growth in numbers of childless couples, beginning in the 1980s. *American Demographics* projects an ongoing trend and predicts that "the number of married couples with children under age 18 will shrink by 12 percent—from 24 million [in 1990] to 21 million by 2000. At the same time, the total number of married couples will grow by 6 percent as the number of couples with no children at home increases by 21 percent."

The empty-nesters are largely married couples between ages 45 and 64, and their percentage is growing rapidly, with a projected 40 percent growth rate—from 13 million in 1990 to 19 million in the year 2000. And a study by the University of Michigan Institute for Social Research reveals that empty-nesters—those whose children have grown and left home—are the most "satisfied" and stress free of all Americans.

At the same time, an increasing number of Americans are choosing *never* to have children. With a strong trend toward later marriage, many couples feel they are "too old" to have children. Others frankly admit they like the economic advantages and relative freedom of being childless. Frequently one or both partners has undergone sterilization prior to marriage (or during a previous marriage). Often both have careers they do not want to jeopardize by having children. In addition, a growing number of couples cite the need for lower population density, crime rates and environmental concerns as reasons for not wanting children.

Ascendance of the One-Person Household

A "family" of one? That, apparently, is what a lot of people want. Postponement or complete rejection of marriage, high divorce and separation rates, and more widows and widowers are all contributing to the rapid expansion of the one-person household. This is the fastest growing household category in the Western world. It has grown in the United States from about 10 percent in the 1950s to more than 25 percent of all households today. This is a trend that still has a long way to go. In Sweden, nearly *40 percent* of all households are now single person.

Both the economic and psychological ramifications of this trend are apt to be quite significant. Marketers are finding both positives and negatives in it. On the one hand, the family-of-one household is less easily targeted with advertising than is the traditional family. After all, just who is it you are reaching in those households—a widow, a young person, someone divorced, someone never married, someone gay, someone heterosexual? On the other hand, all those new households mean many more "units" needing brooms, TVs, dishes, etc. So, on balance, the news is good for business.

But what of the social and psychological implications of all this "loneliness," as some choose to characterize it? The Swedish model may, again, provide some answers. There is certainly no evidence there that this lifestyle has resulted in any increase in suicide, antisocial behavior or mental illness; on the contrary, those problems are declining in that country. Nor is there any evidence of emerging misanthropy. Of all Western countries, the Swedes, according to recent surveys, are the *least* likely to regard themselves as "totally isolated" (less than two tenths of 1 percent).

"So perhaps," writes sociologist David Popenoe, "nothing is really amiss with the new lifestyle; it may be a full expression of the privacy and individualism and freedom that have long been among the dominant values in Western civilization."

If anything, the near future should prove even more conducive to the single-person household as the information and service economies make it easier to remain "in touch" and, in fact, to expand contact with others.

"Mr. Mom" a Reality at Last?

When women began pouring into the workforce in the late 1970s, expectations were high that a real equality of the sexes was at hand and that men, at last, would begin to shoulder more of the household duties, including spending more time at home taking care of the kids. Many women now regard the concept of "Mr. Mom" as a cruel hoax. But, in fact, Mr. Mom *is* slowly emerging. However, he'll never replace Mrs. Mom (or Ms. Mom) entirely. There is overwhelming biological evidence that men simply don't have the ability to be as nurturing and patient with children as women are. This is another one of those anticipated social changes that is viewed as having "failed" only because expectations were unrealistic to begin with.

Men *are* showing more interest in the home and in parenting. Surveys make clear there is a continuing trend in that direction. Granted, part of the impetus for this is not so much a love of domestic work as it is a distaste for work outside the home. But there is also, among many men, a genuine desire to play a larger role in the lives of their children. These men say they feel "cheated" by having to work outside the home so much, cheated of the experience of seeing their children grow up.

As the trend toward more equal pay for women creeps along, gender roles in the home can be expected to undergo further change. Men will feel less pressure to take on more work and will feel more freedom to spend increased time with their families. A number of major corporations are already offering "paternity leave," and such companies as IBM are reporting that a growing number of men have declined promotions that would have robbed them of time at home with their children.

AT&T reports that whereas only one in four hundred of its employees taking family leave was male a decade ago, today that number is one in fifty. And Du Pont notes that in the mid-1980s only 18 percent of its male workers requested part-time work so they could spend more time with their families; today that number is 33 percent.

Mr. Mom has even captured the attention of Madison Avenue. Advertisers have begun downplaying the long-prevailing image of Dad as a bungling idiot in the kitchen and are, increasingly, portraying him as competent and astute. *Progressive Grocer*, a trade journal of the food industry, reports that men are the primary grocery shoppers in 17 percent of all households, up significantly from past years. And another study finds that men take care of nearly *all* the domestic chores in one of every six households, also a considerable change from preceding decades.

The Wall Street Journal characterized Mr. Mom as "a fast-growing minority of men who handle most of the shopping and chores at home." Advertisers, the *Journal* warns, will ignore these men "at their peril. Men control billions of dollars of the nation's $369 billion in grocery sales, and their share is growing."

More "Reconstituted" and Multigenerational Families

More stepfamilies, more households headed by grandparents, more young adults, especially males, staying home with their parents. All of these are definite trends.

The number of young adults ages 20 to 24 who are still living with their parents is now at 55 percent, up from 43 percent in 1963. *Newsweek* examined this issue with an apt headline: YOUNG BEYOND THEIR YEARS. The phenomenon is one of early physical maturation and delayed emotional maturation. America has gone from a country that permitted virtually no time for adolescence to a country in which youngsters enjoy (or suffer) a prolonged adolescence. This is a phenomenon of "all grown up and no place to go."

Today's youth are the product of both overindulgence *and* parental underattention. Many young people now feel, with some justification, that they are superfluous. In stark contrast to the adolescents of decades ago, who had to enter the workforce at early ages to survive (and help their families survive), the youth of today more typically feel they have no real function. This, as discussed in the first chapter, is one of the reasons for the current epidemic of violence and suicides.

Ironically, the tougher economic conditions looming ahead for the youth generation may actually be beneficial, if only to the extent that they create a new sense of urgency among parents, policymakers and the young themselves. The youth generation desperately needs new directions in the form of social and economic programs that will make them more productive, more integral to the community. These needs are beginning to be recognized and some real progress—toward reintegrating youth into society—should be made in the coming two decades.

Some parents, however, are welcoming their adult children back to the fold. Single women, both divorced and widowed, in particular, seem comfortable in forming a new "family" with adult sons who are having trouble finding work. This particular form of reconstituted family seems to work better than some others. There is some reversion to traditional gender roles: the sons enjoy being pampered (having their meals prepared for them, their laundry done and so on) and the mothers are glad to "have a man around the house" again. Marketers, as well as Freudians, have taken note of the new mother-son symbiosis, which, if anything, can be expected to intensify in the near future.

Other forms of reconstituted families, particularly stepfamilies, will also proliferate in the coming two decades. Stepfamily formation increased about 12 percent in one recent five-year period, and it is now estimated that more than 30 percent of all children born in the United States will have a stepparent before reaching adulthood. There is a trend toward better understanding of the stresses created in children by the stepparenting process; this research is expected to make stepfamilies more durable—and less likely to cause trauma—in the years ahead.

The high rate of marital dissolution has created another phenomenon of family reconstitution: grandparents assuming the parental care of their grandchildren. More than 3 million children in the United States now live with grandparents, up 40 percent in just ten years. This trend reflects society's failure to provide sufficient child support in the wake of separation and divorce. As the United States catches up with much of the rest of the industrialized world in providing that support, fewer grandparents will be called upon to raise second families.

More Interracial Families

There are now about 600,000 interracial marriages annually in the United States, a third of these are black-white, nearly triple the number in 1970, when 40 percent of the white population was of the opinion that such marriages should be illegal. Today 20 percent hold that belief.

There is every reason to expect that both the acceptance of and the number of interracial unions will continue to increase into the foreseeable future.

Recognition of Same-Sex Families: Toward Gay and Lesbian Marriage

Family formation by gay and lesbian couples, with or without children, is often referenced by the media as a leading-edge signifier of just how far society has moved in the direction of diversity and individual choice in the family realm. The number of same-sex couples has steadily increased with each census and now stands at 1.6 million such couples. There are an estimated 2 million gay parents in the United States. And while most of these children were had in heterosexual relationships or marriages prior to "coming out," a significant number of gay and lesbian couples are having children through adoption, cooperative parenting arrangements and artificial insemination.

The *Advocate*, a national gay publication, summarizes the situation thus:

> Five years ago, no jurisdiction in the United States granted gay or lesbian couples any of the rights afforded heterosexual couples. Few gay and lesbian political organizations put recognition of gay and lesbian relationships near the top of their agendas. Today, ten cities, one village, and the District of Columbia have adopted domestic-partnerships legislation, and at least six other municipalities have granted certain benefits to gays and lesbians in relationships through administrative procedures. Activists all over the country are fighting in city councils, state legislatures, and the courts for the rights of gay and lesbian couples.

Typical of the new ordinances being passed is the one in Minneapolis which, for the purpose of obtaining benefits, requires same-sex couples to declare that they are "each other's sole domestic partner and neither has a different domestic partner," that they "share the common necessities of life and are responsible for each other's welfare." Where such laws have been passed they also apply to cohabitating unmarried heterosexual couples.

Some of this new legislation provides municipal employees with health and dental benefits for their domestic partners and for sick and bereavement leave in the event of illness or death of a domestic partner.

Other new laws have enabled gay couples and unmarried heterosexual couples to live in neighborhoods zoned for single-family residence. Others provide domestic partners with hospital and prison visitation rights.

While welcoming domestic partnership legislation, gay leaders are pressing for the right to marry throughout the United States. Efforts have been made in Massachusetts, the District of Columbia, Hawaii and elsewhere to achieve this end. Within the next two decades, gays and lesbians will not only win the right to marry but will, like newly arrived immigrants, be some of the strongest proponents of traditional family values.

As Anna Quindlen, writing in *The New York Times*, observes:

> Only 25 years ago it was a crime for a black woman to marry a white man. Perhaps 25 years from now we will find it just as incredible that two people of the same sex were not entitled to commit themselves legally to one another. Love and commitment are rare enough; it seems absurd to thwart them in any guise.

Family of Friends: The Rise of Fictive Kinships

Multiadult households, typically consisting of unrelated singles, have been increasing in number for some years and are expected to continue to do so in coming years. For many, "roommates" are increasingly permanent fixtures in daily life.

In fact, for many, housemates are becoming what some sociologists and psychologists call "fictive kin." Whole "fictive families" are being generated in many of these situations, with some housemates even assigning roles ("brother," "sister," "cousin," "aunt," "mom," "dad" and so on) to one another. Fictive families are springing up among young people, old people, disabled people, homeless people and may well define one of the ultimate evolutions of the family concept, maximizing, as they do, the opportunities for fulfillment of specific social and economic needs outside the constraints of biological relatedness.

The New—More Liberal—Politics of Family

The term "profamily" still suggests a lobby consisting of conservative and fundamentalist religious groups that are staunch defenders of traditional gender roles and are highly exclusionary when it comes to the definition, rights and prerequisites of "family." But the profamily lobby is rapidly changing and will undergo further dramatic alteration in the near future. Moderates, liberals, feminists, gays and many others are now making it clear they will no longer give ground in the discussions about the family.

Allan Carlson, president of the Rockford Institute and author of *The Swedish Experiment in Family Politics*, commented on this trend in *The Wall Street Journal*:

> The GOP has held a near-exclusive claim on the "pro-family" mantle for the past dozen years, albeit with little effect. Family-oriented measures have been on the back burner since the opening day of Ronald Reagan's first term, waiting for the "right moment" that never comes. Smugly complacent, the president's men have asked: "Where else can the . . . conservatives go? To the Democrats?"

Carlson notes that, earlier in this century, conservatives in Sweden made an issue of that country's perception that the family was falling apart and that the nation, as a result, was going to hell. People weren't having babies at the rate they once had, and young couples were not marrying. For all the talk, however, the conservatives did little of any real substance for the family, focusing, instead, for example, on getting the sale and distribution of contraceptives banned for a time. By focusing for too long on "morality" at the expense of the real economic and social well-being of the family, the conservatives ultimately lost power to the Social Democrats.

Once the Swedish liberals decided there was no reason to automatically concede "the family" to the conservatives, the politics of family changed virtually overnight. The liberals came to the economic defense of young couples and fractured families, proposing social reforms that were revolutionary in scope and intensity.

Carlson continues:

> With stunning speed, the "family" became a Social Democratic issue. When new elections were held in 1936, it was that party that was able to posture as pro-motherhood, pro-child, pro-family and pro-birth. In a sweeping victory, the Social Democrats crushed the conservatives and ruled the country for 40 years, enacting policies that significantly shifted responsibility for children from the family to the state.

Might history repeat itself? The growing indifference of the GOP leadership toward the family issue has left the door open to a historic political realignment, signs of which are already evident.

Carlson and others point to the recent emergence of new liberal think tanks and organizations, such as the Institute for American Values and the Progressive Policy Institute, that make family issues their central concern, to the sponsorship by liberals of bills providing for increased income tax exemptions for children, child tax credits and so on.

Attacks on the conservative profamily lobby are increasing. The sincerity of the lobby, similarly, is more frequently being called into question, as it was, for example, by historian Stephanie Coontz, also writing in *The Wall Street Journal*: "Given the unwillingness of that group to support larger reforms, one cannot help but suspect that much of the agitation for 'preserving the family' camouflages an agenda for acceleration of economic and political inequality."

Whether the conservatives will act in time to avoid the fate of their Swedish counterparts remains to be seen. But whatever happens, the politics of family will be distinctly more liberal in the next two decades.

←——— Solutions/Recommendations ———→

What Can We Do About the Breakup of the Nuclear Family?

It's hard to tell how many times we've heard even well-informed health professionals blithely opine that "the breakup of the family is at the root of most of our problems." The *facts* disagree with this conclusion. As the foregoing discussion makes evident, most of the social problems attributed to the dissolution of the "traditional" family (which, in reality, is *not* so traditional) are the product of other forces. Indeed, as we have seen, the nuclear family has itself created a number of economic, social and psychological problems.

As Stephanie Coontz, who has astutely observed that "poverty derives from class, race and work relations, not family ones," notes:

> A program to solve current social problems by recreating "traditional" families would involve staggering Draconian measures—and it would almost certainly fail. To establish the family wage system, in which married men supposedly support all mothers and

> children within self-sufficient families, would require either mandating abortion and birth control for our nation's unmarried women or equipping them with chastity belts, prohibiting divorce except among the rich, obliging unwed mothers to give up their children for adoption, and forcing prospective adoptive couples to accept the black, racially mixed, older white, and disabled children who now cannot find homes. It would also mean prohibiting employers from replacing formerly unionized, male dominated jobs with cheaper female, foreign or part-time labor.

Not quite what the friends of the nuclear family had in mind.

What *can* we do to save the nuclear family? Changes associated with "affluence, secularism, and the strong emphasis on individual development and self-fulfillment" could fuel an evolutionary redirection of the "post nuclear family." Changes could be ushered in by "economic decline, which could force families into a situation of greater self-sufficiency and economic struggle; increased participation in religious institutions, which could generate a greater concern for social responsibility and the continuity of life; a national campaign to reverse low birth rates through the promotion of familism; and the rational calculation that excessive individualism generates social corrosion, with a concomitant decrease in the cultural emphasis on self-fulfillment."

What should we do? We should strengthen those social contracts that ensure the health, well-being and freedom of individuals, including parents, and particularly those individuals who nurture children.

Toward a New Child-care Agenda: Less Day Care/More Parental Leave

Families, in all their diverse new forms, need help, especially when the family, whatever its makeup, includes children. Since the trend is toward even more young mothers entering the workforce in the next two decades (75 percent of mothers with preschool children will soon be working, according to the forecast of the National Council on Family Relations), child-care issues will inevitably gain in urgency and importance.

It is a virtual certainty that government regulation and support of child-care programs will increase sharply over the next twenty years. David Popenoe's summation of the situation in Sweden provides a look at the future:

> Swedish children are born into a society that has an enviable record in its public childcare policies. . . . Conservatives may fault Sweden's attempt to push mothers out of the home and into the work force, but given the fact that almost all mothers now hold outside jobs, the public measures taken in Sweden to care for the children are well in advance of such programs in most other countries. Most noteworthy in this regard is Sweden's parental insurance scheme, which provides either parent of a newly born child up to nine months leave from employment at nearly full salary and another three months at partial salary. Virtually all mothers take this leave in whole or part, and it is shared by 25 percent of the fathers. Indeed, Sweden leads the Western world in its attempts to involve fathers in home and childcare. Following the end of parental leave, Swedish parents have the right to hold their jobs part-time (six hours per day) until their child is between eight and twelve, depending on the community. This is one reason why Sweden has not only the highest percentage of mothers in the labor force but also the highest percentage of women who work only part time. . . . High on the political agenda of Swedish Social Democratic women's groups . . . [is] the goal of a six-hour work day for all workers.

It should be noted that these benefits are available in Sweden not only to married couples but also to cohabitating couples with children and to single mothers. And, though some of these programs are being pared back during relatively difficult economic times, they still remain significant fixtures of Swedish life.

The cost of such social programs has been cited by some in this country as ample reason *not* to implement them here. But there can be little doubt that the benefits to society of such programs far outweigh their costs. These benefits can be measured in terms of both enhanced physical and mental health, children who are more readily educable, reduced domestic abuse, less violence in general, benefits with enormous monetary value to society.

There are numerous measures afloat to provide more day care for the children of working women, but the smart money, long-term, is on the more generous leave-time solutions that have been implemented in Sweden and a few other countries with resounding success. The effects of day care on children are only beginning to be assessed in any meaningful way; the results to date are not entirely encouraging. Even licensed day-care centers are poorly regulated and monitored. And most day care is in unlicensed settings, typically in another person's home.

Many people are shocked to learn that, at this late date, there are still no federal regulations governing day care.

Psychologists are particularly concerned that young children in day care for more than twenty hours each week are more likely to form poor relationships with their mothers and to have psychological problems later in life. Other research shows additional negative results among day-care babies as they grow older: discipline problems, impaired communication skills, diminished ability to complete tasks and otherwise perform effectively in school or at work.

Intriguingly, the worst day-care results have been seen in the children of both the poorest and most affluent. The poorest tend to get day-care services of the lowest quality and the rich tend to expose their children to the *most* day care, which, however high in quality, still has deleterious effects because of its sheer quantity.

There has been a concerted effort to dispute these negative findings—day care is now part of $15 billion-a-year child-care industry—but the findings continue to accumulate. And, in any case, as Pat Wingert and Barbara Kantrowitz, writing in *Newsweek*, observe, "there's little dispute over the damaging effects of the high turnover rate among caregivers. In all forms of child care, consistency is essential to a child's healthy development. But only the lucky few get it."

Results of the National Child Care Staffing Study confirm this. "Turnover among childcare workers is second only to parking lot and gas-station attendants," according to the study's director, Marcy Whitebook. Moreover, the average salaries of day-care workers, very low to begin with, have actually been declining over the past several years.

Further darkening the picture is a Centers for Disease Control report that children in day-care centers are significantly more likely to contract a wide spectrum of diseases, including serious ones such as hepatitis and spinal meningitis.

Day care is here to stay, but it will no longer be viewed as the working parent's panacea. And for very young children it will, increasingly, fall out of favor. It will be subjected to greater regulation and, very soon, to meaningful regulation. Day-care workers will require accreditation, and the industry, in some particulars, will enjoy federal and local subsidies that will help strengthen it.

One such subsidized program is beginning to serve as a national model of what day care *can* be. A fifteen-site network of centers in Pomona, California, provides various forms of child care every day of the year from six in the morning until midnight. The centers are strategically located near major freeway ramps for easy commuter access;

some are situated near learning centers where teen mothers study for high-school equivalency tests. Still others are integrated with Head Start programs and with welfare projects (providing free day care to welfare recipients who pursue jobs or adult education). At other sites, day care is offered in conjunction with counseling related to child abuse, special education and so on.

The Pomona program is considered highly cost effective and is attracting attention around the country. It is sure to be widely emulated over the next several years. Daniel B. Wood, writing in *The Christian Science Monitor*, calls the program "a paragon of the possible for the bureaucratically beleaguered systems in the other 49 states . . . childcare professionals from around the country see [Pomona's] success as proof that effective and affordable childcare is possible."

Even vastly improved day care, however, will not solve child-care problems. Parental-leave programs are apt to have more impact—*and* be healthier for families and, especially, for children. U.S. Representative Patricia Schroeder, Democrat from Colorado, has proposed The Family and Medical Leave Act that provides a working parent with ten weeks of leave to care for a newborn child, an ill child or a newly adopted child. To those who complain of the costs, Congresswoman Schroeder replies: "We're spending billions of dollars protecting the family from the outside [via our huge military budget]. The cost of one missile would protect them from the inside."

Dr. Benjamin Spock has similarly called for taking some of the excesses of the military budget and directing them toward the family realm. He argues for parental leave programs that would keep parent and child together as much as possible, particularly during the child's first five years of life.

Family-leave legislation failed to become law in the recent past, but under the Clinton Administration this has begun to change. Much as liberals perhaps hope that the conservatives will dig in their heels and suffer the fate of their Swedish counterparts, there are signs that the right has read the writing on the wall and will join with the middle and the left to make common cause of the family. Even if the accommodation is not comfortable and complete, it should prove sufficient to advance a new profamily agenda, embracing a number of the Scandinavian solutions.

Judy Mann, writing in *The Washington Post*, states:

> There is a hopeful sign . . . that conservatives are going to be addressing the stresses on modern families more realistically and

> more creatively than they have. . . . This optimistic forecast results, in part from an article by William R. Mattox, Jr., in . . . the [conservative] Heritage Foundation's *Policy Review.* "The biggest problem facing American children today is a lack of time and attention from their parents," Mattox writes, citing a study that found that parents spent 30 hours a week with their children in 1965 and only 17 hours a week in 1985. . . . One of Mattox's recommendations is to dramatically reduce the tax burden on families with children. . . . Further he writes, "policy makers should encourage flexible hours, part-time work, job sharing, and most especially home-based employment opportunities." . . . He suggests that the pattern of sequencing family and career be encouraged "by calling upon employers to give preference in hiring to parents returning to the labor force after an extended stint at home with children," much the way veterans are given preference in hiring when they return to work.

To sum up, with Catholic bishops and gay leaders joining forces to support child-care programs in San Francisco, it shouldn't be surprising if the liberals and the conservatives finally get together on substantive family issues. As the female presence in the workforce continues to grow, so will the trend toward more comprehensive child-care programs, parental leave, part-time work and flexible hours.

The psychological health of the nation should improve as a result of this trend. T. Berry Brazelton, M.D., one of the family's most effective advocates, makes the case for parental-leave legislation in the context of infant mental health. Writing in *The Wall Street Journal*, he declares:

> To form stable attachments and get a good start in life, a baby must pass with its parents through four stages. In the first seven to 10 days of the baby's life, the parents (with the baby's cooperation) must learn how to help the newborn maintain an alert state and pay attention to its surroundings. In the second stage, babies learn to smile and vocalize in return for attention from parents. In the third stage (ages two to three months), the child learns to expect different reactions from each parent and to tell the difference between parents and strangers. In the fourth stage (somewhere around four months) the baby is sure enough of himself and his caregivers to take the lead in building relationships. We have found that the baby "knows" his or her parents by the age of four months and can

therefore "know" that they will return after disappearing for the working day.

To the extent that the "family problem" needs "solving," the seeds of some genuine solutions are being sown today, but with emphasis shifting dramatically in this context from the preservation of the nuclear family to the *protection and proper care of children*.

FOUR

Heart

Kinder and Gentler/ Meaner and More Hateful?

THE TREND The United States today is one of the most heterogeneous cultures in the history of mankind. It has created an almost unprecedented cult of the individual. Despite this combination, it has achieved a high level of social harmony and communality, which must be accounted one of the great triumphs of the human spirit. Current headlines of bigotry and hate notwithstanding, the trend in this country is toward greater, not less, tolerance of minorities, toward expanded, not retracted, accommodation of disparate beliefs. The decline of "traditional morality" has actually contributed to a strengthened ethic of individual accountability and responsibility that benefits society as a whole. The mass media and other tools of the Information Age both distort and amplify this trend, frequently producing the illusion of impending conflagration even as they accelerate the forces of accommodation. Conflict and confrontation will continue to be part of the accommodative process, out of which will emerge a wave of populist reforms, greater accountability of public servants, a new era of volunteerism, a rejection of greed as culturally acceptable, and a more productive and, ultimately, more caring approach to welfare. The trend toward more-enlightened self-interest (or "reciprocal altruism") will lead to a kinder, gentler nation—but also to one that is smarter, tougher and, in many ways, more rational.

Overview

Hope versus Hate

As the sun sets on the twentieth century, pundits are widely decrying the twilight of morality, the decline of tolerance, the ascendance of hate in an environment of heightened expectations and diminished resources. They project for our culture an escalating parochialism that is an echo of the tribal *jihad* they see sweeping the world, fragmenting and shattering nations. Consider these bleak assessments of our future:

- "An epidemic of ethnic hatred is sweeping the world, dismaying and perplexing fair-minded people who are at a loss to explain it." (*Time* magazine)
- "This is where we are in this country; fear begetting fear, hate, hate; revenge, revenge." (Anthony Lewis, *The New York Times*)
- "Hate crimes against Jews are on the rise in the United States . . ." (*The Oregonian*)
- "Reports of anti-gay violence and harassment jumped dramatically last year in six major cities . . ." (*New York Native*)
- "Bias crimes are rising across the nation." (*Money*)
- "This trend is surprising and disturbing to those who have studied prejudicial behavior. . . . Particularly disturbing is the increased prevalence of bigotry on college campuses." (*U.S. News & World Report*)
- "What should disturb the American people is the growing intolerance toward the hungry and homeless." (Raymond L. Flynn, former Mayor of Boston)
- "Overconsumption by the world's richest people is killing the Earth." (*International Wildlife*)
- "Ray Kroc, the late, legendary genius behind the McDonald's hamburger success story . . . said if a competitor is drowning, you should stick a hose in his mouth. . . . Society cultivates and rewards shrewd, cunning, assertive—even exploitative—behavior." (*Christianity Today*)

Relief from all this gloom is seldom part of today's cultural weather forecast but, in reality, much of this psychological smog is a mirage. Not that all is sweetness and light; far from it. Things are bad—but are they really getting worse? What are our points of reference? With what are we making comparisons?

Certainly African-Americans are far better off today than they were throughout the first half of this century, when mental and physical abuse of blacks was—shamefully and incredibly, as we look back now—condoned and even codified in law, taken for granted even by the "well-meaning" mainstream of society.

The same holds true for other minorities. Homosexuality, for example, "the love that dares not speak its name," now speaks its name across the nation, not only on the streets but in the media and at the ballot box. What was widely viewed as a "perversion" in the 1950s, one that was "treated" with imprisonment, banishment and even "corrective" psychosurgery, is today regarded by many as another "lifestyle."

Those who see American pitted against American as never before either don't know history or have forgotten it. The deep and often deadly enmities that once polarized the various immigrant groups in this country are now largely the stuff of memory. What is astonishing is not the differences among us but the similarities, especially given the diversity of national backgrounds.

Certainly when viewed from the perspective of (or in comparison with) homologous societies such as exist in Japan or Western Europe, which so frequently assume a superior attitude, the American landscape sometimes looks like a war zone. The wonder, however, is that ethnic strife is as limited as it is. How remarkably well we've managed under the circumstances comes home to us every once in a while. When a number of foreigners who sought asylum in Sweden, for example, were recently settled in rural areas there, some of the locals greeted them not only with insults but with grenades! What would not have caused so much as a burp in the dynamic body politic of America caused a major case of social dyspepsia in serene Sweden.

Similarly Japan has dealt poorly with the Koreans in its midst, systematically discriminating against them. This is the largest foreign group in Japan—yet it is tiny, making up less than 1 percent of Japan's total population, a percentage that wouldn't raise an eyebrow in the United States.

America is not the worst nation at dealing with issues of tolerance; it is almost certainly the *best*. It has been challenged in this regard as no other country has, and it has risen to that challenge time and again. Moreover, it has derived much of its unique vitality and dynamism from that very challenge.

The trend toward tolerance and accommodation that has been a major evolutionary force in the shaping of this country since its inception continues unabated. The hue and cry that presently attend these issues do not portend resistance to continuing change but quite the opposite. We're paying more attention to these issues than ever before. In an era of pervasive instant information, we want instant results. Awareness is dramatically heightened and so are our expectations. When those expectations fail to be fulfilled with the immediacy all this new awareness seems to call for, we feel frustrated, we declare failure and setback. But those declarations are largely "noise," some of it shrewdly calculated to accelerate desired change; it is as if we must not admit to any progress lest we slow or forestall more of it. Our national "fever" is not a sign of impending demise but of the struggle toward health.

Additionally, we're finally coming to recognize that tolerance is not something that is achieved in a linear fashion; we move up, down, sideways, and sometimes backward before going further ahead. Look behind today's headlines of racial or ethnic strife worldwide, and what do you see? Progress. Take, for example, *Time*'s report that there is an "epidemic of ethnic hatred . . . sweeping the world," under the headline AN OUTBREAK OF BIGOTRY. The body of this report is actually quite thoughtful and it concludes that one of the major examples cited in support of the "epidemic" hypothesis—the desecration of many Jewish graves in France—is not as alarming as it has seemed to many:

> In the wake of the desecrations, 2,000 French Jews applied to immigrate to Israel. . . . But experts on ethnic conflict caution against alarm. Says sociologist Pierre-André Taguieff: "Today antiracism is growing faster than racism. The anti-Semites are marginal."
>
> Underscoring his point, tens of thousands of citizens took part in marches all across France last week to register their disgust with bigotry. In the Paris protest, which drew some 80,000 people, members of all religions and political parties—except [Jean-Marie] Le Pen's [extreme far-right National Front]—rallied together for the first time in recent memory. Even President François Mitterrand was there, marking the first time since Paris' liberation in 1945 that a French head of state has taken to the streets to demonstrate.

Similarly, at the conclusion of its report on the discontent in Japan over the Korean contingency in its midst, *Time* acknowledges: "In fact, discrimination is declining . . ."

But what of the prevalent view that with the "breakup of the family" and the "decline of traditional [and religious] values," there is a diminishing likelihood that we will be a "kinder and gentler" nation in the years ahead? The late Bertrand Russell would certainly take exception to this notion. He once wrote: "The more intense has been the religion of any period and the more profound has been the dogmatic belief, the greater has been the cruelty and the worse has been the state of affairs." One has only to reflect on the hundreds, perhaps thousands, of religious wars and persecutions to find merit in this statement.

Alfie Kohn, in a particularly perceptive piece in *Psychology Today*, surveyed the research literature of the past several decades related to this issue and found no correlation between "piety and pity, between God and good." Or, if there was a correlation, it was more likely to be *negative*. A study of 2,000 Episcopalians, for example, showed "no discernible relationship between involvement [in church activities] and charitable acts. In some cases, a negative relationship appears." Other studies, similarly, showed no significant association between traditional religious beliefs and altruism; nonbelievers were just as likely to "do good."

In fact, in one study of college students, atheists were the only group in which a majority did not cheat on an exam administered under an honor code! And a series of findings have repeatedly revealed that those who attend church are significantly less tolerant of minorities than are nonattenders. Those who are, in the words of psychologist Gordon Allport, "the most indiscriminately pro-religious" are the least tolerant of all people studied. So the decline in traditional religious values cannot be simply understood as a bad sign for tolerance.

These findings coincide in many respects with some of those reported in preceding chapters. Men with the strongest "family values," for example, were found to be the most likely to abandon their families in difficult economies. These "values" all too often become an extrinsic substitute for any genuine intrinsic belief or value system. They are *emblematic*, rather than *felt*. The individualist, with his or her own set of intrinsic convictions, it appears, is actually more likely to be altruistic, cooperative and helping—and is *not* the stereotypical self-serving hedonist. Somewhat ironically, it is the "individualist," as thus defined, who is most likely to support the community movement that has flourished in recent times, a movement that seeks to accommodate the needs of the disabled, the elderly, of recovering alcoholics, minority groups, the homeless and so on.

But after the "Me Generation" of the 1970s and the "Gimme Decade" of the 1980s, many wonder, can we really expect any change of heart? First it must be recognized that those labels were gross oversimplifications of a complex set of social dynamics. Much of the "me" of the Me Generation, for example, was, again, not so much the quest for hedonistic self-gratification as it was the reaction to decades of stultifying and frequently hypocritical social conventions that made marriage and relationships, work and life in general less fulfilling than many perceived these pursuits could be.

And the 1970s, it should be remembered, was a decade in which much of the community movement gathered force, a period in which women, African-Americans and other minorities were given leave, through changed laws and attitudes, to take more power. It was in the seventies that college enrollments soared, with most of the gains accounted for by the working class, minorities and women. By 1980 there was a *ninefold* increase over 1970 in the number of black women psychologists and lawyers, to cite just one example of what this changed atmosphere produced. During the same decade millions of those who had been working at the lowest levels of society had advanced to significantly higher paying jobs. The so-called decade of narcissism and mediocrity was, in reality, one of the most dynamic and liberating periods of the century.

As for the 1980s, there was, unquestionably, an atmosphere of sanctioned greed abroad in the land—but this does not mean that the citizenry in general became more venal and less caring in that decade. It was in the eighties, after all, that many environmental organizations and causes grew by unprecedented leaps and bounds. What was lacking was direction for altruistic impulses at the highest levels of government, and that, undoubtedly, had an enervating, discouraging effect on many.

But not for long, as it turned out. By the late eighties surveys and opinion polls were reflecting the deep dissatisfaction with the "greed-is-good" philosophy on the part of the public. Volunteerism had begun a sharp ascent; students were declaring that money was no longer their primary aim—and this was not just idle chatter; students were increasingly putting their time and talents into studying for the helping professions and, decreasingly, into those traditionally associated with prestige and affluence. Ethics were back in fashion. Tom Wolfe, who had characterized the 1960s in *Radical Chic* and the 1980s in *Bonfire of the Vanities*, saw another change coming: "We are leaving the period of money fever that was the Eighties and entering a period of moral fever," a period *Fortune* magazine has called "the New Altruism."

HEART: Kinder and Gentler/Meaner and More Hateful?

Our Altruistic Capacity: How Deep Is It?

Nancy Solomon and Richard Nalley, writing in *Science Digest*, observe that Charles Darwin "once stated that if a single characteristic of a living thing existed for the sole benefit of another species, it would annihilate his theory of natural selection," which is usually summarized as "survival of the fittest." These authors add that today, "Sociobiologists go a step further, applying Darwin's statement even to members of the same species."

And thus has been born a scientific controversy that frequently appears to go to silly extremes to try to prove or disprove that creatures can be nice to each other. That's putting it in simple terms. Some go to extremes to try to prove that every behavior, every activity of every living thing is ultimately self-serving. Others work just as assiduously to try to show that purely selfless behavior exists in many species, including *Homo sapiens*.

When one of the latter, C. Daniel Batson, reported on his latest, elaborate and, in some respects, ingenious research effort, the results of which he believes show that "not only do we care but also that when we feel empathy for others in need, we are capable of caring for them for their sakes and not our own," his critics were quick to pounce. John M. Martz, for example, responding to Batson's paper in *American Psychologist*, declared:

> Once again, Batson championed his empathy-altruism hypothesis, with its basic premise: We care. And damn us if we obtain any gratification or reward for doing so—we would be terminal egoists whose prosocial behavior is merely instrumental to our own well-being. Enough already!

Enough already, indeed—from *both* sides. The vast middle ground of this issue, which is too often ignored in the heat of this debate, is occupied by scientists, including Darwin himself, who have long accepted the overwhelming survival value of cooperation and reciprocal altruism. If we help others to help ourselves, then fine. But the bottom line is this: "kindness," caring and cooperation appear to be every bit as responsible for our survival as aggression, strength and dominance. In fact, as we've come close to experiencing in the twentieth century, too much strength and aggression can be positively annihilating.

Nobel laureate Herbert A. Simon has persuasively argued (*Science*) that some human behavior is "genuinely altruistic," i.e., devoid of any expectation of reciprocation. "Docility," which he defines as "receptivity to social influence," is a human trait that he says (using a mathematical model) makes an "enormous" contribution to social growth and well-being. Individuals sacrifice—by paying taxes, serving in the military, etc.—for the greater good of society. Thus docility is "positively selected" by the natural forces of evolution. "Altruism," Simon concludes, "either as defined socially or as defined genetically, is wholly compatible with natural selection and is an important determinant of human behavior."

It really should not be so surprising that altruism has so large a role to play in the survival of life. As many researchers have noted, evolution is more concerned with the survival of *species* than with the survival of individuals. Interestingly, and logically, our altruistic impulses are the greatest in times of disaster, when we collectively sense a threat to our survival. Neighbors who have never spoken to one another are suddenly warm and caring buddies in the wake of an earthquake, fire or flood. People who've bickered with one another for years are suddenly solidly united in the face of an external enemy. People who would ordinarily shrink from a shadow suddenly risk their lives in times of war and natural disaster.

Anthropologists argue that self-sacrifice and "heroism" are selected for in nature because these traits help perpetuate the species. In hunter-gatherer days those who went out of their way to rescue others were themselves the most likely to be rescued in return when they got into trouble. This proclivity persists into the present day—and even dead heroes are selected for, indirectly, through the added luster their selfless behavior bestows upon their blood survivors.

Kinder, gentler behavior, however, has immediate benefits for the individual as well as society as a whole. Just how dramatically this can be the case has only recently begun to be appreciated. Animal studies, for example, have found that lower levels of dominance and the ability to give and receive comfort often equate with higher levels of health. And in other studies it has been demonstrated that women are more likely to survive disasters than are men for reasons that have to do with their lower levels of aggression and higher capacities for cooperative behavior.

A long-term study of nearly 3,000 people by researcher James House and others at the University of Michigan turned up a surprisingly powerful correlation between volunteerism and longevity. Men in this group who engage in regular volunteer work were two-and-a-half times less likely to die (during the study period) than men who did no volunteer work.

Other studies have demonstrated that acts of altruism can actually boost our immune responses. Even showing a film in which altruism is featured reportedly boosted an element of immunity in those who viewed it.

Eileen Rockefeller Growald and Allan Luks, commenting on various of these studies in *American Health*, quote researchers who believe "that the opiate system will turn out to modulate altruism." They write:

> That feeling of warmth from doing good may well come from endorphins—the brain's natural opiates, which have also been linked to the highs we feel from running and meditation. Animals given naloxone, a chemical that blocks the effect of endorphins, dramatically increase their attempts to seek out contact with other animals [presumably to try to compensate for the loss].

We know that close and frequent social contact (requiring a dampening of hostility and a boosting of cooperative behavior) seems to benefit health in striking ways. A long-term study of 5,000 people conducted by epidemiologists at Yale and the University of California, Berkeley, for example, showed that those with the fewest human contacts were at least twice as likely to die (during the study period) than those with rich social lives. Many other studies have shown that hostile people who shut themselves off from others tend to have higher incidence of blocked coronary arteries and heart attacks.

Again, evolution appears to favor those personalities that are nurturing and capable of being nurtured.

The growing awareness of the benefits of cooperation and altruism could in itself promote more such activity. Thus the trend toward expanded research in this fascinating field could result in a new trend toward *planned* altruism, a concept that might seem a bit peculiar—not to say a little cynical—at first blush but which need not be a contradiction in terms. As Growald and Luks put it:

> The notion that altruism is good for people could have a profound social effect. We could see a sudden rise of volunteerism. Good Samaritans might cease to be a rare breed. Just as people now exercise and watch their diets to protect their health, they may soon scrape peeling paint from their elderly neighbor's house, collect money for the March of Dimes, campaign for a nuclear freeze, teach illiterates how to read or clean up trash from a public park—all for the same self-protective reason.

Dr. Jonas Salk, developer of the polio vaccine, believes our

> society is at a crisis stage. But he also believes that in such crises, humans manage to produce the knowledge and wisdom necessary to help them choose "the most evolutionarily advantageous path." Our developing knowledge about the health benefits of altruism may be a case in point.

Perhaps, but the human capacity for altruism is deep and abiding. It is not something that has to be induced; it is at the very heart of our collective will to survive as a species.

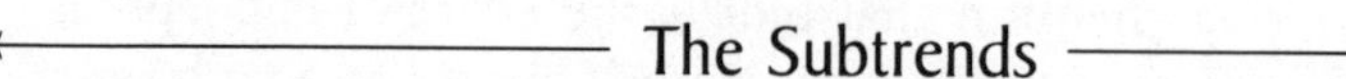

The Subtrends

Increasing Tolerance

Despite all the attention they've gotten recently, bigotry and hate are not what they used to be. It is not "politically correct" to say so but it is clear that *some* of the attention paid to them is part of a calculated effort to achieve what some have called "most-favored-victim" status and thereby to accelerate the advancement of minority-related social causes. It is sometimes easy to sympathize with this impulse, if, like right-minded people everywhere, one believes in genuine equality for all. But the effect of all this distortion, unfortunately, *can be* despair, hopelessness and paralysis.

John Leo, addressing this issue in *U.S. News & World Report*, writes that

> more and more aggrieved groups want to magnify their victim status. This is one of the little intergroup truths nobody talks about: The more victimized you seem, the more political leverage you have. . . .
>
> Crime victims, regardless of their ethnicity and sexual orientation, should complain. The problem is that we have evolved a broad politics of group victimology in which slights and crimes get all tangled up with the social goals of the complaining group. One by-product is elliptical and dishonest debate. . . .
>
> There is no way to overstress how this spread of victimology poisons our politics. . . . It pushes angry people into leadership positions and undermines optimism and balance.

Only the most doctrinaire, agenda-driven activists would seriously argue that African-Americans, women, Jews, gays and many other minorities are not "better off" today than they were in the past. As noted in the opening section of this chapter all have made remarkable gains in the political, social and economic arenas in the past three decades. Much remains to be done, but it is important to maintain a clear perspective lest needless pessimism divert us from a productive path toward further progress. Without hope based in reality there can be no further progress.

Racism, however, remains a pressing problem in this country and will for some time to come. If there is good news, however, it is that our racial "enmities" are not as deep-seated and intransigent as some believe. Our views on these matters are ambivalent and thus mutable; they seem particularly susceptible to guidance, calling attention to the need for real moral leadership at the highest policy-making levels. This is one area, some research indicates, where laws can help change minds.

A few decades ago, African-Americans rode in the back of the bus, infrequently voted, held practically no elective offices and were virtually invisible in businesses and the professions—and the Ku Klux Klan numbered in the millions.

A few decades ago, women stayed in the home and raised children, tended to vote as their husbands dictated (having obtained that right to vote a few decades earlier), held practically no elective offices and were virtually invisible in business and the professions (other than nursing and teaching). Rape and spousal abuse, though even more prevalent than today, were seldom reported and even less frequently prosecuted.

A few decades ago, homosexuals were so effectively oppressed most straight Americans barely knew they existed—and when they were identified, they were usually branded as "criminal" and/or "mentally deranged." Though they could vote, the idea that a self-avowed homosexual might actually be elected to an office was unthinkable.

Too often we only look at the latest headline—or the latest "incident"—as a barometer of the current social climate. Thus, in the wake of the 1992 Los Angeles riots the doomsayers declared these the worst of all times, conveniently forgetting all those earlier incidents, including the bloody riots of 1917 in which 48 people died and 250 buildings were destroyed in racial warfare in East St. Louis (a situation in which entire black families were shot by whites while trying to escape from homes the same whites—none of whom were subsequently convicted—had torched).

Or when a Jewish synagogue is vandalized by anti-Semites, the headlines shout that hate crimes against the Jews are sharply escalating when in fact one survey after another confirms that non-Jewish Americans are more tolerant and accepting of Jews than ever before in our national history and that the evident anti-Semitism of today is but a pale shadow of what existed in the 1920s and 1930s.

Similarly, the intolerance against immigrant groups today gets enormous press, and, in this, many of our social commentators find evidence of newly hardened hearts and contracting social conscience, forgetting the rabid xenophobia of the last century and the early decades of this one. The tired, poor and huddled masses, though never as warmly embraced as some would like to think, get a warmer welcome today than they did at many other stages of our national development.

What astonishes many sociologists and psychologists is just how well we've handled the enormous new wave of immigrants. The Asian population of the United States more than doubled in the 1980s, while Hispanics increased their ranks here by about 50 percent. "Cultural diversity probably accelerated more in the 1980s than any other decade" in the century, according to Carl Haub of the Population Reference Bureau. And those coming here now are more culturally different from the "mainstream" of America than were the waves of European immigrants who came here at the turn of the last century, making the challenge of assimilation that much greater.

The in-migration, moreover, is not just to a few areas but into every state in the country. Pulitzer Prize–winning journalist Stanley Karnow notes that "Asians are just becoming part of the landscape. Where in the past they were odd and exotic, now they are accepted."

Fox Butterfield, writing for *The New York Times*, makes these supporting observations:

> In Birmingham, where eating out long meant barbecue, there are now 60 Chinese restaurants.
>
> In Huntsville, Korean managers at the Korean-owned Gold Star television factory give orders to their American workers.
>
> And here in Bayou La Batre, at the tip of Mobile Bay, a third of the old Cajun fishing village's 2,600 inhabitants are now Vietnamese or Cambodian.
>
> In a state that a quarter-century ago was a symbol of racism, these new settlers are a wave of immigrants that has increased the Asian-American share of Alabama's population by 124 percent in the last decade, according to figures recently made public by the Census Bureau.

For the most part, as in times past, these immigrants are bringing new vitality to America—and, far from displacing Americans born here, they are revitalizing businesses and neighborhoods increasingly abandoned by the "natives." As pointed out in a preceding chapter, the new wave of immigration is expected to be the salvation of New York City and some other major urban centers that have been abandoned by the middle class in recent decades.

Certainly there is still trouble ahead. Intolerance, fascism and bigotry will continue to rear their ugly heads for years and probably decades to come. Groups that foster hate and discrimination will continue to seize every opportunity to oppress target minorities. Under the disingenuous banner of "no special rights," for example, religious fundamentalist and other right-wing groups will continue to try to deny homosexuals equal protection under the law—and will, no doubt, do so with some intermittent, temporary success. This will not, however, be due to genuine intolerance on the part of the public (a strong majority of which supports equal rights for gays, as demonstrated in poll after poll) but to a phenomenon of calculated distortion on the part of antigay lobbyists and initiative writers.

The cyclical nature of social change has been described by legal philosopher Ronald Dworkin, author of *Law's Empire*, thus: "Questions considered easy during one period become hard before they again become easy questions—with the opposite answers." Ideas that change the fabric of society are considered radical in one period and taken for granted in another, working their way, Dworkin explains, through this process:

> They appeared in law school classrooms and law review articles, then as lawyers' arguments in particular cases at law, then as judicial arguments in dissenting opinions explaining why the majority opinion, reflecting the orthodoxy of the time, was unsatisfactory, then as the opinion of the majority in a growing number of cases, and then as propositions no longer mentioned because they went without saying.

Cycles explain why we currently find it difficult to conceive of a time in which women were denied the vote, African-Americans were denied basic civil liberties and interracial "mixing" was a crime.

A New Wave of Activism, Idealism, Volunteerism

The 1980s deserved being called the "Gimme Decade" far more than the 1970s deserved being characterized as the "Me Generation." But as the "decade of greed" came to a close, those who profited appeared to be "getting religion" even faster than the S & L's were tumbling. Cynics saw in this simply more self-serving behavior. But, at a deeper level, change was in the works, creating a new trend that is likely to continue at least for some years.

As early as 1988, the media began declaring a change in the social weather. *U.S. News & World Report*, for example, announced "Idealism's Rebirth":

> Just when the evidence suggests that traditional American idealism is languishing, countervailing signs are cropping up. . . . Americans are starting to feel uncomfortable with the unbridled pursuit of their private interests and are volunteering for a widening array of community-service activities. . . .
>
> The percentage of young and single people who volunteered for some service activity dropped sharply between 1980 and 1985. But a Gallup-Independent Sector survey . . . shows that the trend has reversed in the past two years. . . .
>
> At the same time, volunteer activities are thriving outside the schools, sponsored by local governments, corporations, churches and other nonprofit organizations. . . .

Polls and surveys indicate that about half of all adult Americans now do regular volunteer work, an average of five hours a week—a situation *Time* calls "astounding . . . even allowing for the number of people who lie to pollsters." And among younger people volunteerism is closer to 60 percent and, in some groups, even higher—dramatic increases over the past two decades.

Here are some highlights of the "new idealism":

- The Peace Corps is making a comeback, with more volunteers and more funding.
- The Campus Outreach Opportunity League (COOL), which was started at the University of Minnesota a few years ago, has now spread its volunteer spirit to more than 450 campuses nationwide.
- The largest groups of volunteers are no longer the elderly and the well-to-do but people in the most productive and busy years of their lives—ages 35 to 49. As *Time* notes, "Certainly the most eager and conspicuous new recruits are the yuppies."
- The annual survey of the nation's college freshmen (conducted by the Higher Education Research Institute and the University of Califor-

nia, Los Angeles) shows a continuation of the trend that started in the late eighties: today's students are *far* less interested in business careers today than they were in the mid-eighties and, instead, are shifting toward the health, teaching and other helping professions; concomitantly, continuing a three-year trend, they consider themselves more "liberal" or "far left" than at any time since the close of the sixties and the dawn of the seventies.

- After seventeen consecutive years in which surveys of students showed *increasing* commitment to the goal of "being very well off financially," this trend reversed, beginning in 1990.
- Ethics is suddenly a "hot" subject for study at a growing number of college campuses.
- Social work, after more than a decade of decline, is back in vogue. Enrollment in the more than 550 social-work programs in the United States—and the number of programs continues to grow—is up as much as 33 percent in many centers over a year earlier. Ann Hartman, dean of one such program at Smith College, comments: "I think it's an antigreed movement. People are repulsed by the callousness they've been seeing. They're thinking about the professions and services again, rather than making a million bucks in business."
- United Way officials say the 78 million baby boomers, soon to arrive at the peak of their earning years, will boost charitable giving to an unprecedented high.
- Business books and many other self-help books are de-emphasizing "looking out for number one," stressing, instead, ethics, accountability, cooperation. One of the most successful business-oriented books in some time has been Stephen Covey's *The 7 Habits of Highly Effective People*, in which the "character ethic" is said to be the key to success.
- Student activism is widely reported to be on the rise, with such human rights groups as Amnesty International, for example, now active on more campuses than ever before (Amnesty alone is active at more than 2,700 high schools and colleges in the United States).
- The number of students who say they believe it is "essential" or "very important" to become personally involved in programs to help clean up environmental pollution has more than doubled since the mid-eighties.
- Polls indicate that a majority of Americans are willing to make sacrifices to help preserve the natural environment and undo some of the damage that has been done to it. A recent Roper poll, for example, showed that 65 percent of Americans reject the idea that economics

should come before environment, and nearly a third of those polled call themselves "active environmentalists." Membership in many environmental organizations has more than doubled in recent years.

- There are a number of indicators that the "greed-is-good" philosophy of the eighties was an aberration and that Americans are rejoining the "traditional" conviction in this country that wealth is only as good as the ends to which it is applied; most Americans now reject as a worthy goal "wealth for wealth's sake." Additionally, *Fortune* reports, "Donald Kanter, professor of marketing at Boston University and coauthor of *The Cynical Americans*, detects growing antipathy toward wealth made 'too easily' or 'too fast.'" As Tom Mathews, also commenting on this trend, observed in *Newsweek*: "Americans don't have anything against getting rich, but the old role models were John D. Rockefeller with his oilfields or Henry Ford and his cars—men who used money and power to create something new, not fast-buck wizards."
- In 1980, 26 percent of Americans believed the government was doing "too little" to improve conditions of African-Americans. Today that number has increased to more than 37 percent.
- Numerous studies indicate that Americans, contrary to what many believe, do *not* vote in their own economic self-interest. Changes in economic status do not correlate in any significant way with voting patterns.

The New Accountability

Well before the elections of 1992 it had become apparent to pollsters and politicians alike that the public was beginning to demand more accountability on the part of its elected officials and others in positions of public trust. This trend continues and is part of the new ethic that contributes to a more altruistic, idealistic era. But it is also one of the subtrends that indicate that the "new altruism" has its tough, pragmatic side.

As the middle class in particular began to perceive that it was losing ground it reacted against the excesses of the eighties that so conspicuously enriched what *Newsweek* has called the "plutocracy of corporate raiders, junk-bond artists, greedy-gut parvenus and their political collaborators." Fed up with the "greed-is-good" crowd, the public began to demand reform. In the process, it has also begun to acknowledge that it, too, needs to be a more active and responsible part of the governing process.

Several of the political targets of all this outrage voluntarily removed themselves from contention before they could be voted out in the last election. Others were swept aside in the balloting. The reaction was not as great as some had predicted but it was significant, nonetheless, and a mistrust of those with entrenched power is likely to continue for many years as the system struggles with reform.

By the end of the eighties the public was thoroughly disenchanted with politics—with nearly 60 percent saying they feel shut out of the process altogether. From there disgust with the status quo continued to build, making it easier for more "nontraditional" candidates, especially women and those with little or no previous experience in politics, to gain footholds. The political action committees that have previously helped maintain an incumbent reelection rate of an astonishing 95 percent came under attack and will suffer further erosion of public trust in the future.

More Women, More Elderly, More Altruism

The aging and "androgynizing" of society will have significant influence on tolerance and altruism. Both women and the aged are more likely to support social-welfare programs. Women are less tolerant of racial discrimination, political corruption, militarism and environmental degradation than men, according to a variety of studies.

Reflecting on these demographics and studies, sociologist Alice S. Rossi has concluded, "The future of Western societies seems far less dismal [than some have predicted]. . . . Indeed, the prospect is bright that an aging and androgynous society holds the potential for becoming a society that is more humane and more caring than any Western nation yet has been."

Solutions/Recommendations

Toward a More "Communitarian" Future

Individualism, unquestionably, has reinforced our society with unique resilience and vitality. But as we grow in numbers and the challenges facing us as a nation and a society become dramatically more complex, the need to balance individual rights with community-oriented responsibilities becomes more acute. In recognition of this there is a growing movement of "communitarians" who are intent upon balancing the needs of the community with the freedom of the individual. They argue with some persuasiveness that in recent years the individual has become so protected that society has suffered.

An editorial in *The Responsive Community*, the journal of the American Alliance for Rights & Responsibilities, a communitarian organization, explains the problem this way:

> . . . while people with AIDS must be protected from invasions of their privacy and from job and housing discrimination, the community must be protected in its efforts to curb the spread of the disease to others. While drug dealers' civil rights must be observed, the community must be provided with constitutional tools that will prevent dealers from dominating streets, parks, indeed, whole neighborhoods. While high school students must be protected against wanton expulsion, places of learning must be able to maintain the social-moral climate that education requires.

Another case in point might be hate speech—language that incites people to practice intolerance, discriminate and/or exert physical violence against target groups. On the one hand are the rights of the individual, on the other, the well-being of the community. Or, to cite another example, violent TV programming for children. Here the freedom of the individual to sell whatever programming he or she sees fit to sell must be balanced against the welfare of the community.

The communitarian argues that we have to apply common sense to each situation, weigh the consequences of restricting a particular freedom and calculate the costs to society of failing to so restrict, and then reach a balanced decision. In effect, the communitarian is arguing for us, as a society, to take more responsibility, make reasoned judgments and rely less on simplistic, black-and-white, all-or-nothing standards and distinctions.

Sociologist Amitai Etzioni believes that communitarianism is something that must be *taught* more than legislated—and a great many others agree with him. As he observed in *The Futurist*, "No society can have enough police and auditors and inspectors to make it decent, so you have to have a sense . . . that certain things just aren't done." To instill a sense of social responsibility we need, in Etzioni's words, a new "moral infrastructure." He believes that the place to start building that infrastructure is in the schools, via a renovated concept of civics.

Others who argue eloquently for an accelerated shift toward communitarianism are Robert Bellah, Richard Madsen, William Sullivan,

Ann Swidler and Steven Tipton, authors of *Habits of the Heart* and *The Good Society*. In an adaptation of their work in *Commonweal*, they assert that "the individual is realized only in and through community." They continue:

> It is tempting to think that the problems that we face today, from the homeless in our streets and poverty in the third world to ozone depletion and the greenhouse effect, can be solved by technology or technical expertise alone. But even to begin to solve these daunting problems, let alone problems of emptiness and meaninglessness in our personal lives, requires that we greatly improve our capacity to think about our institutions. We need to understand how much of our lives are lived in and through institutions, and how better institutions are essential if we are to lead better lives.
>
> . . . the culture of individualism makes the very idea of institutions inaccessible to many of us. We Americans tend to think that all we need are energetic individuals and a few impersonal rules to guarantee fairness. Anything more is not only superfluous but dangerous—corrupt, oppressive, or both. Americans often think of individuals pitted against institutions. It is hard for us to think of institutions as affording the necessary context within which we become individuals; of institutions as not just restraining but enabling us; of institutions not as an arena of hostility within which our character is tested but an indispensable source from which character is formed. This is in part because some of our institutions have indeed grown out of control and beyond our comprehension. But the answer is to change them, for it is illusory to imagine that we can escape them.

Anthropologist Mary Douglas declares: "The most profound decisions about justice are not made by individuals as such, but by individuals thinking within and on behalf of institutions."

There is some encouraging evidence—found in some of the changing attitudes discussed earlier in this chapter, as well as in the changed rhetoric of the politicians—that what Bellah et al. hope to achieve may not be out of the question: "an American public philosophy less trapped in the clichés of rugged individualism and more open to an invigorating, fulfilling sense of social responsibility."

There is a sense, in the writings and reflections of many communitarian social commentators, that we are on the brink of rediscovering, through volunteerism in particular, the empowering potential of institutions that are at the heart of *community*. They believe we are on the verge of an era of rebuilding institutions at the heart of our social infrastructure, an era that may rival that of Franklin Roosevelt's New Deal. Among the evidence are calls for a national volunteer service and community-based efforts designed to help repair our torn social fabric (discussed below).

Reform Welfare

It is clear that Americans are as eager as ever to help others in need (for example, a measure that would have slashed welfare benefits was defeated in California in 1992); it is equally clear that they are fed up with "help" that doesn't really help or that, in some instances, may actually make things worse. A trend toward fundamental change in public welfare has been building for some time and will intensify in the next several years until genuinely productive assistance programs are in place. In general, these changed programs will be more *preventive* and less *interventive* than at any time in many decades. Emphasis will be placed on health care, education, job training and community-based initiatives. At the psychological level, there will be a subtle but very real shift from an attitude of "they owe it to me" to "I owe it to myself to better my lot."

Signs of this changed attitude were already emerging in the mid-1980s. Lena Williams, writing in *The New York Times*, in 1986, observed:

> In a major shift of thinking, many black leaders are openly debating whether black Americans should rely more on their own initiative and efforts in solving critical problems long attributed to racism.
>
> For years blacks and their allies supported aid programs that benefited the poor and members of minorities as an effective mechanism to reverse years of discrimination. Cautious about taking positions that would undermine those programs, they often muted discussion of the degree to which blacks had to assume responsibility for some of their own problems.
>
> But gradually, although there has been scant public notice, questions are being raised about whether to put more emphasis on self-reliance and less on governmental, administrative or legislative measures.
>
> . . . John E. Jacob, executive director of the National Urban League, said, "In concentrating on the wrongs of discrimination

and poverty, we may have neglected the fact that there is a lot we can do about our own problems ourselves."

Recently those concerns were echoed by Charles S. Robb, former governor of Virginia, who urged shifting the focus from racism to "self-defeating patterns of behavior among blacks." Coming from a white politician so prominent in the Democratic party establishment and a potential presidential contender, his comments added fuel to the debate.

Even Jesse Jackson allowed that Robb's "positions are headed in the right direction." In 1992 Americans elected president a candidate who expressed much the same philosophy—supported by a political platform that sought significant welfare reform, emphasizing more self-responsibility and job training.

I hasten to add that the trend is *not* toward government stepping entirely aside. It will not and *cannot* if real reform is to be achieved. But "Big Government" proved it couldn't do the job by dumping poorly directed funds on the poor, as it did in the 1960s and 1970s. Those funds, some have charged, amounted to little more than "hush money" allocated like bribes to quiet the underclass (recall the urban riots of the 1960s) and assuage the guilt of the more affluent. For many, welfare became a self-perpetuating condition, enervating community initiatives that might have contributed to real urban renewal.

But if Big Government failed, so did the private sector which, in the 1980s, made a great deal of noise about rebuilding the inner cities through programs that were to stimulate entrepreneurial vision and investment. Both approaches excluded, in effect, direct and meaningful participation by the very individuals they claimed to target, one by asking them to do too little, the other by asking them to do too much.

It is clear now that elements of both approaches will be required to achieve meaningful reform. As former HUD Secretary Jack Kemp put it, "Let's stop assessing blame and . . . begin to look for a synthesis between the left and the right as to what to do."

The old, unproductive debate over whether economic disparities or welfare perpetuated dependency and poverty is, mercifully, droning off into the inaudible range. It is increasingly accepted that both have played roles in creating an underclass in our society.

Federal involvement in welfare, the data suggest, will increasingly be oriented toward job-training programs that may, in some instances, stand alone and, in others, be optional components of community-based efforts integrating private and public input. That "welfare-to-work" programs can pay off has been amply documented. The

Manpower Development Research Corporation of New York, for example, has shown that programs that put "welfare mothers" to work far more than paid for themselves in reducing long-term welfare dependency among those who participated. Even allowing for the one third of the welfare poor who have physical and mental disabilities sufficient to exempt them from these programs, the savings welfare-to-work programs can achieve are enormous, not only in terms of dollars saved but also in terms of enhanced productivity, social unrest allayed, lives and psyches salvaged and community spirit lifted. The resolve and money required to launch these job-training programs, so vital to rebuilding our economic and social infrastructures, are substantial, but the payoff will be even greater.

Other federal efforts are likely to focus on programs that support single and working mothers so that more of them don't fall into full dependency. Coming soon will be legislation that forces men to pay court-mandated child support. The United States lags far behind most countries in Western Europe in this regard. The burden of welfare will continue to fall on the states, cities and communities. There, much of the effort will be directed toward revamping the schools, rebuilding the inner cities, creating job-training programs and rescuing the youth. And why will all this "altruism" come to pass? Because the alternative—to do nothing, to accept the status quo, to permit further deterioration—will cost far more and will imperil not only the quality of life but lives themselves in *all* social and economic strata. The fact that there *are* solutions and that they not only work but can often save money means we will ultimately avail ourselves of them on a concerted and comprehensive scale.

There is evidence, moreover, that the public is already rapidly maturing in its collective attitude toward these issues. Whereas urban riots have generally resulted in public outcry for more police, more "law and order," the reaction to the Los Angeles riots of 1992 was quite different. Polls found that significant majorities of both blacks and whites believed job training would do more good than more police in curbing further urban violence. Americans are more ready than at any time in decades to face the complexities real solutions require.

Saving the Inner Cities (and Rescuing the Young)

In the wake of the Los Angeles riots, the public and private sectors exhibited a new willingness to work together to find solutions for the nation's troubled inner cities. In reality, this was a trend that was already developing, though the riots were certainly a catalyst for acceleration.

There are some measures that the federal government can spearhead. Despite opposition, there is still some support for new federal job programs and a national youth corps devoted to improved health and public services. Proposals are being weighed in both Republican and Democratic circles to pay for the college educations of those who will agree to work in the troubled inner cities as police, teachers and social workers. Surely such a program is at least as much in the interests of society and its "national security" as programs that have paid for the college educations of those who assumed leadership and technical positions in the military.

A public job corps, recalling some of the programs of the New Deal, is also under discussion. The aim is to rebuild urban infrastructure—streets, bridges, hospitals, libraries, parks, recreational facilities, schools. Mary Jordan, writing for the L.A. Times—Washington Post Service, notes such a program "while correcting infrastructure problems . . . also would create badly needed job histories for thousands of inner-city residents."

A job-oriented national youth service has a successful precedent in Franklin Roosevelt's Civil Conservation Corps (CCC), launched, with overwhelming congressional support, in 1933. This innovative program put 2.5 million out-of-work youths into public works.

Neal R. Peirce, writing for the Washington Post Writers Group, declares:

> Many of the . . . young people who went through the CCC would later describe it as an immense skill-and-confidence builder, a turning point in their lives akin to direct military service. . . .
>
> One would like to see hundreds of thousands of youths in just such programs [today]. And it could happen. The Commission on National and Community Service, created by Congress in 1990, is just getting ready to make about $60 million in expansion grants to some of the country's best youth-service programs.

Peirce and others believe that it is best for the federal government to encourage the expansion of existing state and local programs rather than launch an entirely new monolithic federal project. The federal government could help provide funding and help establish standards for the program but leave administration and fine-tuning of programs to the communities involved.

Senator Harris Wofford of Pennsylvania, a strong advocate of nationwide youth service programs, says, "I'm sick and tired of the patronizing social service approach—treating young people as problems, dangers, menaces. We need to turn them around and let them discover themselves as resources."

Peirce, Wofford and others propose using military funds and personnel in youth service. They suggest that as the military is downsized some of the best talent there be redirected to the youth service and that some military bases scheduled to be phased out be converted to youth training centers. Peirce notes that most of the successful existing programs "involve tough calisthenics, uniforms—real demands on kids—often the first constructive discipline they've ever experienced."

A consensus is gradually building to the effect that *self-help*, carefully encouraged by public and private funding, is the key to revitalizing our urban centers. Robert A. Rankin, in a Knight-Ridder News Service series called "Hope for Cities," notes:

> Typically a private philanthropic foundation gives seed money to get a community group rolling, then government grants [state or federal] sustain the enterprise.
>
> Such outside support is essential, but it is equally important that outsiders not take over. Inner-city communities themselves must generate ideas, leadership and grass-roots support . . . or the programs will probably fail like others before them. . . .
>
> "The thing there's no stomach for anywhere anymore is large, [Washington, D.C.] Beltway-driven, bureaucratic programs," said Paul Grogan, president of the Local Initiatives Support Organization, a non-profit group. "But only national leadership can elevate the best of these ideas and give them enough force to make a difference. . . . I would view the welter of successful local experiments as direction-finders for national policy."

Here are examples of some of those "local experiments" that are working.

The New Futures School in Albuquerque, New Mexico, helps pregnant teenagers and adolescent mothers break the cycle of poverty, abuse and welfare through education and training in parenthood. Knight-Ridder reports that whereas 80 percent of all teen mothers have a second pregnancy within two years of the first, only 9 percent of those at New Futures do, and 75 percent of them get their high school diplomas, compared with less than 50 percent of teen mothers nationwide. Moreover, babies born to girls who are the product of New Futures are far healthier than those born to teen girls nationally. There are 50 percent fewer premature and low-birth-weight babies born to the teens at New Futures. The program, now more than two decades old, is funded by the local school district, by private grants and by a nonprofit division of the school that raises money through everything from sponsoring golf tournaments to selling textbooks.

In Saginaw, Michigan, a group of black men involved in business, law, the ministry and education, have launched GAP—The Growth and Afrocentric Program—to help instill pride and self-esteem in young boys growing up in Saginaw's ghetto. "So far," reports Knight-Ridder's Patricia Chargot, "what the men in the program have accomplished is nothing less than dramatic change in the behavior and self-esteem of 200 boys . . . on Saginaw's ravaged east side." The rapidly expanding program has established a Council of Elders to provide the young with a sense of community, role models, tutoring and sources of support in times of personal crises. School and law-enforcement officials report disciplinary problems are down and believe the new program will have a significant impact on crime reduction and community rebirth.

In Indianapolis, Eastside Community Investments, Inc., a non-profit agency is providing business training and financial aid to help restore a shattered community. It is a public-private undertaking that has helped the community develop industrial parks, new housing, day care, home-ownership programs, job-training facilities and so on. Its funding comes largely from neighborhood institutions.

In Baltimore's devastated Sandtown-Winchester district exists an oasis of hope, an experiment in urban renewal funded by private and city money. Forward-looking Baltimore Mayor Kurt Schmoke teamed up with renowned city-saver James Rouse, described by reporter Rankin as "the legendary developer whose record of reviving dead zones in American cities is unparalleled." They fired up the Sandtown community and involved hundreds of locals in a project that seeks to restore the neighborhood from the inside out. The number of new and rehabilitated homes is already in the hundreds—and crime rates have fallen in the restored areas, which are further buttressed with job training, health care, day care and counseling facilities all under one roof for easy access and coordination.

Other ideas that deserve vigorous investigation and trial include "new enterprise zones," proposed by Jack Kemp, endorsed by President Clinton and others. In these inner-city "zones" private enterprise will get tax incentives to provide businesses that hire local people.

Equally important are proposals to help revitalize inner cities by improving public transportation in and out of the central core (so that, among other things, inner-city citizens can commute to the suburbs where nearly 70 percent of the jobs are today); by rethinking low-cost housing to provide for smaller, more scattered and liveable complexes; and by offering tax and interest-rate incentives to promote more and better rentals and encourage home ownership. All of these initiatives portend some movement toward a renewed, more caring urban environment.

Reduce Homelessness

Why is there so much homelessness today and what can be done about it? Estimates of the number of homeless vary from a few hundred thousand to more than 3 million. Everyone agrees the number has been growing at an alarming rate and that children, many of them under 5 years of age, constitute a large part of the homeless population. The National Coalition for the Homeless reports that families with dependent children constitute 40 percent of the nation's homeless.

Factors contributing to the growth of homelessness include economic ills, a long-term trend toward "deinstitutionalization" of mentally disturbed and handicapped people, urban decay and, in some cases, poorly conceived "urban renewal" that displaces the poor. Lack of adequate child support, increased female poverty, lack of adequate health care and sex education for the young, drug abuse and alcoholism and, especially, lack of adequate affordable housing are also cited.

Martha R. Burt and Barbara E. Cohen of the Urban Institute, whose research into homelessness is leading edge, conclude (in *Social Problems*):

> Homelessness in late twentieth-century America is a sign that "safety net" programs for the prevention of extreme destitution have gone astray. Solutions to homelessness must rest on a clear recognition of the multi-faceted nature of the problem, and the application of approaches tailored to the specific needs of the homeless and near homeless.

Their research indicates that "The rise in the presence of homeless families toward the end of the decade [the 1980s] is primarily a phenomenon of women's poverty." As that becomes more clear, support will further intensify for programs that help single mothers, force fathers to pay child support, provide better day care, encourage more equality in the job market and so on.

Other studies make it clear that the retreat in the 1980s from public housing has had disastrous effects. In that decade funds allocated for such housing dropped from $32 billion to $7.5 billion annually. Legislation in the works should reverse that trend in the next decade. And with funds increasingly being allocated to projects with strong community input and control, linked with job training and other support systems, the homeless tide should begin to turn before the end of the decade.

The general assumption, supported by some polls, is that Americans are hardening their hearts toward the homeless. But this certainly is not the case. Polls indicating "public resentment" toward the homeless are largely a function of semantics. More in-depth polls and surveys make it clear that the public does *not* want to turn its back on the homeless. Both liberals and conservatives support programs that will help lift the poor out of homelessness. What people deplore are programs that do nothing to rehabilitate the poor but merely maintain them in a state of poverty.

Many of the innovative approaches being directed toward the revitalization of the inner cities will also impact favorably on the homeless. But there are many pilot projects under development that specifically set out to rescue the homeless population.

Here, too, Jim Rouse, whose work in Baltimore was noted earlier, has been a pioneer. His Enterprise Foundation has been especially successful in bringing government, private enterprise and communities together to reduce homelessness in many cities throughout the country. Rouse, long before others were thinking in like terms, had the vision to realize that if homeless people were to get off the streets they'd have to be given the opportunity and the responsibility to guide their own destinies.

He found ways to build good housing at low cost and to do so in a context of comprehensive community self-help that included health care, job training, child support and the other components of a social infrastructure crucial to long-term self-maintenance.

The Enterprise Foundation grew out of Rouse's experience with Jubilee Housing, a Washington, D.C., project that, with volunteer effort and both private and public fund raising, turned decaying ghetto buildings into clean, safe, tenant-run, low-cost living units. Now the foundation has a large field staff to help communities help themselves. As F. Barton Harvey, deputy chairman of the foundation, put it, writing in *The Humanist*:

> In its bottom-up approach, the Enterprise Foundation seeks to stimulate individual and local initiative, find better ways of achieving neighborhood goals, evaluate the cost and benefits of different programs, and be entrepreneurial. . . .
>
> Enterprise now works with seventy neighborhood groups in twenty-seven cities. . . . Instead of obstacles, it has found remarkable opportunities to build a new national system, linking groups through shared goals, holding up one group's solutions to another, and acting as a national clearinghouse to provide knowledge and experience.

As stereotyping of the homeless as simply "lazy bums" looking for handouts diminishes, Americans can be expected to open their hearts to this segment of the population. The media have been helpful, giving the subject heavy and, for the most part, thoughtful coverage. Many Americans have expressed surprise and heightened concern upon learning, for example, that so many children and families are homeless—more than at any time since the Great Depression—and that, according to some surveys, more than 20 percent of the homeless work at part- or full-time jobs, or that, according to a National Institutes of Mental Health study, 50 to 65 percent of the homeless have completed high school and 25 to 30 percent are college graduates.

Most want to find work but because of economic conditions, physical or mental health problems, financial disaster, family crisis or other circumstance have fallen so far below the "safety net" society has traditionally provided that they cannot, without help, bounce back.

The Los Angeles riots of 1992 were only the most recent reminder that America cannot move forward as a two-tier society, with 34 million people, constituting a frighteningly large underclass, living in poverty.

The survival value of altruism is becoming starkly evident as we approach the twenty-first century.

Teaching Tolerance

We are not *born* haters. We *learn* to hate. There is a great deal that can be done to *prevent* intolerance and hatred and even, though with more difficulty, to *unlearn* these corrosive attitudes and behaviors once they've taken root. The realization of this is helping to create a most welcome trend toward teaching tolerance, in the schools, in the inner cities, even among politicians and statesmen.

A number of school systems, in recent years, have begun providing racial and ethnic "sensitivity" training for their faculties and their students. In New York City, for example, a new "multicultural curriculum" incorporates material related to racial and ethnic relations and issues of tolerance into regular course work. History, reading and literature classes, for example, introduce the works, achievements and progress of minorities of every kind.

Many police departments are also requiring both recruits and veterans to participate in training sessions and seminars, often led by members of the minority groups under discussion. Studies indicate that such programs diminish the "depersonalization" of minorities that facilitates so much intolerance.

State and city governments are joining the battle, too. Seattle, for example, is attempting to fight hate crimes, bigotry and intolerance with a sophisticated commercial campaign on TV. Thousands of posters and brochures accompany the campaign; the multimedia effort portrays the many facets of hate and makes clear Seattle will aggressively prosecute perpetrators of hate crimes. Numbers are provided that can be called to get further information or report harassment, violence and other hate-related crimes.

Even some hardened practitioners of intolerance, it appears, might be susceptible to sensitivity training. When several Klansmen were named in a lawsuit for attacking participants in a civil-rights march, the judge ordered them to enter into a long dialogue session with leaders of the march, including Joseph Lowery, president of the Southern Christian Leadership Conference, which had sponsored the march.

"All of us," Lowery commented at the conclusion of the experiment in reconciliation, "had a feeling that a great deal of repentance took place today."

In other intriguing experiments that deserve follow-up, a new breed of "political psychologists" is attempting to understand and reconcile the animosities and intolerances that separate *nations* and endanger life throughout the world.

The 1,400-member International Society of Political Psychology has been particularly active in this context, setting up unofficial meetings between hostile factions and states, sometimes, according to observers, paving the way toward *official* accommodations of opposing views that wouldn't otherwise have been achieved. These meetings, between Israelis and Arabs, Americans and Russians, among others, have taken place at Harvard's Center for International Affairs, The Esalen Institute in Big Sur, California, and elsewhere.

Newsweek has referred to these meetings as "international group-therapy sessions" in which there is a growing realization that enmity is a *psychological* concept and, as such, is amenable to psychological treatment and *cure*. The American Psychiatric Association (APA) has joined in, as well, seeking to find new ways to break down the fears that create "them" and "us." These "sessions" have made promising progress in getting opposing groups to respect one another's right to exist, a crucial first step in the direction of tolerance. A hopeful example of this came in the summer of 1993 when Israel and the PLO (Palestine Liberation Organization) signified their intention to coexist peacefully.

Just as we have no genetic predisposition to violence, neither do we have any intrinsic need to hate. Indeed, as we have seen, only through cooperation and tolerance can we survive as a species. As we are becoming increasingly conscious of this central truth, our future prospects brighten.

FIVE

Life

More Respect/Less Respect?

THE TREND Notwithstanding those visions of mankind sliding down a "slippery slope" of situational ethics, abortion, euthanasia, capital punishment, legal and black markets in organs, fetal tissue and made-to-order babies, genetic engineering, eugenics and the wholesale destruction of entire animal species, *more*, not less, respect for life is likely in the next two decades and, barring some calamity of remarkable proportions, well beyond. Indeed, respect for life has steadily increased since the birth of the United States, concurrent with increasing knowledge of life processes and consequent control of our biological destiny. Greater understanding has created greater *choice* and, thus, the opportunity as well as the need to exercise greater responsibility and, ultimately, greater morality. Though some will persist in misperceiving choice as "sin," others—the majority—will accept it as both the burden and the reward of a new epoch in human evolution, recognizing that where there is no choice there is no real morality, nor any genuine opportunity for life-enhancing growth, adaptation and change. The transition from our perception of ourselves as passive objects of evolution to active participants in it will not pass without the raising of many grave doubts and longing backward glances. This will be particularly evident in the next two decades as we are called upon to exercise our collective judgment in the best utilization of rapidly expanding technologies that can, increasingly, not only prolong life but also alter it according to our desires. At the threshold of "participatory evolution," mankind finds itself a fledgling and sometimes fearful and reluctant creator—but a creator, nonetheless, and one more in awe of the life forces it now actively helps shape than it was when it was but passively shaped by them. Like a passenger who suddenly becomes a driver, mankind must now pay far closer heed to the engines of life and the "rules of the road" along which safe, productive and nurturing life proceeds. Even in an unfolding universe of "choice," there are barriers, aggregates of natural law and "moral tension" that cannot, without negative consequence, be breached.

Participatory Evolution: Will We Be Master or Slave?

Aldous Huxley, in his novel *Brave New World*, predicted a "biological revolution" that he said would create the promise and peril of "genetic predestination," human-directed evolution of life. But rather like those prognosticators who miscalculated that the resolution of the Cold War was at least a hundred years away, Huxley predicted the "brave new world" of participatory evolution for six hundred years in the future!

When it comes to life and our perception of it, the changes over the past few decades have been and will continue to be quick in coming, profound—and not always welcome.

David Rorvik, writing in *Omni* more than ten years ago, observed:

> The late Nobelist Dr. Edward L. Tatum has called the growing ability of *Homo sapiens* to engineer the genetic future of the species "the most astounding prospect so far suggested by science." Caltech biologist Robert L. Sinsheimer terms it "one of the most important concepts to arise in the history of mankind." He adds, "For the first time a living creature understands its origins and can undertake to design its future."
>
> Not everyone is sanguine about what all this portends for mankind. To some, genetic engineering is a monstrous affront to God and nature. . . .
>
> Some of the bio-engineers themselves have serious qualms about man's headlong rush into creation, fearing that we now have the

> ability to create but not the wisdom to know what, when, or whether to create. "Our ignorance is profound," declares Nobel Prize winner George Wald, urging a moratorium on much of the current gene tinkering.
>
> "Have we the right," asks Columbia University biochemist Erwin Chargaff, "to counteract, irreversibly, the evolutionary wisdom of millions of years in order to satisfy the ambition and the curiosity of a few scientists?"

But, as Rorvik noted in 1980, it was no longer just "a few scientists," but a multitude. Rorvik predicted that genetic engineering would be "the next big growth industry, potentially bigger than the semiconductor industry," and that it was unstoppable. He—and many others he quoted—worried about abuses, the use of reproductive and genetic breakthroughs to create babies to order, utterly defect free and all depressingly alike; to screen out "undesirables" and even to engage in covert "recombinant warfare," producing test-tube viruses and other "bugs" that selectively attack specific ethnic minorities. In the same article he warned that genetic screening could be used to deny "bad risks" insurance, to deny people employment on the basis of detected environmental vulnerabilities and so on:

> These . . . developments portend an invasion of privacy that may ultimately provide "scientific" bases for discrimination, alienation and exclusion. . . . Genetic screening, for all its potentially positive contributions, may eventually serve as a means of declaring certain "genetic types" dangerous, useless, inefficient, or obsolete. . . .
>
> These new technologies, I fear, will not make man more noble, more compassionate, more aware of his own diverse mystery, but rather more malleable, more tolerant of social and environmental decay. The "super race" whose advent so many have feared will not be the forced irrational product of a mad dictator's dreams but the cost-analyzed, market-tested, pragmatic product of profit-oriented scientist-businessmen. Blue eyes and blond hair won't be a fraction as important as the ability to endure stenches, stress, verminous food, crowding, industrial pollution, boredom, and depersonalization.

Though some of those who sounded the alarm a decade or more ago have since modified their pessimism, many—properly, in my view—

maintain a taut "moral tension" with respect to the use of these technologies.

Famed biologist Salvador Luria (*Science*, 1989), for example, cautions that our expanding genetic knowledge may "invade the rights and privacy of individuals" and lead to a "program to 'perfect' human individuals by 'correcting' their genomes in conformity, perhaps, to an ideal, 'white, Judeo-Christian, economically successful' genotype." And, Robert Wright, writing in *The New Republic* in 1990, warns of imperiled health insurance and civil liberties and a "complicate[d] ethics of human reproduction."

Robert A. Weinberg, writing in *Technology Review* in 1991, shows us "The dark side of the genome" project, a massive multibillion dollar effort to map and analyze the entire DNA sequencing that makes up a human being. Weinberg worried that, in as little as ten years' time, we may already know so much about the human "recipe" or "genome," as our genetic blueprint is known, that genetic tests will permit parents not only to screen their prospective progeny for serious defects that are *sure* to arise if a pregnancy is carried to term but also for milder and far less certain defects that may, nonetheless, tempt parents to get perfection by aborting any embryonic or fetal "product" that falls short of the desired mark.

And not so much later, he adds, we'll be able to screen for eye color, gender, body shape and so on—leading to even greater temptations and still more trivial justifications for "corrective" abortion.

When, ultimately, we can tell everything—or *think* we can tell everything—through genetic analysis, then, he continues, we will be the victims of "genetic determinism," defined by what our genes predict for us, "shackled," in Weinberg's view, by our "pedigree."

> Such a surrender to genetic determinism may disenfranchise generations of children who might come to believe that genes, rather than spunk, ambition, and passion, must guide their life course. . . .
>
> In coming years, we will hear more and more from those who . . . embrace a new astrology in which alleles rather than stars determine individuals' lives. It is hard to imagine how far this growing abdication of responsibility will carry us.
>
> As a biologist, I find this prospect a bitter pill. The biological revolution . . . has proven extraordinarily exciting and endlessly fascinating, and it will, without doubt, spawn enormous benefit. But as with most new technologies, we will pay a price unless we

anticipate the human genome project's dark side. We need to craft an ethic that cherishes our human ability to transcend biology, that enshrines our spontaneity, unpredictability, and individual uniqueness. At the moment, I find myself and those around me ill equipped to respond to the challenge.

It is just such concerns as these that make one more optimistic about the future and our continuing high regard for life in all of its diversity. The very prevalence of these concerns, both within and without the world of biotechnology, improves the chances that we will make carefully considered choices following much public debate. If only as much concern and public involvement had been evidenced in the early stages of our nuclear technologies. And if only the Nuclear Age had promised to be even a fraction as life enhancing as the Biological Age does.

Few would disagree that health care in general is today vastly improved over what it was one hundred, fifty, and even ten years ago. Already there are tens of thousands of beneficiaries of our new genetic and reproductive technologies. There is little sense in the argument that "life" has been diminished, cheapened or otherwise compromised by man's "interference," an interference that has conquered infertility previously declared intractable and provided the first truly promising approaches to detecting, preventing and treating the most dire genetic diseases, as well as cancer and numerous immune disorders. Even many of those with the most foreboding concede that we are on the verge of breakthroughs that will result in unprecedented benefits for mankind.

As Robert Wright, whose fears were noted earlier, points out, "It will be a pathetic comment on civilization if the world's societies can't arrange things so that the good that comes from genome research outweighs, at least narrowly, the bad."

It seems likely that we will circumvent some of the more obvious potential abuses. Insurance companies, for example, may attempt to use genetic screening to weed out "bad risks." So might employers. But will society stand by inertly in the face of such developments? Events of the past several decades strongly suggest this assumption is unjustified. There has been and continues to be a strong trend toward worker protection and in favor of diminished—not increased—discrimination against the handicapped.

Again, it comes down to making choices—and society has long recognized that choices that profoundly divide rather than unite the populace are ultimately destructive to all.

Society will almost certainly "arrange things" so that genetic screening doesn't do more harm than good. Indeed, with respect to insurance, many observers believe that if nothing else revolutionizes our insurance system (by replacing it with universal coverage), genetic screening surely will. The easiest—and most cost-effective way—of obviating the potential abuses outlined above is to mandate insurance for everyone.

More Signs of Life—and Respect for It

Certainly there are hard issues—and choices—ahead for society related to the "sanctity of life." But even with regard to abortion, capital punishment, euthanasia, care of the aged, environmental decay and traffic in organs, other body parts and fetal tissue, there are vital signs of life and sustained or increasing respect for it. While all of these topics will be dealt with in greater depth in the Subtrends section, I'd like to make some prefatory remarks about some of them here.

In reality, few people are actually "for" abortion, in the sense that they advocate it. Yet, the majority in this country *favor* it as a legal option, under broad circumstances. Our society as a whole has made a choice—and that choice favors, for the most part, established life over potential or incipient life.

Is abortion, then, the first step, as the self-declared "prolife" forces claim, down that "slippery slope" where, at the bottom, there is a morality so relative and "situational" that life, stripped of any intrinsic value, is utterly debased and devalued? Society says no and holds that, on the contrary, established life—and particularly the life of girls and women—would be more significantly debased by an absolutist "life ethic" that forbade abortion under most or all circumstances. In the view of the majority, a policy allowing abortion is more life enhancing than life denigrating. There is no credible scientific evidence that this policy has promoted disrespect for life in any other context.

Some have claimed that "increased sentiment" for euthanasia—"mercy killing"—represents the *next* step down the "slippery slope" toward utter disrespect for life, but, in fact, euthanasia has been debated in various cultures for centuries and is not an *inexorable* step up *or* down.

In our own society, the current tension over euthanasia is a product of medically prolonged life (a phenomenon that is itself surely the product of genuine prolife forces) unattended, in too many cases, by adequate *quality* of life. This is a new phenomenon that requires a new set of choices. The vast preponderance of evidence to date suggests that society is prepared to be thoughtful, cautious and responsible in making those choices and, to the extent that it favors euthanasia under some circumstances, it is, the same evidence makes clear, for the purpose of alleviating terminal suffering out of respect for *meaningful* life.

It is highly unlikely that, contrary to what some have suggested, the aged will become the equivalent of the unwanted unborn in coming decades, if for no other reason than the fact that we *all* are eventually destined to join the aged and that, in addition, this segment of the population is, as a percentage of the whole, rapidly growing in size and political power. It is safe to say that the aged will award themselves *more*—not less—respect in coming years.

The scientific literature, moreover, gives us some reason to believe that as we age—and expect to live increasingly longer—we assume a concomitant "longer view" of life and thus also a more "consequentialist" ethic.

This could bode well for the environment. Indeed, there are growing signs that we are becoming increasingly sensitive to the fragility of life, across the spectrum, upon which we ultimately depend for our own collective and individual existences. Respect for life appears to be growing in direct proportion to our understanding of it.

The subtrends that follow move from current "hot-button" life issues, such as abortion, euthanasia and capital punishment, toward topics that will increasingly dominate ethical and policy debates in the next twenty years: care and rights of the aged, environment, reproductive technologies, genetic interventions and the "brave new world" of *guided evolution.*

Abortion: A Quieting of the Old Debate, a Quickening of the New

It is not the purpose or within the scope of this book to argue the ethics of abortion. It is fair to state, however, that abortion has not, by any objective, verifiable standard, caused a decline in what can be called "respect for life." There is no correlation, for example, between the incidence of abortion in our society and, say, murder, assault, child or spousal abuse or infanticide. Nor can abortion be shown to correlate with promiscuity or unethical business practices or environmental disregard.

On the contrary, the "prochoice" forces have tended to be those that are more inclined to favor environmental protection, oppose nuclear proliferation, oppose capital punishment and favor universal health care and assistance to the needy and the homeless.

Indeed, the "prochoicers" are part of the core constituency that has long lobbied for economic equality for women, and for the whole agenda of family and child-care support that most other Western nations have long since embraced but which is still largely unrealized in this country: parental leave, extended day care, mandated and enforced child support and so on.

Thus, to the extent that the self-described "prolife" forces have ignored or actively opposed these life-enhancing social positions and innovations, it could be argued that the antiabortion position correlates with an "antilife" attitude in several contexts.

Abortion, in any case, as noted in a preceding chapter, will decline in incidence as a new era of advanced contraception progresses. Within the next two decades, effective, safe male contraceptive "pills," as well as even more revolutionary vaccines that prevent conception, will be achieved. Prior to that, "morning after" pills that are abortifacient at the very earliest stages of embryonic development will further dim the current debate, no matter how much some will continue to insist that an abortion is "murder" at whatever stage it is carried out.

But a new debate can be expected to rise in intensity as abortion begins to be used more frequently (but still in numbers insufficient to reverse the overall decline) in the coming two decades as the vehicle of a kind of crude eugenics. As genetic screening becomes more refined and is more widely available, more prospective parents will opt for abortion to terminate fetuses found to have serious genetic defects.

This new debate is likely to become particularly heated when abortion is used to end those pregnancies in which genetic screens determine that the offspring will be of the "wrong" sex, body type, hair and eye color and so on. It seems likely, however, judging by the current warnings against such scenarios, that society will take a generally unfavorable view of this use of abortion. And it is safe to say, judging by what is being written today (and by whom), that many of those who favor legal abortion as typically used today will *oppose* it for these applications.

In any case, it appears again that this particular use of abortion will be relatively short lived, largely obviated by increasingly sophisticated genetic testing that will be able to predict probable genetic outcome *before* conception.

But even if some "trivial" use of abortion persists—and it almost certainly will—can that prospect outweigh the enormous countervailing benefits of genetic screening and the incalculable alleviation of suffering it will effect? I'll have more to say about genetic screening later in this chapter.

Finally, it is worth noting that through the decades of legal abortion in the United States the literature related thereto has not become increasingly more callous and uncaring. On the contrary, if anything there has been *more* concern voiced by prochoice forces in the context of calling for more productive alternatives to abortion, e.g., more and better sex education, beginning in elementary schools, more and better contraceptives and wider availability, especially among teens, more social and financial support for single mothers—all generally opposed by those on the other side.

Capital Punishment: More Support in the Short Term, Less in the Long Term

It used to be that liberals reliably favored abortion and opposed capital punishment; conservatives, at the same time, generally opposed abortion and favored capital punishment.

Today those lines are not so neatly drawn. There are some religious conservatives (still a distinct minority within that group) who disapprove of both abortion and capital punishment. And there are now more and more so-called double-death Democrats, liberals who favor both abortion and the death sentence.

There is, unquestionably, a trend toward greater support for capital punishment in this country, a trend that runs starkly counter to the worldwide trend. But this is a trend with many a countercurrent and ambivalent eddy. It is also one that I predict will be relatively short lived. There is nothing in the trend that signals a fundamental shift toward disrespect for life. Even given the currently rising sentiment in favor of the death penalty, we'll have to go some distance to match the zeal we had for capital punishment in frontier days.

Since 1976, France, Norway, New Zealand, Cambodia, Australia, Haiti, Namibia, Romania, the Philippines, Nicaragua, Denmark, the Netherlands, East Germany and Portugal have all abolished capital punishment.

"The U.S.—alone among Western democracies—is defying the trend," writes John Horgan in *Scientific American*:

> Indeed, since the Supreme Court ended a 10-year moratorium on executions in 1976, Americans have embraced the death penalty with a vengeance. Recent polls show that 75 percent of the public supports capital punishment, up from 57 percent in 1972. . . .
>
> Thirty-six states already have death-penalty statutes, and pressure is building in [others] . . . to jump on the bandwagon . . . more than 2,300 [prisoners] . . . are on death row. . . . Lawmakers at the state and federal level have proposed a welter of bills to expedite executions and to extend their reach. . . .

Some—but not all—favor capital punishment because they believe it deters others from committing capital crimes, principally murder. As the overwhelming evidence that capital punishment does *not* act as a deterrent becomes more widely known, support for the death penalty will erode among this particular subgroup.

Researchers William C. Bailey and Ruth D. Peterson (*American Sociological Review*) have thoroughly studied the effect of executions on subsequent homicide rates and have concluded that there is none:

> For periods ranging through one year after executions, the overall effect of executions on homicide rates was essentially zero . . . [and] this analysis provides little reason to question the consensus reached over the last two centuries by most criminologists that capital punishment does not provide an effective deterrent to murder.

Some researchers are finding that capital punishment, and the publicity surrounding it, actually seem to encourage *more* murder. Criminologist William J. Bowers has reported, for example, that, in New York State, there was an *increase* in homicides (by an average of more than two) in the month after an execution. These findings held up in a study that covered more than half a century—from 1907 to 1963.

Bowers and others believe that capital punishment may have desensitizing and brutalizing effects that help promote more murder.

Others have favored capital punishment because they believe it is more cost effective than life imprisonment. That assumption is false, a fact that, as it becomes more widely known, will also cool some of the ardor for capital punishment. Given the appeals process that commonly attends the long march to the gallows, the electric chair or the gas chamber, legal killing typically costs more than *four times more* than imprisoning someone for life. A movement toward diminishing those appeals is expected to result in cutting an average two years at most off the process in each case.

Of course, some believe that capital punishment is called for even if it isn't cost effective and even if it doesn't deter others from killing. These advocates of the death penalty seek retribution. Revenge, they say, is reason enough to execute. This, however, is far from the majority opinion.

It appears that support for the death penalty is much softer than the polls suggest. There are a number of reasons for this, and they have a great deal to do with the public's respect for justice and for life.

Once again, one has to be mindful of how public opinion polls are *worded* in terms of interpreting what they—and their results—really mean. Implicit, if not explicit, in some polls on this issue is the idea that capital punishment can help curb our high crime rate—one of the highest in the world. This, of course, elicits a lot more support for the death penalty than some other approaches might.

In fact, in a recent poll in which respondents were asked if they favor capital punishment (with no alternatives or modifications provided), 75 percent of those responding said yes. But, then, when respondents were given choices (either the death penalty or life imprisonment without the possibility of parole), support for capital punishment plummeted to under 50 percent. Support falls further (to under 30 percent) when the convicted is required not only to serve a life sentence but also to financially compensate the family of the murder victim.

Additionally, as Richard L. Worsnop (*Editorial Research Reports*) has noted, a number of researchers and crime experts believe that the public's *statements* in support of capital punishment do not necessarily reflect the public's real *convictions* and "*feelings*" about it; furthermore,

> poll results and campaign oratory may only hint at the complexity of popular opinion about capital punishment. Some analysts say support for the death penalty is so high because it is perceived as a symbol of toughness on crime. Other evidence suggests, these analysts say, that people's gut feelings about actual executions are a good deal more ambivalent.
>
> David J. Gottlieb, a University of Kansas law professor and death penalty opponent, says available data clearly indicate that people favor the death penalty more in the abstract than in actuality. "It's almost impossible to reconcile the support for the death penalty with the relative infrequency of executions in any other way," he says.

Worsnop points out that only 132 executions had been carried out between 1976 and 1990, averaging fewer than 10 a year, and that 70 percent of these were carried out in "just four of the thirty-seven states" where capital punishment is legal (Florida, Texas, Louisiana and Georgia). In the other states, Worsnop observes, "There seems to be a deep-seated reluctance to carry out a sentence of death except in the most extraordinary circumstances."

A good deal of that reluctance accrues from a revulsion over the taking of human life. But, in addition, the public is also aware of the potential for the most grievous form of injustice: executing someone wrongfully convicted in a capital case. One survey, Horgan reports, shows that "in the past 18 years, at least 27 people condemned to death have later been found innocent by a higher court." That's a considerable number, and, he adds, "others have not been so lucky. From 1900 to 1985, at least 23 Americans were executed for crimes they did not commit, according to a 1987 report in *Stanford Law Review*."

Many believe that the numbers are actually considerably higher than this. But, in any case, these grim statistics help show why the public is properly ambivalent about the use of the death penalty and why some believe the appeals process needs to be strengthened, not weakened.

There is another life-respecting reason why the public feels deeply uneasy about the actual implementation of the death penalty. The statistics reveal a strong racial bias in that implementation. Simply put, whites who kill blacks do not get the death penalty; blacks who kill whites *do*. Between 1976 and 1991, not a single white who has killed a black has received the death sentence, let alone been executed. In that same period, thirty-three blacks were executed for killing whites. As Horgan sums it up: "84 percent of those executed since 1976 murdered a white person, although half of the murder victims in the United States are black."

It was just such concerns that caused the Supreme Court, with public opinion in agreement, to ban capital punishment with rulings to that effect in the late 1960s and early 1970s. These rulings came during a period when, as the *Economist* recently noted, "There had been a lot of discussion on the ethics of capital punishment," it was seen to be racially discriminatory, sometimes arbitrarily and unjustly applied and ineffective in curbing capital crime.

Worsnop has commented insightfully on the cyclical nature of the public's relationship with capital punishment:

> History suggests . . . that opinion on capital punishment in the United States is subject to cyclical swings over long periods. Sup-

porters and opponents of the death penalty both seem to fight harder and win more converts when the opposing view is accepted as conventional wisdom. As in the case of an incumbent office-holder, people evaluate a state's philosophy of criminal punishment on the basis of perceived effectiveness. If the person or policy fails this test, voters will seek out an alternative.

Thus, a sharp increase in executions could trigger popular revulsion against the death penalty, especially if murder rates fail to drop significantly as a result. Televising of even a few executions might have a similar effect, leading perhaps to the repeal of capital punishment laws in a number of states.

The current cycle favoring capital punishment (with qualifications and considerable ambivalence, as we have seen) is, above all else, the result of frustration over our persistently high crime rate. The politics of retribution, as argued in chapter 1 of this book, are doomed to failure. When that failure is amply manifest and more productive policies are implemented, the current trend toward increased use of capital punishment will be reversed.

In the meantime, there is nothing in this trend that suggests a growing collective disregard for human life. On the contrary, it is part of an anguished—if, as the evidence would suggest, misguided—effort to preserve and safeguard human life.

Better Health Care, Longer Life, More Respect for the Aged

Whatever the flaws and inequities of our present medical system, few would deny that we, along with a few other countries, have achieved a level of health care unprecedented in human history. And we are on the verge of an even more life-enhancing era, a revolutionary shift from interventive to *preventive* medicine.

The most striking consequence of medical advances is longer life. This is having a remarkable impact upon the aged, their place in society and the respect accorded them. And, in turn, their greater presence, as we have seen in some previous chapters, will have a profound impact upon society itself.

The baby boom is about to become the "senior boom," or as *Newsweek* put it, the "geezer boom." Melinda Beck, writing in that publication, notes that "the generation that once counseled not to trust anyone over 30 will begin turning 64 in 2010. By 2030, the entire baby boom—77 million people, one third of the current U.S. population—

will be senior citizens." Only one in every twenty-five Americans was 65 or older in 1900. Today it's one in eight. By 2030, it will be one in five.

Four-generation families will be the norm rather than the rarity as early as the year 2000, according to the Census Bureau. "Even now," as *Newsweek* has noted, "for the first time in history, the average American has more living parents than children—and that is already changing the family psychologically, emotionally and financially."

There is some truth to the criticism that we are extending life without at the same time extending quality of life. But this notion has become considerably exaggerated—to the point where many imagine that *most* of the aged will be bed-ridden, unproductive and senile, taxing our medical system to the point of nonremedial bankruptcy. But, the fact is, even at the present time (without factoring in future medical advances that will make advanced age even more tolerable), American men who reach 65 can expect to live an additional 15.4 years, during all but two of which they will be in relatively good health, free of major disability. Women at age 65 can expect to live even longer—20.5 years—and enjoy 16.2 years that are active and potentially productive.

Many believe that the "Geritol Generation" may not be the economic downfall of the nation in the early decades of the twenty-first century but, rather, its *salvation*. For already industry is worrying about the "baby bust" generation that follows the baby boomers. There are dire projections of labor shortage, especially among skilled, educated workers. Now, it appears, industry and the aged can solve their problems simultaneously: the seniors, living longer and in better health and with more time on their hands, can fill those jobs economists are so worried about. The boomers will delay retirement or perhaps even return to work in significant numbers. (We'll explore this situation in more depth in the following chapter.)

Meanwhile, a number of sociologists and psychologists are predicting that as the boomers age and have a longer period in which to contemplate and come to terms with death, they will help promote a more consequentialist worldview—one that stresses the interrelatedness of all life and, thus, greater respect for it.

At the same time, society, as a whole, will have more respect for the aged. As Melinda Beck observes, "As a greater portion of the population turns elderly, old age itself may lose much of its stigma." She quotes Dr. T. Franklin Williams, former director of the National Institute on Aging: "We're going to see more and more second and third careers." And Paul Hewitt of the Retirement Policy Institute: "You'll see wrinkled people in advertisements, but they'll be happy. They'll be enjoying a quality of life."

More Respect for the Dying and for Death Itself

We are at an awkward place in medicine at the end of the twentieth century—able to sustain terminal patients for prolonged periods of time and capable of maintaining individuals who are essentially "brain dead" indefinitely in a state of suspended animation. The breakthroughs that would prevent or cure, or at least place in remission, many now terminal conditions loom just ahead, but—for now, there are many instances in which life is being prolonged without real *meaning*.

It is out of this predicament that much of the current debate over euthanasia (or "mercy killing" or "withholding of artificial life support" or "death with dignity") emerges. This is a debate that will, in some circles, match or surpass the abortion debate in intensity over the next two decades. On the one side are those who charge that euthanasia, if widely legalized, will soon provide an excuse for murdering not only the terminal and the intractably suffering but also those who come to be viewed as "excess" or "inconvenient." That "slippery slope" again. On the other side are those who say euthanasia is an expression of respect for those who prefer death to prolonged and painful dying.

In one opinion poll after another, Americans come out strongly—by margins of six to one in many surveys—in favor of letting individuals decide for themselves when they want to die. These polls, however, generally relate to patient-directed withdrawal of life-support systems rather than to more overt, doctor-assisted deaths. Even among most religious groups, the majority favors some right-to-die policies.

About 70 percent of Americans also believe that family members or other preappointed "proxies" should be allowed to stipulate a withdrawal of life-support systems for terminal individuals who can no longer communicate. Those stipulations can be made through "living wills," documents that spell out what a patient wants doctors and family to do—and *not* do—in the case of terminal illnesses or disability.

Suicide to end acute pain associated with terminal illness or incurable disease or disorder is supported, under varying circumstances, by about 50–55 percent of the population, up from 40–44 percent in 1975. Interestingly, a good deal more—about 70 percent—*say* they believe it is acceptable for a spouse to kill his or her mate in the event that mate is experiencing great pain due to terminal illness. Yet, only 33 percent say they can actually imagine themselves taking a life under these circumstances.

American ambivalence toward "mercy killings" became further manifest in 1991 when residents of Washington state defeated an initiative, by a 54-to-46 margin, that would have allowed doctors to give terminally ill patients fatal substances or, upon request, to kill them with lethal injections. Yet, prior to the actual vote, polls had shown only 27 percent opposed to the initiative and 61 percent in favor, about the same that favored the initiative in a nationwide poll.

It seems that the public is behaving here a bit as it does on the capital-punishment issue. Public pronouncements aren't entirely reflective of "gut feelings." An analysis of a majority of past polls and many of the related studies and surveys suggests that the public overstates its support for doctor-assisted death in order to vent its frustration and anger over a medical-care system that it does not believe is responsive to its needs and desires.

Peter Steinfels, commenting on the Washington state vote in *The New York Times* asserted:

> . . . The vote on the proposal sent several messages. One was that voters, when their minds are wonderfully concentrated, will probably put the burden of proof on those proposing a departure from civilization's deeply entrenched belief that doctors should not kill.
>
> But another message was that people want to assert control over dying because they profoundly distrust contemporary medicine's capacity to respond to terminal illness or protracted, painful debilitation.

The latter is clearly true, or the initiative would never have made it to the ballot. And the former is undoubtedly true, as well. Americans are struggling with *choice*. They want a humane, sensible policy that will allow the terminally ill and suffering to die—if that is clearly the wish of the patient. But they are also keenly aware of the potential for abuse when others—such as doctors—are permitted to actively participate in those decisions.

Defeat of the Washington state initiative was widely attributed to the lack of safeguards in the proposed legislation. Plainly stated, "Plenty of people are worried," says Arthur Caplan, director of the Center for Biomedical Ethics at the University of Minnesota (*Christian Science Monitor*), "that a doctor or their relatives might dispatch them."

Additionally, prominent bioethicist Leon Kass (quoted in the same publication) notes that "people are beginning to see what this means, not only for the elderly but for those who are alone or impoverished and already short-changed by the health-care system." Dr. Kass's point is a particularly sharp one in view of the fact that 30 million Americans have no medical insurance. Will they—in health crises—be considered more readily for euthanasia than those who can pay to sustain life?

Just such concerns may have been on the minds of Californians who, in 1992, rejected a "right-to-die" measure that many had also predicted would pass.

Safeguards that will begin to take these concerns into consideration will be built into some other electoral initiatives, and it is almost certain that, beginning in the near future, some states will sanction doctor-assisted euthanasia. Most of these states will almost certainly require at least one "second opinion" from another medical doctor. Others might implement ethical review boards to deliberate each case, particularly if allegations of abuse become widespread.

George D. Lundberg, M.D., editor of the *Journal of the American Medical Association* (quoted in the *Los Angeles Times*), calls this "a real tough area" but predicts: "I think in the next century death without pain and with dignity and perhaps even at a prearranged time will be the norm. But I hope that we do not get there quickly because there is a tremendous gulf of philosophical experience that runs counter to that."

Lawrence J. Schneiderman, M.D., director of Medical Ethics and the Humanities at the University of California, San Diego, School of Medicine, writing in *The Humanist*, pleads for society to keep euthanasia a carefully considered "special case." Schneiderman says: "Medically administered death must be as painless as possible for the patient and as anguishing as possible for the physician," which provides another expression of the need for "moral tension" that we've spoken of in relation to a number of these life issues.

Of course some, such as Derek Humphry, founder of the euthanasia-promoting Hemlock Society and author of the bestseller *Final Exit*, believe we need to move more quickly. His view (as expressed in a column in the *Los Angeles Times*) of bioethicists is less than enthusiastic:

> Let me be frank: I have a vested interest here. The bulk of this nation's scores of so-called ethicists are against euthanasia, which I support. The basis of their opposition appears to lie in ancient history (the Hippocratic Oath, for instance) and an ingrained fear of breaking tradition.

> Reformers they are not. While they come over on television as seemingly independent voices, their salaries are invariably paid by institutions that reflexively support the status quo.

And Dr. Jack Kevorkian, a retired pathologist, has made headlines around the world with his "suicide machine," a device that dispenses lethal drugs. Charged with murder for using the "machine" to help chronically ill people die, Dr. Kevorkian was exonerated by Oakland County Circuit Judge David Breck, in an action brought against him in Michigan. The judge went so far as to declare: "For those patients, whether terminal or not, who have unmanageable pain, physician-assisted suicide remains an alternative."

Another Michigan judge, Gerald McNally, who had earlier dismissed similar charges against the pathologist, has stated: "There is a place for this in society. You can't put this in dark alleys. . . . Unless we deal with it, we're going to drive it underground."

It seems unlikely, however, that the public will widely endorse doctor-assisted euthanasia in the case of those who are *chronically* but not *terminally* ill. Prosecutors are appealing the Kevorkian decisions.

In any case, what is generally defined as "death with dignity" has *not* been forced into the "back alleys." It is already widely permitted in hospitals throughout the land. According to a recent American Hospital Association report, 70 percent of all the 6,000 deaths that occur daily in hospitals in the United States are "somehow timed or negotiated with all concerned parties privately concurring on withdrawal of some death-delaying technology or not even starting it in the first place."

And, according to a survey carried out by *Physicians' Management*, about 60 percent of all U.S. physicians have withdrawn life-support systems from terminal patients and more than 90 percent have complied with patient and family requests not to resuscitate terminal patients.

"Ironically," writes Elizabeth Rosenthal, in *The New York Times*, "as fears of the process of prolonged death escalate, doctors say the care of the dying has actually improved and they are far more likely now than ever before to honor patients' wishes to forego aggressive treatment."

Part of this new willingness is due to the 1990 U.S. Supreme Court ruling that made explicit the right of the individual to refuse treatment. The ruling also asserted that life-sustaining technologies could be withdrawn where there is "clear and compelling evidence of the individual's wishes."

One development that may both complement and help hold in check or reduce the need for euthanasia is the hospice movement, which provides a supportive and, often to quite a successful degree, a pain-free environment for dying individuals. A number of observers increasingly express the belief that the hospice movement may blunt the headlong rush into legalized suicide and doctor-assisted euthanasia.

We'll have more to say about the important hospice movement in the final section of this chapter.

Americans are beginning to change their attitude toward death. This is healthy. It does not mean that we are embracing death but, rather, we are beginning to see it as an important, integral part of human experience, to confront it.

Until quite recently, the trend throughout most of the twentieth century was in the opposite direction—toward *denial* of death. As Graham Turner has noted in the *Sunday Telegraph* of London, "A century ago, only five percent of the population died in a hospital. The dying were cared for at home. Their deaths did not cause families to shrink from their very presence."

Now, he continues, most people die in hospitals. Parents, in recent times, have been "so determined to shield their children from death that they will not even allow them to attend Grandma's funeral . . . we flee from any intimation of mortality."

That appears to be changing, though, in part because of the aging of the baby boom population. Perhaps because of its sheer size and the volume of its internal "feedback" mechanisms, *most* life issues stand out in sharper relief for this segment of our culture.

Herman Feifel, in a paper called "Psychology and Death: Meaningful Rediscovery" (in *American Psychologist*), lists, among those "urgent social issues" that he says are associated with presently shifting attitudes about death, the following: "abortion, AIDS, and euthanasia, and such destructive behaviors as drug abuse, alcoholism, and certain acts of violence." Though these things are not positive in themselves, our ability to adapt to them and cope with them *is*. "Recognition of personal mortality," Feifel concludes, "is a major entryway to self-knowledge."

Many studies have shown that those who come to terms with death earlier in life usually have a more upbeat, positive psychology. David B. Wolfe, in his book *Serving the Ageless Market*, which many businesses have found enlightening, notes that an acceptance of mortality is positively correlated with a more mature, long-term worldview that encourages altruism, volunteerism, respect for life and the environment. And Wolfe finds that the baby boomers are coming to grips with issues related to death seven or eight years earlier than people normally do in this culture.

Forbes has also taken note of this trend. Our mortality, the magazine observes, is, increasingly, being used to sell products. Even here, however, psychologists and sociologists find something positive. Some of these ads are reminding us that life is short and precious and that we should make the most of it. Additionally, some advertising is beginning to portray the *real*, rather than the ideal. Nike, for example. As *Forbes* describes it:

> A new ad for Nike athletic shoes shows a near-perfect nude with the headline, "Yes, this is a goddess." Then comes the cold shower. "But, you are not a goddess and you aren't ever going to be a goddess so maybe you should just get used to it. . . . Someday, since you are human, you will notice your body has changed and your face has changed and your kneecaps look more like Winston Churchill than ever before." The ad goes on to suggest that it might just be worth strapping on a pair of running shoes anyway, and the hell with looking like Kim Basinger.
>
> "This is the first time we addressed the issue that if you don't come face to face with your mortality, it's going to come face to face with you," says Janet Champ, the ad's copywriter. . . .
>
> Nike reports receiving upwards of 45,000 calls praising the new down-to-earth tone—the most responses to any of its campaigns yet.

All of this should hearten John Baker, the Bishop of Salisbury, who has lamented that Western cultures have shrunk, unhealthily, from death: "What we're doing by pushing the thought of death away is robbing ourselves of its power to make our lives what they are meant to be."

Death, then, can be life affirming—or, at least, facing it, accepting its inevitability, coming to terms with it and using those terms to help us establish priorities, can be.

A Growing Consciousness of the Interrelatedness of All Life

In the last chapter, we explored the explosion of interest in the environment in recent years. Our collective consciousness is unquestionably focusing more sharply than ever before upon the interrelatedness and inter*dependence* of all life. A "global consciousness" that some say really began with those first images of Planet Earth, as seen by our astronauts from space, is growing and expanding—and this trend seems to be intensifying with particular rapidity right now. That intensification will almost certainly continue into the foreseeable future, as the nature of our environment continues to be explored.

Indeed, concerns about environmental decay and related population growth are likely to provide what amounts to a new "external enemy," something for a majority to rally against now that the Cold War has thawed. At the same time, these concerns will also, undoubtedly, produce internal divisions which, at times, will break along traditional conservative/liberal lines.

In any case, some have suggested that in the next two decades, the battle cry will not be "ban the bomb" but "ban the *population* bomb." Nor will such cries be from fringe groups only. Already, the "extreme" of a few years ago is the "mainstream" of today. And the trend is again away from denial—in this case denial of environmental destruction and thus, once more, death—toward active confrontation, a movement which, however dire our condition may be, will help dispel some of the feelings of helplessness and hopelessness that diminished our responsive capacities in the recent past.

The statements that have been made about population pressures and threats to our atmosphere and food and water supplies are no longer being made just by the "alarmists." These are now mainstream *and*, increasingly, *grass-roots* concerns and as such signal a shift from denial to confrontation, raising hopes that we may still be able to act in time to avert at least the most disastrous of the scenarios that have been put forth and blunt the negative impact of some of the others.

It is fortuitous that the Cold War, which both diverted us from and contributed to these environmental woes, ended when it did. The world's people are now directing much more attention and energy toward these life-and-death issues. Encouragingly, even the peoples of Third World countries now rank environmental concerns second only to economic issues, according to a Gallup poll. In fact, the poll indicates the citizens of all but two countries, India and Turkey, say they put environmental protection *above* economic growth. Nor was there the expected finger-pointing between developed and undeveloped nations, with the former acknowledging overuse of resources and the latter acknowledging exploding population growth.

Add this dramatic raising of consciousness at the grass-roots level to the recent shift in "establishment" positions on the environment and there is real reason to hope for a new era of life-consciousness. Recently, the National Academy of Sciences joined with Britain's

Royal Society to issue a surprisingly strong statement, warning that "the future of our planet is in the balance. . . . If current predictions of population growth prove accurate and patterns of human activity on the planet remain unchanged, science and technology may not be able to prevent . . . irreversible degradation of the environment."

Academy leaders said they issued the statement to "stimulate debate among scientists, decision-makers and the public." They called upon nations to take a variety of measures to curb population growth and called as well for fundamental behavioral changes to avoid catastrophe.

There are, of course, still vocal skeptics and naysayers who insist all is basically well.

But, as Ross Gelbspan notes:

> These voices are increasingly in the minority. And as evidence has accumulated, the tide of the debate has swung increasingly toward those who believe that the Earth's ability to withstand untrammelled human activity has reached the breaking point.
>
> Dr. Stephen Schneider, a leading atmospheric researcher with the National Center for Atmospheric Research in Boulder, Colorado, said recently, "It is journalistically irresponsible to present both sides as though it were a question of balance. Given the distribution of views, with groups like the National Academy of Science expressing strong scientific concern, it is irresponsible to give equal time to a few people standing out in left field."
>
> [Then] Sen. Al Gore . . . added, "The overall weight of evidence [of global warming] is so clear that one begins to feel angry toward those who exaggerate the uncertainty."

What a turnabout! Just a few years ago, it was those who were sounding these warnings who were said to be doing the "exaggerating" from "out in left field." But the public saw the gravity of the situation much sooner than many of the policymakers.

The case of Vice President Al Gore is instructive in this context. When Gore's book *Earth in the Balance: Ecology and the Human Spirit* was published, many of his colleagues in government said its message was so "radical" it would doom his political future. The book proposes a "Global Marshall Plan" to help save the planet and heal a "dysfunctional civilization" addicted to unfulfilling and destructive consumerism. It is packed with specific, often (at least in the short term) painful cures for our current ills, including measures that stringently tax and otherwise penalize waste, pollution and destructive agricultural and energy-producing practices throughout the world. It also proposes a number of persuasive incentives for international cooperation.

Far from being "out of touch," as some charged, Gore's book struck a responsive chord in the public, which made it a bestseller—and Gore's political fortunes were enhanced.

Still, the battle for the "public mind" on this issue is far from over. Stewart L. Udall, former Secretary of the Interior, and W. Kent Olson, writing in the *Los Angeles Times*, foresee something of a "holy war" between conservationists and a coalition of certain conservative and fundamentalist elements:

> Now that global communism has imploded, far-rightists need a domestic target, and so the color green has become red. Patrick Armstrong, a director of Our Land Society, asserts that environmentalism wants "to destroy or at least badly cripple industrialized capitalism." Ron Arnold [spokesman for the "Wise Use" movement, which, among other things, calls for more mining and drilling in our national parks] nominates environmentalism as "The [next] great wave of messianism to hit the planet after . . . Marxism-Leninism." The John Birch Society has rung in, ranting about Marx and "planned" federal seizures of 26 million acres of timberland in the Northeast. Never mind that such plans do not exist.

In some of the literature of what Udall and Olson call the "Me First!" movement, environmentalists are portrayed as anti-American, anti-Christian and, frequently, "satanic." One "Me First!" spokesman charges that "preservationists are . . . worshipping trees and animals and sacrificing people." The same individual refers to nature preserves as "scenic gulags."

A good deal more of this should be expected in the coming decade, but, as we've seen, the scientific, public and moral tides are very much in the "Earth First," rather than the "Me First," direction. As Udall and Olson observe: "But this too shall pass. A certifiable conservation ethic, evolved over centuries, has rooted itself irrevocably in our culture and is growing globally."

The Traffic in Humans and Human Parts (Babies, Organs, Tissue for Sale)

We shall treat this topic only briefly since the primary controversy in this context centers on the new "commerce" in human eggs and sperm and related reproductive technologies, discussed in the pages that follow.

The fear is that we will soon, quite literally, commercialize the human body, making what some have called "sacred products" into "profane products," marketing body parts the way we do, say, automobile parts. Is this another sign of growing disrespect for life and indicative of a trend?

The facts suggest that the answer to both questions is no. That people and their body parts, to put it crudely, have potential intrinsic commercial value is not an idea originating in or confined to the present era. It is almost certainly the case, in fact, that there is *more* respect for life than at any previous time.

As Elizabeth C. Hirschman, Professor of Marketing in the School of Business at Rutgers University, points out in *The Journal of Consumer Affairs*:

> Both historically and currently, there are several markets in which humans and human components are exchanged for money or other economically valued resources. In the past, persons were sold into slavery and women in the United States were considered chattel property of their husbands until the 20th century. . . . [There was] a thriving market in human cadavers and body parts for medical dissection . . . in both France and England from the 1790s through the 1840s.
>
> . . . prior to the 1920s, illegitimate and orphaned babies were commonly viewed in an instrumental, economic fashion. Often such infants were sold to "baby farms," where most perished due to a lack of adoptive parents. During the 1920–1930 period, babies were culturally redefined as sacred entities, valued for their sentimental and emotional qualities. By the 1950s a severe shortage of adoptable infants resulted in black market prices of $10,000.

It is true that today, as the shortage of adoptable infants continues, there remains a brisk market that essentially trades in human life. But no one can reasonably deny the social progress that today leaves almost all of us incredulous of those earlier eras in which blacks were slaves, women were chattels and infants and children could be sold to "baby farms" and committed to child workhouses.

And, in contrast with the eighteenth and nineteenth centuries, we go to great pains today to regulate the medical uses of blood and organs, a "commerce" that the public increasingly views as *life enhancing*. Federal laws strictly govern these uses and prohibit "free-market" commercialization of body components. Concurrently, bioethicists and others continue to argue against relaxing the rules under which organs may be used for study or transplantation. There is no credible evidence of any "deterioration" in moral values in this context.

More controversy has erupted around the use of fetal tissue in medical experimentation and transplantation. One of the fears here is that as more uses for fetal tissue are discovered, we will become more tolerant of abortion. Given the large number of abortions, however, this argument fails to persuade. In short, there is currently no lack of fetal tissue nor any shortage on the horizon, despite a projected decline in abortions.

Increasingly, fetal tissue will be viewed in the same light as donor organs, to be used for appropriate medical applications when the proper permissions are obtained. The enormous, life-giving benefits that can accrue from use of this tissue (in Parkinson's and, many expect, Alzheimer's diseases, to name just two of many potential applications) will outweigh any cultural uneasiness over the issue.

As Professor Hirschman of Rutgers concludes, "commercial markets in human blood, organs and reproductive components do not so much put a price on life, as they permit the expenditure of economic resources to *enhance, prolong, or create life.*"

More "Test-Tube" Life

In the 1950s, 1960s and even 1970s, those who proposed starting human life in the "test tube" were frequently considered crazy or criminal. By the late seventies, early eighties, there was a dramatic transformation in this context, as millions of infertile couples came to view the new in vitro (literally, "in glass," meaning in laboratory dishes, test tubes and other containers) technologies as their salvation.

Women with missing or diseased fallopian tubes but functional ovaries could, for the first time in history, become pregnant and successfully carry a baby to term by having their eggs surgically removed, fertilized by their husbands' sperm in a laboratory container and then implanted in their wombs. Variations on this theme have followed with, for example, the transfer of an embryo from one woman to another, the use of "surrogate mothers" to carry babies to term for women who cannot, for medical reasons, do so themselves and so on.

Again, our society increasingly views these new technologies as life enhancing and, in this case, literally life *creating*. With infertility now afflicting a rather astonishing one in six married couples in this country, the demand for in vitro conceptions and related technologies will continue to accelerate. And so will the technologies themselves.

We've already reached the point where we can successfully combine selected eggs and sperm in the laboratory, incubate the resulting embryos and then freeze them for future use, at which point they are thawed and implanted in surrogate wombs. Some envision something akin to "seed catalogues" in which prospective parents "shop" for the embryo of their choice, paying heed to such things as gender, skin, eye and hair color, projected IQ, body type, predisposition to disease and so on.

Such visions, fanciful and/or deplorable though they may seem to some, are likely to be realized in coming decades, either in legal or black markets. Already, some of those who make use of artificial insemination go to some lengths to ascertain—and select—donor characteristics. Indeed, there has been in existence for some years the Repository for Germinal Choice, more commonly referred to as the "Nobel sperm bank" since its founder prefers to dispense only the semen of Nobel laureates (but has expanded to include the sperm of other exceptionally accomplished donors).

Concerns about these technologies are raised on multiple fronts. There is the fear that many couples, desperate to have children, will proceed without being capable of giving truly informed consent. The consent forms, which are supposed to clearly explain all the possible risks, are considered inadequate and difficult to understand by many.

In vitro fertilization (IVF) carries with it a number of risks, not the least of which is failure. Only nine out of one hundred IVF procedures lead to a live birth, and, along the way, there is an increased risk of ectopic (tubal) pregnancy, miscarriage, multiple pregnancy, adverse reactions to drugs used in the process and risk of death from anesthesia.

Sometimes in a desperate effort to achieve a pregnancy *several* fertilized eggs are simultaneously implanted into a woman's womb, in the hope that at least one will survive. Occasionally, *all* survive, and suddenly, a woman finds herself carrying more embryos than she can safely sustain and deliver. Then she is faced with "pregnancy reduction," the need to destroy some of the embryos so that one can be carried all the way to term. Certainly couples need to be advised of such possibilities in advance.

Additionally, there is the problem of what to do with embryos that are created in the laboratory but not implanted. Most of these are now frozen and stored. Prolife forces argue that destroying frozen embryos is the same as abortion. Others argue that since the embryos have never been implanted they represent only "potential" life. Most IVF clinics now attempt to reduce their potential legal liability by asking their clients to stipulate what is to be done with any excess frozen embryos in the event of the couple's deaths or divorce.

Such matters have already begun finding their way into courts, just as the surrogate-mother issues did some years earlier. Now divorce courts have to decide to whom they should entrust custody of not only the children but also the couples' frozen embryos!

Kathryn Pyne Addelson summarizes (in *Social Problems*), some of the ethical and legal dilemmas we're facing now and in the near future:

> At present, the legal issues surrounding the uses of IVF are daunting. If the embryos are transferred to a woman other than the one who contributed the ovum, we may have one of the difficult questions of surrogacy. Can binding surrogacy contracts really be drawn up? What happens if the surrogate mother wants to keep the child? Other legal problems center on the frozen embryos and their place in the family or social system. If the biological parents divorce before using them, are the embryos to be dealt with in the property settlement or in a child custody arrangement? If the biological parents die before using them, are the embryos heirs to the family fortune? Does their grandmother have responsibility for them?

The Vatican, meanwhile, remains opposed to IVF, artificial insemination by donor, surrogate motherhood, embryo freezing and almost all of the new reproductive technologies. Many other religious bodies, however, have made exceptions, and public opinion polls show that even among Catholics the use of these techniques to overcome infertility finds favor. Some polls of the general population show support for IVF running "as high as 90 percent." As Arthur L. Greil observes, in *The Christian Century*, "appeals to moral rights and wrongs are less convincing when we believe we can change our condition through technical know-how."

Technology often changes morality. And our technical ability to overcome a significant amount of previously intractable infertility is, our culture now declares, *good*. The majority perception is that technology is acting positively—in the service of life—in this context. This view is given further, tangential, support by the use of these technologies to help perpetuate endangered species.

The technology will advance rapidly in the next two decades, during which period the legal and ethical debates will accelerate apace. It is likely that legislation will manage to contain, though probably not eradicate, serious abuses, all of which will, nonetheless, be regarded as "worth the price."

More Human-Directed Life

As noted in the opening passages of this chapter, we are entering an era of "participatory evolution," as our ability to "edit" our genetic script gradually increases. Those who fear that we will too lightly assume the role of "creator" might be at least fractionally reassured to learn that for every word written in encouragement of these developments there are at least ten written in warning or caution. There have been three decades of detailed debate before even the first, halting steps have been taken—and that debate will, if anything, intensify in coming years.

Indeed, so much has been written and said concerning the *peril* of the "biological revolution" that most of us lose sight of its remarkable *promise*. Nobel laureate James Watson, writing in *Science* about the significance of the Human Genome Project, designed to map and sequence the DNA that is the "blueprint" of mankind, declares, "A more important set of instruction books will never be found by human beings." And he adds:

> When finally interpreted, the genetic messages encoded within our DNA molecules will provide the ultimate answers to the chemical underpinnings of human existence. They will not only help us understand how we function as healthy human beings, but will also explain, at the chemical level, the role of genetic factors in a multitude of diseases, such as cancer, Alzheimer's disease, and schizophrenia, that diminish the individual lives of so many millions of people.

In past eras, there was enormous reluctance to learn "too much" about the workings of the human body and mind. Surgery, psychiatry, internal medicine, organ transplantation and so on have all been impeded by such fears. Now, even many of those who say we should "go no further" look back with incredulity and sometimes contempt on those periods in our history when we shrank from attempting to understand more about the human condition, in all its intricacy. The motivation to search for deeper self-knowledge is powerful.

The new genetic research will first lead to an identification of single-gene defects, the source of more than 3,000 inherited disorders. This, in turn, will lead rapidly to diagnostic tests for these gene defects and, later, to therapies to correct many of them. These therapies will include drugs and "genetic surgery" to replace or remove missing or conflicting genetic instructions. Still later, more complex multigene defects, related to such illnesses as cancer, arthritis and other autoimmune diseases, heart disease and so on, will be elucidated, leading, in turn, to highly sophisticated diagnostic, preventive and interventive measures.

We have already discovered the complete or partial genetic loci of a number of disorders. And we have tests that can detect certain genetic defects that may lead to disease later in life. Within a decade, the list of disorders we will be able to detect will expand considerably. There will be an uncomfortable, transitional period in which such tests, absent effective therapies to deal with what they reveal, may invade privacy and, in a very real sense, terrorize their recipients, who, in many cases, "would rather not know." But, in very short order, these discoveries should lead to more effective treatments, making the tests sought after, rather than feared—in the same way that so many of us today eagerly have our cholesterol levels tested to see whether, and by how much, we need to alter our lifestyles.

More than anything else, our new understanding of the basic building blocks of life that make up our genes and chromosomes will enable us to shift, dramatically, from treating disease to *preventing* disease. Caltech biology professor Leroy Hood, commenting on this (*Fortune*), remarks:

> I don't think most biologists even begin to understand how profoundly the whole art of biology will change when we [accomplish the objectives of the genome project]. . . . The findings will have an incredibly important impact on medicine. We'll be able to design a protein, for example, that can bind specifically to a lung cancer cell and kill it. In 15 years we'll have identified at least 100 genes that predispose people to diseases, and we'll have figured out how to circumvent their bad effects. So when a baby is born 20 years from now, a genetic profile will say that this person is susceptible to these diseases, and here is what to do to prevent them.
>
> Medicine will thus shift from a reactive to a preventive mode. Everyone would go through life essentially avoiding all the diseases that he would naturally be predisposed to. In addition, in 20 years virtually all autoimmune diseases—rheumatoid arthritis,

> multiple sclerosis, the most common forms of diabetes—could be circumvented. . . .

Evidence is already accumulating that we will soon find some and, perhaps, eventually all of the genetic roots of alcoholism and other addictive disorders, as well as an impressive range of mental disorders, making life, through resulting gene therapies, not only livable but pleasurable and productive for millions who languish in their afflictions today.

We should not be disturbed that, despite all this promise (which will no doubt prove in some respects to be exaggerated, and in others, much underestimated), there remains so much pessimism. Certainly there are real risks, and that pessimism may prove preventive. And, as we become more familiar with these technologies, some of their fearful mystique will fall away and we will find that we can as easily imagine the benign as the malign.

Yes, as we have so often been warned, we *could* ultimately use these technologies to discriminate, possibly to eliminate even those "defects" that contribute to creativity, to instill a heartless aggressiveness or worker "drone" mentality in the populace, to create a deadeningly "perfect" monoculture. But *why* would we pursue these ends, the actual effect of which would be to undermine, not enhance, our survivability as a species? Why cannot we more readily imagine scenarios in which we work to promote the genetic bases of creativity, cooperativeness and vitalizing diversity, all of which, demonstrably, strengthen our abilities to survive? The answer is, we can and we will because survival interests us more than anything in the world.

Solutions/Recommendations

Universal Health Care

The most effective thing we can do to produce a social and psychological atmosphere respectful of life is to provide health care for every citizen. Numerous polls show that Americans, by large majorities, want a national health insurance plan and are willing to accept higher taxes to pay for it, if that is required. And, contrary to what many believe, the young—ages 18 to 29—are the *most,* not the least, willing to make financial sacrifices to fund such a program, even though most believe their elders would make more use of it.

In reality, a program of national health insurance will *save* money in the long run by creating a healthier, more productive and more motivated populace. Lack of "equal access" to medical care in this country is a source of alienation, disenchantment, pessimism and divisiveness among large segments of the population. The implementation of comprehensive national health coverage is a primary goal of the Clinton administration.

This is an issue that is rapidly evolving and highly controversial. Many conservatives, previously resistant to anything suggestive of "socialized medicine," will have to join with moderates and liberals to arrive at an acceptable plan, the full implementation of which should be in place within a few years. Look for the emergence in the program of special attention for children, adolescents and expectant mothers.

An Expanded Hospice Movement

While universal health care can go a long way to enhance respect for the living, an expanded hospice movement can be a powerful vehicle for bringing more respect to the dying. The hospice is the best alternative to needlessly—and often cruelly—prolonged medical intervention and to "active euthanasia," or "mercy killing." The hospice provides, as much as possible, an environment that frees the dying individual from both physical *and* psychological pain. It withdraws life-sustaining technologies and treatments but provides pain relief and a psychological and, if desired, spiritual support system that can seldom be achieved in a hospital or typical home setting.

The hospice option, moreover, frees doctors, spouses and other relatives from the sometimes perceived necessity of becoming active participants in the death of a patient or loved one, a participation that can have psychologically disturbing consequences, in some cases, for years to follow. Many now believe that an expanded hospice system can diminish support for active euthanasia, and in fact, most religious faiths are increasingly advocating hospices among their own followers.

Hospitals, too, are becoming more ardent supporters of the hospice concept. Hospitals in a number of states have now contracted with a for-profit organization that provides the needed services and is no doubt a harbinger of more such businesses to come.

Undoubtedly, not all hospice care will measure up to the ideal, and more regulation and carefully monitored standards will be required. But the hospice movement, whatever its shortcomings, seems to many to be fraught with fewer perils than active euthanasia. And there is no doubt that the trend toward an expansion of this useful concept is a strong one. Since its emergence in the 1970s, the movement has grown to more than 1,500 programs, serving 200,000 people at any given time.

Teaching Environmental ABC's

Remember the zealousness of some "antinuclear" parents during the height of the Cold War? Some of their critics said they were making a religion of ideology and psychologically scarring their children by emphasizing the terrifying possibility of imminent nuclear annihilation. Well, it turns out that those children, according to psychological studies, were actually able to cope *better* with such fears than were children who were "protected" by their parents from exposure to these issues. *Most* children, it turned out, were frightened by the prospect of nuclear war, but the children of the activists felt more empowered and more positive precisely because they and their parents were striving to stay informed and to actively oppose nuclear proliferation.

Similarly, there is evidence that the children of environmentalists are better equipped to deal with the realities of a world in which population growth and resource depletion increasingly impact on all aspects of life. We need to incorporate more environmental studies into public education, beginning even at the preschool level, emphasizing the delicacy and the precision with which the various "systems" that regulate and interrelate all life operate.

Will this come to pass? It seems likely, given the gathering consensus among major mainstream scientific organizations, that our environmental crises are rooted in our psychology and that "the battle for the planet" will be lost or won in the human mind.

"A hopeful sign," note Stewart Udall and W. Kent Olson, "is the landmark 'Joint Appeal by Religion and Science,' recently crafted by 115 leading scientists and theologians who 'accept our responsibility to teach [about] the environmental crisis and what is required [morally and scientifically] to overcome it.' "

While increased environmental curricula can be expected in the immediate future, overt efforts to curb population growth will be somewhat slower to emerge, though many will be talked about in the next several years—and, with the passage of time, they will come to seem less radical.

Planned Parenthood of the Rocky Mountains, for example, started a program in Denver that may one day be emulated throughout the country and, perhaps, many parts of the world. The "Dollar-a-Day Teenage Pregnancy Prevention Program" *pays* teens not to get pregnant. The teens check in at a local center regularly—with the added benefit that they meet each other and form a support group. The project has been successful in preventing many pregnancies—and thus abortions—and only costs $365 per teen girl a year, compared with an average $13,000 annual cost per teen pregnancy for Colorado taxpayers.

The program is working so well that other communities in Colorado, Maryland and California are copying it.

Noel Perrin, a teacher of environmental studies at Dartmouth College, calls the Denver program "the best idea I've heard in a long time" to curb teen pregnancies. Even if young women were paid considerably more not to become pregnant—on an escalating scale of $600 to $1,200 for each nonpregnant year, Perrin calculates—the program would be highly cost effective. If 90 percent of *all* American girls who reach puberty this year were enrolled in such a program and were paid to stay in it for the next five years, the total cost, including administration fees would, Perrin says, be about $10 billion—"less than the state of California alone will spend on Aid to Families with Dependent Children in one year."

Perrin concludes: "This plan decreases abortion, saves taxpayers money and plainly benefits the young women it serves—while at the same time making a start toward keeping the planet habitable."

That such plans are being proposed, let alone implemented, suggests the growing strength of the environmental movement. Until recently, environmental groups shied away from the population issue, fearing attack by well-organized right-to-life forces, which usually see population control in the same light as abortion. Reports Joe Alper in *Science*:

> But in the wake of Earth Day '90 and the enormous publicity that surrounded it, environmental groups seem to have acquired new political confidence. Says Diane Sherman of Zero Population Growth: "Many of these [environmental] organizations have gone through a skirmish or two with the [right-to-life] groups and found that while they can be scary, they're just a vocal minority."

Ultimately, it appears that "quality of life" is more important than "right to life" in our society.

The Need for Vigilance

Finally, among pressing life issues, we need to keep a firm grip on the genetic research that both promises and threatens to transform us in a variety of ways. The new reproductive technologies that are already in wide use also need monitoring, not necessarily to further restrict them but to provide more useful guidelines and better informed consent.

Daniel Navot, M.D., director of In Vitro Fertilization and associate professor of obstetrics, gynecology and reproductive science at Mount Sinai Medical Center in New York City, says, "The technology is advancing much more rapidly than ethicists and lawyers can keep up with."

Lori Miller Kase, writing in *Health*, adds:

> The federal government is no help. Rather than regulate the use of reproductive technology through funding, it has effectively avoided the issue through a clever catch-22: It cannot conduct or support human IVF [in-vitro fertilization] research without the sanction of a special ethics advisory board, but that board was disbanded in 1979, and the Bush administration [showed] no interest in reconstituting it. Without any clear guidance, patients are being forced to decide for themselves. And by the time many patients resort to IVF, they are so desperate to conceive that the question "Will we have a baby?" supersedes all others.

Clearly, a high-level advisory board needs to be reestablished. And it needs to be empowered by giving it some meaningful control over funding of IVF research and facilities.

This kind of advisory input and regulatory control is even more vital with respect to the rapidly advancing gene work. Fortunately, the Human Genome Project provides a logical locus for such oversight. A significant proportion of the project's funding is directed toward ethical issues, but there is still a need for a more highly visible and unified regulatory body to help inform the public about the progress, prospects, promises and perils of this work. Other countries, notably Britain, France and Germany, are ahead of us in this context.

As biologist Robert Weinberg sums it up in *Technology Review*:

> Policies governing the use of genetic information need to be debated and put in place early . . . not after problems emerge. Bioethics is already a thriving cottage industry, but the problems many of its practitioners wrestle with—issues like surrogate motherhood and *in vitro* fertilization—will be dwarfed by those surrounding genetic analysis. The groups organizing the human genome project have already assembled experts to confront the

ethical, legal, and social dimensions of this work. But these individuals have yet to plumb the depths of the problems.

Again, part of the problem has been the categorical opposition of "right-to-life" groups to this research. As government moves away from a close association with that position in coming years, more meaningful public discussion of regulation aimed at preventing potential perils will emerge. That will be good news for life, both as we live it now and as we will live it in the near future.

SIX

Satisfaction

More Content/Less Content?

THE TREND On the eve of the twenty-first century, though beset by economic difficulties and braced for a future of diminished material expectations, Americans are—and will remain—among the most psychologically satisfied people on the planet. Indeed, even as discontent with government continues to grow, attaining a level unprecedented in the last fifty years, personal satisfaction, as evaluated by a number of potent signifiers, continues to flourish. For Americans, more than for most people, the Enlightenment dream persists as reality: the expansion of human liberty and the freeing of the human spirit pervades the collective consciousness as the natural order of things. Americans are among the most optimistic and hopeful of all peoples, and hope is the very engine of adaptation. Thus, at a time when many pundits are declaring the American Dream dead, a majority of Americans account themselves in some respects *more* satisfied than ever before. Moving from a quantity-of-possessing to a quality-of-life course will bring greater, not less, satisfaction. In the years immediately ahead, the goal of many Americans will shift from *being well-off* to *well-being*. What some are calling "the New Realism" embraces a gathering tide of anticonsumerism and a set of new priorities that focuses more on personal freedom and self-actualization, more on health, both physical and mental, and less on wealth. Nor is this simply a reaction to the economy of the early 1990s. It is a trend that should persist for a decade, and probably much longer, due to dramatically altered economic and generational realities. The less-is-more prescription for satisfaction is, in some of its manifestations, here to stay. The American Dream is not merely being "downsized," it is being fundamentally redefined.

Overview

"Satisfaction" versus "Happiness"

As I considered the meaning of this chapter, it seemed to be: "How *happy* are we?" Yet, when I investigated the "happiness" literature, I found psychologists and laypeople alike so divided on the meaning of the term that, ultimately, it bordered on the meaningless. By contrast, I found abundant data suggesting that "satisfaction" is a far more stable and useful concept in terms of evaluating "quality of life." This same conclusion was reached in an ambitious national study carried out by the Russell Sage Foundation. Its researchers noted that, going back to the Greek philosophers, scholars have struggled to satisfactorily define "happiness."

They observed (in *The Quality of American Life: Perceptions, Evaluations and Satisfactions*) that "happiness has rather central connotations involving short-term moods of gaiety and elation that are quite different from the core meaning of satisfaction." And though there is some significant overlap of the two concepts, it is possible, and commonplace, for people to be "happy" about a number of things (such as a new car or a bank balance or a sunny day) and still be quite dissatisfied with their lives. "Young people are more likely to describe their lives as happy than older people, but are less likely to say that they are satisfied with life," say the Russell Sage researchers. They add:

> Level of satisfaction can be precisely defined as the perceived discrepancy between aspiration and achievement, ranging from the perception of fulfillment to that of deprivation. Satisfaction implies a judgmental or cognitive experience, while happiness suggests an experience of feeling or affect. . . .
>
> The second consideration which recommended the use of satisfaction as our basic concept was our concern that our data have relevance to public policy and our conviction that measures of

> affect would seem less realistic to practically minded people than measures of satisfaction. Legislators and decision-makers are well accustomed to thinking in terms of satisfying public needs. . . .
>
> Finally, the concept of satisfaction was attractive because of its adaptability to a study design which sought a series of measures from separate domains of life rather than a single global measure. . . .

These researchers make it clear that the task is to try to assess the "experience of life" rather than just the "conditions of life," as has so often been done in the past:

> Because we are accustomed to evaluating people's lives in terms of their material possessions, we tend to forget that satisfaction is a psychological experience and that the quality of this experience may not correspond very closely to these external conditions of life. If there were a close and universal relationship between the level of material possessions and the quality of life experience, there would, of course, be little point in undertaking a study of the kind in which we are here engaged.

Money and material success define only one of many "life domains" that help determine our overall level of psychological satisfaction. In many studies, physical and mental health are regarded as the most important elements of psychological satisfaction, followed by the quality of one's interpersonal relationships (marriage, friendship, family life, romantic attachments, etc.). Work, where one lives, and the quality of one's community and government typically occupy the next rungs down the satisfaction ladder, at the bottom of which are religion and, contrary to many expectations, financial status. Americans have a long tradition of tenaciously separating financial health from psychological health. This isn't to say there is not confusion between the two—but considerably less in this culture than in some others. Perhaps this helps explain why, despite all the sour feeling over government and the economy, Americans remain as optimistic and satisfied as they are.

The Upside of "Downshifting"

The term "downshifting" was coined by writer Amy Saltzman (author of the book *Downshifting: Reinventing Success on a Slower Track*) to reflect a trend discussed in a previous chapter: the movement among many professionals to delay or even forego advancement in their work in order to spend more time with their families and friends and pursue other interests they perceive to be life enhancing. Saltzman stresses that downshifting is not a new term for "dropping out." On the contrary, in many ways it implies greater engagement, rather than resignation and isolation—but greater engagement outside the workplace, which heretofore has been so dominant a part of most lives. "Downshifting," Saltzman writes, rejects the typical definition of success "in narrow self-interested terms" and is driven by the growing awareness that "the fast track shackles us to a set of standards and rules that prohibit us from leading truly successful, happy lives."

That an increasing number of Americans agree with her is attested to by a number of recent polls. One of these—a *Time*/CNN poll—found that 69 percent of those surveyed want "life to slow down." Nearly 90 percent said it was "more important these days to spend time with their families" than pursue promotions, more money, greater financial and career-related success. More than 60 percent agreed that finding time to enjoy life is becoming increasingly difficult.

Sarah Ban Breathnach, writing in *The Washington Post*, sees the "downshifting movement [taking] hold across the country" and quotes psychologist and marketing researcher Ross Goldstein as characterizing this as "one of the most powerful trends I've ever seen. I think this goes all the way down to our bones." Goldstein perceives three reasons for downshifting: an adverse reaction or backlash to/against the rampant consumerism of the 1980s, the persistent economic downturn and the aging of the baby boomers. Consumerism failed to deliver happiness, let alone satisfaction. Recession helped necessitate downsizing of expectations, and, Goldstein points out, "Sixty percent of baby boomer households have children under age 18. Your priorities change when you have children to take care of."

Among the new priorities: making time for both children and aging parents, getting involved in community activities and politics, substituting personal growth for professional advancement. Increasing volunteerism, a trend noted earlier in this book, is one outcome of this; growing interest in environment is another.

Goldstein says his research indicates that downshifting represents a more "permanent" change. "There's something that happens to people when they go through a recession and when they go through a life-stage change—it fundamentally changes their values. There is value in simplifying your life," and once that value is perceived, he believes, people will not soon let it go. There is evidence from previous economic downturns and from the Depression that this is, indeed, the case. The changes that are taking place are likely to persist and even intensify for some time, certainly for at least the next decade. And, in this instance, they may persist longer given the fact that the baby boomers are so powerful and pervasive a presence and given the prediction of so many economists that our nation may be in for a period of prolonged material decline.

Rabbi Harold Kushner, author of such best-selling books as *When Bad Things Happen to Good People* and *When All You've Ever Wanted Isn't Enough*, believes that another generational issue will help perpetuate the downshifting trend: "I think young people in their late twenties and early thirties, and this has been said by others," he told *The Washington Post*, "represent the first generation of Americans who cannot count on being better educated and more successful than their parents." Thus, he adds, "What I am finding is that a lot of young people from fairly successful families are saying, 'The only way that I avoid feeling like a failure as compared to my father is to redefine success in more personal, more spiritual terms.' "

The upside of all this is that "success" and "satisfaction" are being redefined in a way that should prove more beneficial to our collective psychology, to society as a whole, than did some earlier definitions. Kushner believes that success will, increasingly, be defined by "the right values," rather than by the "right job" or the "right car." Integrity, he says, will take precedence over income through the 1990s and beyond. And to be considered "smart" one will figure out ways to spend time with family and friends on weekends and *not* bring home work from the office.

In an article called "The Graying Yuppie: Reality Zaps the Baby Boomers" (*New York*), writers Stephen M. Pollan and Mark Levine observe that as the boomers gradually abandon what some call their "sense of entitlement," society stands to gain:

> This shift away from materialism will benefit not only boomers but the rest of society. Faith Popcorn, founder and chairman of a future-oriented marketing consultancy, Brain Reserve, sees a dramatic change taking place: "People will begin to be happy with less. They will become more interested in ethics. They'll go to church; they'll get involved with causes; they'll grow their own vegetables. There will be a return to salons—people will get together in groups to talk and enjoy each other's company. They'll be involved in teaching, recycling, and their community. Rather

than doing things that cost a lot of money, they'll look to do things that offer gratification to the soul. People will toughen up and become more self-sufficient. We'll turn into a nation of survivors.

Perhaps some of these forecasts are a bit overblown—but the best evidence suggests the gist of them is correct. And what is particularly surprising—and encouraging—is that Americans are increasingly willing to accept a particularly painful form of "downsizing" in order to create a better and more satisfying society: they are willing, under appropriate circumstances, to accept *higher taxes* toward that end. This represents a psychological shift of significant magnitude.

A recent Gallup poll reveals what Richard Harwood, writing for the LA Times–Washington Post Service, calls a "portrait of the American electorate" that belies the stereotyping of our society as "a balkanized mess" in which various minorities and interest groups flail at each other and seldom agree on anything: "the country is far more unified than it often appears in its perception of contemporary problems and their possible solutions." Americans, he adds, are "prepared and eager to enter into a period of social reform and renewal with a government that will tax people fairly, demonstrate its own competence and encourage self-reliance."

That, at any rate, is what this particularly detailed poll indicates. Large and diverse segments of the population would support higher taxation to help cure our economic ills, reduce the deficit and get more people into productive work. Those willing to be taxed at higher rates to achieve these ends include Republicans (63 percent), Democrats (64 percent), whites (59 percent), blacks (58 percent), Hispanics (65 percent). Additionally, some 88 percent of Americans surveyed say they would do volunteer work to help get the nation back on the right track economically. Rather than let the failure of government diminish their own life satisfaction, Americans are eager to use the strength of their personal optimism and satisfaction to make government itself more satisfying—even if it means some economic sacrifice right now.

Today's reality is in sharp contrast with what was widely predicted for these economically troubled times. The baby boomers, we were told by many, would become more conservative as they desperately clung to the remnants of the American Dream—and conservatism in general would grow in strength. Yet several polls conducted for *USA Today*/CNN in early 1992 clearly demonstrated that the public was, if anything, in a mood to be more adventurous and less traditional than ever before, favoring, for example, "college loans to everyone in return for either military or nonmilitary service," "strengthening environmental regulations, even if it hurts business conditions," "a national health-care system paid for by new taxes," "providing condoms to public high school students to help reduce the spread of AIDS" and "strengthening affirmative action laws for women, blacks and other minorities."

It is time for us to abandon the notion that "hard times" automatically mean hardened hearts, reactionary politics, scapegoating and declining satisfaction. As has been demonstrated in several preceding chapters, Americans continue to find greater satisfaction through increased freedom to experience life in an environment of diversity nearly unparalleled in the world. Whatever serious problems may yet confront them, women, African-Americans, gays, Hispanics, other ethnic minorities, the elderly, even white males are today able to pursue their dreams with greater latitude and tolerance than at any time in the history of our country, freed as never before of social and psychological constraints and conventions that previously confined most of us.

The Psychologizing of Satisfaction

We need to look at what researchers have called the "social indicators," in order to try to assess relative states of satisfaction. But simply to quantify such things as dollars spent on health care for various subgroups, crime rates, employment, per capita income, divorce rates, population growth, leisure time and so on is insufficient. Increasingly, researchers are, as the Russell Sage researchers have noted, trying to find relationships between psychological change and social change, in pursuit of more meaningful conclusions.

Whereas many surveys, for example, on job satisfaction were once skewed heavily in favor of wages, promotions and monetary ancillary benefits, they have only recently begun to focus on how people *feel* about their work. We're now aware of the fact that a high level of salary satisfaction can coexist with a high level of job stress or job boredom. For a time we imagined the Japanese were among the most satisfied workers of the world, given the zeal with which they applied themselves to their work. It was only when the surveys became more "psychological" that we discovered the Japanese are actually among the *least* satisfied peoples of the industrialized world, particularly in terms of their ability to relax, experience pleasure and find satisfaction in their interpersonal relationships. Similarly, in this country many top management people express "great satisfaction" at having achieved their goals, yet, upon more subjective probing, admit to feelings of isolation and loneliness "at the top"; a surprising number opt out or down in pursuit of something more rewarding.

Paul Thorne, director of a British corporate-psychology consulting firm called Psycom, notes (in *International Management*) that this more subjective approach to defining happiness and satisfaction has achieved respectability only in recent years. Now, he adds, there is a "flood" of treatises on the topic. Among the many he cites is the recent book by Mihaly Czikszentmihalyi of the University of Chicago, *Flow, the Psychology of Optimal Experience.* "Flow," as Thorne summarizes it, is defined "as the state of involved enchantment that lies between boredom and anxiety," a definition that he says could "also be taken for happiness" but which perhaps serves even better as a definition of satisfaction at its psychological roots. Thorne continues:

> Czikszentmihalyi says anyone can reach flow every day. It's only a matter of attitude. The components of happiness appear to be: keeping busy, being useful, having and being among good friends, being well organized, but not expecting too much, having control of your life, emphasizing the positive and eliminating the negative. Clearly, happiness lies in you and how you see your world, not what it is. Imagine that your joy is in reaching for goals, rather than achieving them, and you should be happier longer.

While we don't agree with all of this (altering one's attitudes, for example, can be among the most difficult of all challenges for some people), the foregoing passage is instructive for its emphasis on the subjective and the relative and for pointing out science's new resolve to deal with these issues in assessing satisfaction in the experience of life.

Psychology these days is even emboldened to examine that once taboo subject "pleasure" in search of a more psychologically informative view of "satisfaction." Part of this boldness accrues from the fact that anthropology has begun to make a science of the study of pleasure.

Asked by Alvin P. Sanoff (*U.S. News & World Report*), "What does the way a society deals with pleasure tell us about the nature of that society?" noted anthropologist Lionel Tiger replied:

> Certainly, some communities appear to have a much more open attitude to various kinds of pleasure. One of the fascinating things about the United States is that, notwithstanding its Puritan heritage, it is a place where people can probably find as wide an array

of pleasures legitimately enjoyed as anywhere in the world. I think this is one of the peculiar, unexamined political results of the Constitution and the Bill of Rights.

I believe that there is some reason for evaluating a society on the basis of how much domestic personal pleasure it allows its citizens. The lack of personal pleasure in the Soviet system may explain why the whole Communist scheme was doomed. And I think that the Japanese are going to have a major intellectual task in trying to reassess the value of private, as opposed to public, experience. It is interesting to speculate on what would happen if we looked at countries not in terms of their gross national product, but in terms of a different GNP, their gross national pleasure.

Interestingly, "pleasure," as perceived here, is almost interchangeable with "freedom."

As we examine various of the "social indicators" and "domains" of satisfaction in this chapter, we will strive to do so in the context of GPP (gross personal pleasure), GNP (gross national pleasure) and such other "subjectives" as control, attitude, connectedness, expectation, process, usefulness, "enchantment" and freedom of being. Even then, however, we must acknowledge that the science of determining satisfaction remains a fledgling and, often, still floundering pursuit. As psychologist Carol D. Ryff of the University of Wisconsin, Madison, has pointed out (in *Journal of Personality and Social Psychology*):

> Prior attempts to predict why some Americans are happier [or more satisfied] than others have focused almost exclusively on sociodemographic variables (i.e., education, social class, age, ethnicity, marital status). These studies have repeatedly demonstrated that, even in combination, such variables account for little of the variance in well-being . . . there is a clear need for enriched theoretical guidance in attempts to identify . . . the mechanisms by which these influences occur. Perhaps looking beneath the broad social structural factors to the life experiences and opportunities they afford or deny would provide a more promising avenue for explanatory research.

The Domains of Satisfaction

Pollsters, researchers and news organizations are constantly trying to define elements of what they alternately call happiness, satisfaction and the American Dream. Results vary, depending upon a number of variables, principally the target population and the nature of the questions. The trend in recent years appears to be toward focusing on "mastery" and "control" as crucial psychological underpinnings of satisfaction. In a study carried out by Margaret Hellie Huyck of the Illinois Institute of Technology (*International Journal of Aging and Human Development*), "the sense of control" in various life situations varied by gender and age. Perhaps one of the most interesting aspects of this and related research is the suggestion that the relative importance of the various "life domains" (e.g., marriage, job, child rearing) is determined, probably to some significant degree, by the extent to which the individual perceives he or she *can* achieve mastery/control in each. This may help explain why in a period of diminishing economic expectations domains related to financial success slip in importance and others, free of those expectations, assume greater importance.

Overall, however, "a sense of control" in matters related to work remains more important to men than to women; but now there seems to be growing importance assigned to matters of health, especially among younger and middle-aged men; for older men there is an especially strong importance assigned to marriage and relationships, a finding that supports the data cited in a preceding chapter suggestive of the emergence of a more androgynized, "romantic" older male. An instructive finding by Margaret Huyck is that as men approach the latter stages of middle age (with middle age defined as 43–56) the importance they assign to work in assessing overall "sense of control" and satisfaction may have more to do with their ability to *distance* themselves from it than to feel engaged in it: "These older men are, in fact, less psychologically engaged with work; apparently if they are pleased with this reduced level of involvement, they can retain (or perhaps even gain?) a sense of control in life." Thus, when one man says he is "satisfied" with his work he may mean something quite different from another man making the same statement—a pitfall often overlooked in satisfaction surveying.

Women remain more concerned with mastery in interpersonal relationships, particularly those with a spouse or "significant other." There has, however, been a shift, in the past two decades in particular, toward women assigning more importance to job and career mastery as a significant correlate of life satisfaction. Health is also becoming much more important to women as a source of satisfaction, especially for younger women and those in early middle age. This is thought by many researchers to represent a significant change that has been developing over the past two decades—to the extent that women who do *not* participate in health-enhancing activities now often view this, as Huyck notes, as "a personal failure or an inability to organize their lives to incorporate such activities." For older women, control seems especially focused on having and making the most of leisure time, which they, more than men, view as a reward for "dues paid." Aging men, on the other hand, several researchers concur, are decreasingly interested in retirement and leisure.

Attempting to get closer to the real psychological roots of satisfaction, Carol Ryff, quoted earlier, developed six new "theory-guided" measures of psychological well-being: self-acceptance, positive relations with others, autonomy, environmental mastery, purpose in life and personal growth. She examined the importance of each in terms of different age and gender groups. Although, as she notes, further assessment and validation of these new measures will be needed, they overcome some of the inadequacies of many previous measures.

Until better methodologies and measures, of the sort under development and investigation by researchers such as Huyck and Ryff, are fully developed and clarified, we can expect to be exposed to a continuing onslaught of less-scientific observations, frequently based upon arbitrarily selected and defined domains of satisfaction. Even here, however, there tends to be some useful convergence in findings, even if the findings are not always given an informed interpretation.

In a recent Gallup poll conducted among randomly selected subscribers to *Money* magazine, for example, the conclusion was that "the dream seems to be shifting back to . . . less materialistic moorings." In reality, surveys designed to probe more deeply had demonstrated that even in the 1970s and 1980s little genuine life satisfaction was derived from "materialistic moorings." Still, there was the perception in the eighties, much of it media driven, that money could buy satisfaction—and, in that sense at least, this poll has correctly reflected a perceptual shift that has some significance in itself. This poll, again like so many others, even skewed as it is toward more affluent individuals, shows some of what those more in-depth studies have long revealed, that "the dream" has more to do with good health and good interpersonal relations than with being able to retire early or enjoy such luxuries as new cars, travel and vacation homes, all of which rank at the bottom of the *Money* list. "Happy home life," good educations for the children and "competent, affordable health care" come in at the top. Midway down the list of "dream" elements are a job that pays well, having children, being married and living in a secure community.

It was from such polls and studies, as well as from the self-categorizing nature of the data that emerged from our computer searches, that we developed the broad categories of satisfaction that are examined in the Subtrends section of this chapter, which follows. These, too, are arbitrary and by no means all-inclusive, but they do serve to summarize the most evident trends of concern to most Americans.

Subtrends

As noted above, much of the data needed to fully assess life satisfaction are not reported. Better measures are being developed that will eventually enable us to more meaningfully assess the quality of our lives. In our pursuit of some enlightenment in this context, for now we are still for the most part confined to an examination of various "social indicators"—but we can, at least, apply more psychologically probing questions than we were profitably able to apply in the past. The best available data emphasize such indicators of satisfaction as health (both physical and mental), job satisfaction and various economic concerns, generational issues, community/government, religion/spirituality, leisure, aging, interpersonal relations, privacy/personal space, sense of place, tolerance/diversity and security. These are reflected and analyzed in the subtrends that follow.

The Shift from Wealth to Health

The association between wealth and satisfaction has been greatly exaggerated in this culture. Financial security certainly plays a part in the American Dream but, for some two decades now, physical and mental health have been supplanting wealth as central, and, indeed, preeminent elements in the truly satisfied life. In fact, health now appears to be even more important to Americans than home and hearth. Good health, more than anything else, is now perceived to be that element of life experience which imparts the strongest feeling that we are masters of our own destinies and thus best able to participate in the unprecedented freedoms available to us.

Two or three decades ago, we viewed the pursuit of fitness as something of an indulgence and even an eccentricity, the luxury of those with "nothing better to do." Today's attitude, increasingly, puts health before work *or* play. Recall those lonely long-distance joggers of the early 1970s, then the subject of bafflement and scorn. That seems like a million years ago. But if a certain amount of affluence and expanded leisure time helped contribute to the fitness revolution, it is clear that the revolution grows in power today independent of those factors. Medical discoveries—the knowledge that we can do more today to prevent illness, intervene successfully when it occurs and, in general, maintain good health—have undoubtedly contributed, as well. But there is another factor that has been more important.

The "health movement" is an integral part of the change that emphasized individual freedom, especially in a sexual/social context, beginning in the latter part of the 1960s. The enormous cultural shifts of that period, reverberating through the 1970s, enabled the still relatively repressed American to focus much more attention on his or her body. To a certain extent, it can accurately be said that today's emphasis on fitness is one of the benefits of the sexual revolution, which gave us permission to be more conscious of our own bodies. In a very literal sense, our bodies gained in social currency and thus it benefited us, as it had not in some time, to make the most of them. (There were, of course, those who, instead, used them to excess—but that, for the most part, was but a temporary phenomenon, an excess that occurred in reaction to a prolonged period of body repression.)

A number of researchers have noted that the rise of feminism in the 1970s did a great deal to promote women's consciousness of their bodies and health. Women who are now in early middle age show much greater interest in health—and depend far more upon it for satisfaction—than did preceding generations. As researcher Margaret Huyck puts it, "psychological investment in health seems to be a route to a sense of control for the younger middle-aged women." She explains:

> The interviews clarify this finding: many of the younger women in this sample were heavily involved in exercising, jogging or serious walking, and reading about positive health care. They talked enthusiastically about how the Women's Movement led them to assume a kind of responsibility for their own health care that they had previously ignored, and they were articulate about insisting they would not suffer the kind of physical frailties their mothers had taken for granted. Women who were not engaged in these kinds of health-monitoring and health-preserving activities often mentioned this lack, discussing it in terms of a personal failure or an inability to organize their lives to incorporate such activities.

For older women, the situation is different. Health remains an important component of satisfaction but not for the same reasons. Having been denied the benefit of coming of age in a more sexually and physically "open" era, these older women's "psychological investment in health," Huyck finds, "seems to mean the kind of preoccupation that accompanies serious health problems, not the kind of enthusiastic preventive care exemplified by the younger women." If the older woman can get through her later decades with no more than what she has come to expect to be the "normal" amount of disability for a woman of her years, then she derives some sense of control and satisfaction—at, very clearly, a lower level of expectation than that harbored by today's younger woman.

To a somewhat lesser but still significant extent, the same holds true for men. Younger men and those in early middle age are much more health oriented than older men. Men, who have previously so identified with their work, are now, increasingly, identifying with body fitness and overall health. Interestingly, they perceive themselves to be more productive and happier in their work if they concurrently perceive themselves to be more physically fit. A closer examination of this finding suggests that a strong feeling of health and fitness makes work generally more psychologically tolerable.

Older men, from late middle age onward, place less emphasis on health than do their female counterparts. Instead, they concentrate on relationships with spouses and significant others. This, however, may be due in part to a variant on the "resignation" factor that is at work in older women, as well—except that here the resignation that death is in the offing is more marked for the somewhat shorter-lived male. The older woman hopes she can "get through" without too many ailments; the older man thinks, "In the time remaining, I better make the most of what really counts."

Even though women in general enjoy greater longevity than men, they also suffer greater morbidity, that is, they suffer more illness, especially of the lingering, chronic variety. And it has now been well documented that, in many contexts, women receive inferior health care to that available to men. As the perception of this grows, there will be further shifts in health-care delivery and perhaps more emphasis on health in assessing levels of life satisfaction among both men and women. Recent research has already begun focusing not merely on life expectancies and "years-of-life-remaining" at various ages but also upon "well-years-of-life" and "quality-adjusted-years-of-life" remaining. In these equations, women are now found by researchers Robert M. Kaplan, *et al.*, Department of Community and Family Medicine,

University of California, San Diego, to have only a *three*-year advantage over men. Findings like these may bring older men and women closer together in their perceptions of the relative value of health in advanced age.

There is no doubt that "health consciousness" continues to be on the rise and that the health-conscious declare themselves more satisfied with life. But is this simply something people *say* that may or may not be true? Studies that have sought answers to this question provide evidence that the expressed satisfaction is genuine. Shulamith Kreitler and Hans Kreitler, for example, in one of the most probing inquiries into this issue, report (in *European Journal of Personality*) that individuals who scored high on health orientation also scored higher on measures of such positive emotions as love, joy and contentment and lower on such negative emotions as depression, anxiety and fear. They note "the emphasis of the health-oriented individuals on a positive internal atmosphere," adding that this "is manifested in the predominance of positive emotions . . . and positive daydreams, and also in the inhibition of negative emotions and negative daydreams."

On the other hand, this study also found higher levels of health orientation among men to be associated with higher levels of hostility and jealousy. It is thought, however, that the jealousy revealed in this study is in the "social-comparison" rather than the "romantic-envy" category and that it relates to a component of male competitiveness that is heightened among the more fitness oriented. Similarly, the "hostility" revealed was thought to be related primarily to "energy, initiative, and assuming the 'fighting spirit' with regard to conditions inimical to one's well-being."

Because physical health has assumed so large a role in what produces satisfaction, the demand for universal health insurance and affordable, good-quality health care for all can be expected to intensify.

Improved *mental* health, in particular, can be expected to impact very positively on perceived levels of life satisfaction in the next two decades. Enormous progress has been made, in the recent past, with respect to the treatment of several major categories of mental illness. It is estimated that nearly 35 million Americans suffer from some form of mental disorder, and though only about 20 percent of them are currently being treated, this represents improvement over previous decades. Visits to psychiatrists and psychologists increased more than 10 percent between 1985 and 1990, and between 1983 and 1989 the number of clinical psychologists practicing in the United States increased 27 percent; the number of psychiatrists increased 13 percent in the same period.

Lewis L. Judd, M.D., former director of the National Institute of Mental Health, recently observed, "The pace of progress in neuroscience is so great that 90 percent of all we know about the brain has been learned in the last ten years." We expect to learn even more by the end of the 1990s, so much in fact that Congress and the president declared this the "Decade of the Brain." Perhaps the most important perceptual change that is occurring is that, as Dr. Judd puts it (in *USA Today*), "mental disorders are real." New discoveries and technologies are, he says, making that abundantly clear:

> New imaging technologies, such as positron emission tomography (PET) and magnetic resonance imaging (MRI) scans, permit us to see structure and activity in living human brains. These have provided graphic evidence that severe mental illnesses are associated with visible brain dysfunctions. For example, studies using MRI, which provides exquisitely detailed pictures of brain structures, have revealed developmental brain abnormalities in children with autism and adults with schizophrenia, disorders once attributed to poor parenting. Mental disorders' roots often are as biological as those underlying any physical ailment.

And, in fact, several of those biological roots have been found and understood, and corrective pharmacological interventions have been formulated. Several disorders that, only a few years ago, were still poorly understood and could only be treated with drugs that suppressed or masked symptoms, often attended by serious side effects, are now treatable with highly specific drugs that zero in on specific biological activity, such as brain chemicals called neurotransmitters. By correcting errors in the production, flow and metabolism of such biological chemicals these drugs can—and do—restore millions of people, many of whom were previously intermittently hospitalized throughout their lifetimes, to full, productive lives. Dr. Judd cites four major mental disorders in which dramatic progress has been made in a relatively short period of time: major depression, panic disorder, manic-depressive illness, and obsessive-compulsive disorder. And, as Dr. Judd adds, "the best is yet to come," as brain research accelerates.

Of course, not all mental distresses will be amenable to psychopharmacological intervention. Nor should they be. Loneliness, for example, at one level, might be viewed as a symptom of sociological illness, rather than an individual illness. In other words, it can be a useful indicator of what needs to be done to "cure" an ailing society. Loneliness is, in fact, one of the most pervasive sources of mental distress in our culture. Studies cited by Benedict T. McWhirter (*Journal of Counseling & Development*) show that at least 10 percent of the general adult population suffers from significant loneliness, women more often than men. Particularly vulnerable are single adolescent mothers of low income, alcoholics, the elderly, high school and college students.

What is hopeful is the fact that loneliness, for the first time, is being taken seriously as a mental disturbance, worthy of study in its own right. As McWhirter observes, "Traditionally seen as part of more encompassing issues of psychological distress, such as depression and anxiety, loneliness has only in the last decade or so been described as a unique clinical problem."

There are other reasons to hope that loneliness will be less prevalent among Americans in years to come.

Toward More Satisfying "Connections" at All Stages of Life

Next to health, we place the highest importance on interpersonal relationships, our sense of "connection" with others, in assessing our respective levels of life satisfaction. Many of the issues related to this subtrend have been explored and analyzed in preceding chapters related to relationships and the family, in all of their rapidly changing forms. Contrary to the received wisdom, as the traditional family continues to evolve, people are *not* retreating into states of disenchantment and isolation. On the contrary, the increasingly sanctioned freedom to explore and form "nontraditional" connections contributes to a greater sense of social engagement and satisfaction. Cross-gender communications appear poised for some real breakthroughs, providing hope that there will be, in the next two decades, a movement toward genuine détente between the sexes. And romance is expected to bloom in older age, as well, as the population ages and men in the second halves of their lives attend to the intimacies that they so often neglected in the first half.

As previously noted, the one-person household is the fastest growing household category in the Western world. Some 25 percent of all households in the United States are of this type, up from 10 percent in the 1950s, and in Sweden, this category accounts for nearly 40 percent of all households. Sweden is the most single-oriented nation on earth; yet its people, as demonstrated in well-designed studies, feel the *least* isolated and lonely. Swedish society, for all its singleness, is one of the most socially engaged in the world. America's movement in the same direction should provide for more satisfying possibilities.

Our perception of how satisfied we are, at each stage of life, has to do with our feeling that we are fulfilling some useful social role, that our "connections" are productive and needed links in the social fabric. Thus, as traditional roles, such as gender roles, begin to lose their meaning in a world where, for example, both men and women must work, some people are temporarily "displaced" or psychologically dislocated. Older women who did not participate in the workforce and who suddenly find themselves widowed with no children at home, for example, are often cast into a kind of roleless limbo wherein dissatisfaction naturally flourishes. Thus the replacement of old, outmoded macroroles with more dynamic microroles should also engender greater satisfaction in coming years; indeed, there is evidence that this has already begun to happen on a large scale. Women are no longer restricted to the roles of "wife" or "mother." Increasingly, they can assume the multiplicity of roles men have long been able to choose from. Similarly, boys and men are no longer expected to conform so rigidly to "masculine" behavior, attitudes and roles, expanding the spectrum of life experience for them, as well. Acceptable role options have increased for nearly everyone.

The nation's young people have, perhaps, been the most disadvantaged in this context. The nation's relative affluence, as noted in an earlier chapter, has helped rob many of our youth of any meaningful role identity, and numerous studies indicate that the epidemic of adolescent suicide in this country can be directly attributed to this. "Putting it succinctly," says Edward A. Wynne of the University of Illinois, Chicago (*Report of the Secretary's Task Force on Youth Suicide*), "[French sociologist Emil] Durkheim proposed that, in Western society, suicide is an affliction largely caused by not feeling immediately needed by others." Interestingly, suicide is more prevalent among more advantaged white youth than it is among disadvantaged minority youth. Why? Because the former, given everything but a useful role to play in life, feel more isolated and worthless than do their counterparts in even some of the most distressed ghettos, where survival itself, often via gang "families," provides the role. Ironically, to *some* extent, more difficult economic times may be psychologically beneficial by obliterating some of the boredom and isolation of leisure among upper-middle-class and more-affluent youth. Additionally, the current movement away from consumerism and materialism toward greater investment of time and energy in community activity and volunteerism may also benefit these youths. For the disadvantaged young, the answer appears to be better health care, better education, better job training, all of which appear more likely to materialize as we perceive such programs to be in our national self-interest.

In part, the importance of youth dissatisfaction, to the extent that it persists, will be diminished by the mere fact that America is so rapidly graying. The "youth culture" and the "baby boom" are about to be supplanted by the "geezer boom," the dimensions of which have been explored in previous chapters. At one time, not many years ago, the pundits were predicting a gloomy new century peopled with dour, demanding old people, sick, isolated, depressed and generally down on life. Surveys fail to confirm movement in that direction, and, in fact, significantly more middle-aged people today find life "exciting" than did in the 1970s. In some studies, certain segments of the elderly are found to be among America's most satisfied people.

In fact in a recent study carried out by the Commonwealth Fund, 61 percent of those Americans over age 65 accounted themselves "very satisfied" with life in general. This exceeds the level of satisfaction expressed by seniors in such countries as Japan, West Germany and Britain. In a *Los Angeles Times* poll, about the same percentage of Americans over 65 said they are very satisfied with life, compared with about 50 percent equally satisfied between the ages of 18 and 49. This survey found far less depression among old people than among young people. Nor are the elderly as fearful as frequently portrayed; they are less fearful than surveys indicated a decade ago and today are no more afraid to take evening walks alone in their neighborhoods than are the young or the middle aged.

The trends that favor increasing levels of satisfaction in advanced age include: the sheer numbers, increasing the political, economic and social importance of this subgroup while, at the same time, diminishing the stigma of aging; medical advances that will finally not only prolong life but increase the quality of the years added; fewer lonely aging women as male longevity catches up with that of females; more active roles for the aged as the consequences of the "baby bust" provide opportunities for both senior men and women to stay in the workforce longer and, in fact, often to move on to more challenging jobs at a time when they previously expected to be relegated to permanent retirement.

This surprising opportunity to remain connected to meaningful work will be especially satisfying. As Stephen M. Pollan and Mark Levine (*New York*) observe, many baby-boomers have made a conscious effort all their lives to find work they enjoy. And when they reach 65, they're facing perhaps another twenty or more years of life. As longevity has increased, retirement has turned into an extended period of inactivity that often results in mental and physical deterioration. The petrified retired couple living in an adult housing project in Florida, who spend all day discussing their various physical ailments and then go to dinner at 4 P.M. to take advantage of the "early-bird special" are familiar—and dismal—role models.

"The parents of baby-boomers lived linear lives punctuated with events like retirement," notes [Ross] Goldstein of Generation Insights. "Boomers, on the other hand, have led cyclical lives, starting over and over again. Retirement for them won't be the definitive event it was for their parents . . . they'll continue to work in some way: part-time, as a consultant, a volunteer, or as an entrepreneur. Not only because they'll want to but because the economy will need to keep them in place."

The corporate world seems prepared to accept this new attitude. Though they are laying off highly paid senior staffers, corporations are also turning around and hiring even older individuals. "Age isn't the factor that it once was," says Dale Klamfoth [senior vice president of Drake Beam Morin, Inc., a human-resources consulting firm]. "Companies are learning that older Americans are a tremendous resource offering a great deal more experience and stability for just about the same money."

To the extent that satisfaction depends upon meaningful connections, the coming decades look promising for most segments of our society. Though the current generation of young people is the first expected to be less materially well off than its parent generation, the psychological environment in which it matures is expected to be one that places higher value on nonmaterial goals that at any time in decades. The repertoire of roles available to minorities is expanding, and the elderly, particularly by the end of the 1990s, will be better connected than at any time in this century.

Work and Leisure: Radically Altered Perceptions and Realities

Satisfaction with our work is an important element in the assessment of life quality. To some extent this is related to financial security, but, more important, it relates to the sense of mastery and control, to the perception that we are achieving something that is creative, productive, useful. The most satisfying work affirms the most positive images we have of ourselves.

Right now American dissatisfaction with work is very high. In part this has to do with economic recession, cutbacks, job uncertainty and the fact that average real earnings, rather than advancing, have actually receded to where they were in 1961! About 75 percent of all Americans were in the middle-income category just ten years ago; now that percentage has declined to about 65 percent and is still sliding.

Noted sociologist Daniel Bell (*The World and the United States in 2013*) asserted in 1987 that, "Sociologically, the most significant [current and ongoing] development is the breakup of the idea of the middle class." He elaborates:

> The term "middle class" was always amorphous, yet possessed a psychological reality in the self-definition of most persons in American society. But there are fewer anchorages today for such self-definition. The breakup of the traditional family has meant that the real incomes of the middle class have become skewed; these divergences will continue. Home ownership, the most important anchorage of the last forty years, has become difficult to achieve. The rising costs of services, particularly for working women, raise questions as to what is a "middle-class" standard of living. Cultural and social identifications may become more important than occupational status (except for those at the top . . .) as a source of cohesion and psychological identity.
>
> We may see, equally, a new politics whose dimensions cut across each other and make continuing groupings difficult. The most important social change in this regard is the new role of women. On the professional level, women are concentrated more in the health and teaching and public sector professions than are men, and employment in those areas is highly dependent on public funding. Generational politics becomes more important: the elderly are now an increasingly cohesive bloc whose interests are largely untouchable. The increasing mobilization of the minority groups is more certain. Regional issues will become more salient. The polarization of society based on educational cutoffs may increase populist sentiments. The down-sizing of the manufacturing corporation and the spread of more small businesses will increase the hopes and the expectations of independence for many persons, yet the short half-

life of many small firms and the upheavals in corporate structures will intensify the insecurity of employment and incomes.

Within ten years, Bell, backed by an abundance of persuasive data, believes we will have this four-tiered socioeconomic structure, which, in fact, is already rapidly taking shape: an upper middle class of professional and managerial workers, comprising about 25 percent of the population; a middle class of technical, administrative support and skilled workers, representing 35 percent of the population; a service class, being about 25 percent of the population; and an underclass of about 15 percent, comprising individuals with no steady employment, doing odd jobs, menial labor, and the like.

The news is, by no means, all bad. Some of it will mean *greater* job satisfaction for many Americans. As Bell has noted, the demise of the middle class is not quite as clear cut as it may sometimes seem. Women, for example, as they assume more political power, can be expected to provide themselves, through the public sector, with more satisfying work, just as the elderly may do. Minorities may also benefit in a new era of populist government reform (see the next subtrend for a further discussion of this).

In the past two decades the biggest shift has been in the reduction of manufacturing jobs and the even more dramatic increase in service-related jobs (in restaurants, janitorial capacities, hairdressing, etc.). What this has meant is that young workers, in particular, those with only high school educations have had to shift from relatively high-paying jobs in factories and the like to relatively low-paying service jobs. This trend will continue, bringing with it, for this group, less overall job satisfaction. But, at the same time, there will also be an increase in much higher paying professional and managerial services. And, as already noted, the perceptual shift that is already accommodating a downsized economy will, to some significant degree, buffer the negative effects of some of these changes.

There are still other reasons to expect that many Americans will find greater—rather than less—satisfaction in work in the years ahead. One important reason relates to child care. As America catches up with some other Western nations in providing parental leave, better day care and child support, American parents, whether singles or couples, will be able to balance child rearing with work in ways that are presently foreclosed. This major cause of job dissatisfaction will thus be significantly reduced.

Meanwhile, there is evidence in recent years (represented by an increased number of research papers and surveys) that businesses, industries and government are all interested in improving the "quality of work life" as the most effective means of enhancing worker productivity and reliability, as well as consumer receptivity to products and services. As M. Joseph Sirgy of Virginia Polytechnic Institute and State University notes (*Journal of Business Research*), "Business in general is beginning to realize that its responsibility to people extends beyond meeting certain market demands and generating employment. Business's responsibility is also to contribute to the quality of life of its employees and the community." The change here is quite fundamental, Sirgy makes clear. Whereas many businesses used to come up with a product and *then* try to make it acceptable to the public, they now, increasingly, "engage in research in order to understand human needs and wants, and to deliver goods and services that can satisfy important needs in such a way as to enhance quality of life of a certain consumer segment, while not debilitating the quality of life of other publics." In short, both with respect to employees and consumers, businesses have discovered the economic value of "quality of life," both as a market guide (a major determinant of what things to produce) and a management credo.

Similarly, Charles C. Manz of Arizona State University and Roger Grothe of Unisys Corporation (also *Journal of Business Research*), note that "Contemporary work organizations have faced a revolution in the nature of values held by the modern-day workforce." They describe those workers who will be between their late 30s and their late 50s in the year 2000 as a values-oriented "vanguard" that business will have to please if it is to succeed. These are the workers who have previously been described, they observe, as the "now generation," "the new breed," "the 60's kids," etc.:

> These individuals . . . grew to maturity during a time of unprecedented prosperity and social turmoil. Campus unrest, the controversial Vietnam war, affluence, and societal conditions in general that seemed to stimulate a revolution of changing values and mores in the United States, were among the major pressures with which they were confronted. As an apparent consequence, they have displayed a set of life/work values that is very different from that of their parents and grandparents. Their combined impact on society and industry appears to be staggering and poses significant challenges for our transition to a new century.

Greater present job dissatisfaction does not reflect working conditions that are worse than in previous periods. By most objective standards, work conditions today for most Americans are *better* than ever. The change has been in values and *perceived* work benefits. What once sufficed to satisfy no longer does so. Emphasis has shifted from wages and monetary benefits to the *content* of work itself, from "getting in the hours" to feeling that the hours are "worthwhile."

General Motors and many other major corporations are taking this change in worker psychology very seriously. They are heeding the warning that *Business Week* sounded more than ten years ago: "U.S. industry must reorganize work and its incentives to appeal to new workers' values, rather than try to retrofit people to work designs and an industrial relations system of 80 years ago."

Numerous experimental programs being tried in several industries are all aimed at making work more meaningful. Some emphasize greater worker independence and self-management linked with more responsive incentive mechanisms. Research indicates that worker motivation is enhanced with the perception that the business in question has a beneficial social and environmental agenda. Thus efforts are being made to merge business goals with ideas and objectives that the individual worker regards as "self-actualizing," with aims that reinforce the worker's ideal image of himself or herself.

Yet another factor that will continue to enhance work satisfaction in some quarters is information-age technology, which frees some to work at home or at other locations away from the central office. Though "telecommuting" has not revolutionized business and work to the extent that some were predicting, it continues to have an impact, one that will be more firmly felt in coming decades. Ultimately, its impact will be quite dramatic. The Travelers Companies of Hartford, Connecticut, describes telecommuting as "the art of moving information rather than people to accomplish work." The telecommuter uses hardware, software, faxes and other telecommunications devices to work on the road or out of the home. Companies, such as Travelers, that use telecommuting, say they save in numerous ways: absenteeism is greatly diminished, investment in centralized facilities can be significantly reduced, rigid "shifts" that reduce worker satisfaction and productivity can be eliminated—and the ability to recruit top talent from anywhere in the world is greatly enhanced.

But as Larry Hilderbrand, writing in the Portland *Oregonian* observes, "Telecommuting is more than eliminating or reducing the rush-hour traffic for some employees. Workers can enjoy alternative workstyles and lifestyles, opportunity for more creativity and productivity, save money on clothing and meals, and provide [home care for children and the elderly]. . . ."

Telecommuting is an irresistible force, Hilderbrand observes, because:

> Employers want access to labor; increased productivity; and lower or no net increase in costs, including for offices, parking, recruiting, training, sick leave and family leave.
>
> Employees want some stability; work satisfaction; to live where they choose; less stress; less personal-time-consuming commutes; greater control of their lives; more time with their families.
>
> Society wants less traffic congestion; improved air quality; wiser land use; less energy consumption and less dependence on foreign petroleum sources; and to hold down the costs of roads, bridges and transit systems.

On another but related front, it appears that changing—and more flexible—ideas about leisure and retirement may also have the effect of making life more satisfying in years to come. The primary change has to do with a blurring of the line between work and leisure. In the extreme, work has been viewed as servitude, something to be endured, a necessary evil. Leisure, in this dichotomy, is a period of temporary respite, an interval in which to pack as much activity as possible—with the result that not much enjoyment derives from it, either. To a lesser extreme, this pattern has prevailed in much of our work culture for decades—a pattern that has weakened as people have consciously sought work that is more satisfying in and of itself.

Much has been made in the press recently of the "overworked American" and the "loss of leisure." It has been pointed out that the cavemen had more leisure time than we do today. In fact, hunter-gatherers, it is estimated, had to spend less than twenty hours a week to procure the food they needed to sustain themselves, whereas, in agricultural societies, it has taken more than sixty hours per week to achieve the same end. More recently, the picture has become more clouded. Claims that Americans are working longer hours today than they were in the late 1960s don't appear to stand up under close scrutiny. These claims have factored in the time people spend "working" at home on such things as fixing leaky faucets and taking care of children. And the statistics get skewed by the baby boom bulge.

Economists Thomas Juster and Frank Stafford of the University of Michigan have studied the issue in depth and conclude: "We don't see any evidence that people work more hours." On the contrary, their findings indicate that American males have actually reduced their combined on/off-job work hours in recent times. The same is true for women, whose increase in paid work has been more than offset by reductions in unpaid work hours at home.

As Stephen Chapman of the *Chicago Tribune* notes, "In an age of clothes dryers, telecommuting, Domino's pizza and waxless floors, Americans still don't have all the leisure they'd like. . . . But if you really think you work harder than your parents did, try telling them that."

As for retirement, many have found it to be more stressful than work. The rush to early retirement that has been evident in recent times will soon reverse, not only because older people, as already noted, will be needed in the workforce but because the "vanguard" workforce discussed previously is in a position to find work more rewarding. As this group ages, it will seek to keep some presence in the workforce, if only on a part-time basis. Telecommuting will be a particularly potent facilitator of this trend, enabling seniors to spend more time with family and friends in locales generally associated with retirement while maintaining that presence in the workforce.

Satisfaction and the Sense of Community/Security

One of the life domains that has considerable importance in terms of perceived life satisfaction is "sense of community," encompassing factors related to government, neighborhood diversity and cohesion, population density, privacy and permanence. In one way or another all of these factors impinge upon the individual's sense of *security*. At present, this is another one of the domains in which Americans experience significant dissatisfaction. The trend may continue in the short term. But there is evidence that Americans will rebuild their collective sense of community in the next two decades.

Sense of community, research indicates, begins with perceptions about national government and works down to the grass roots. Even the residents of the most prosperous and orderly communities experience some insecurity and instability in periods of widespread disenchantment with national government. When people feel the nation is "going wrong," they feel their own communities are imperiled. That is what has been happening for several years throughout the United States. This has resulted in a pervasive desire for fundamental change in government. In polls asking people whether they want more or less government, the results are often in favor of *less* government. But those results are contradicted by more detailed and probing surveys which demonstrate that a strong majority of Americans actually want *more* but *better* government, that is, more responsive to community needs. Indeed, the desire for that kind of government is more intense than at any time in two decades.

The most detailed surveys support the idea that Americans want grass-roots, populist reforms that will help restore the cities, reinvigorate rural and suburban areas, rebuild a decaying infrastructure (roads, bridges, schools, etc.), provide jobs and job training and extend health care to all, regardless of income. Not since the post-Depression, New Deal era has there been so much sentiment for this kind of government presence in our lives. Even the desire to put able-bodied welfare recipients to work is in concert with the *new* New Dealism. I referred earlier to some of the government programs Americans, mostly by very substantial margins, favor, including college loans to anyone who will agree to military service or some national rebuilding program, and national health care paid for with new taxes if necessary.

By a 13-to-1 ratio, according to a CBS–*New York Times* poll, Americans view government-directed economic restoration as the number one "national security" issue. With the evaporation of the Cold War and the "Red Menace," our top "external enemy" has become the faltering economy. Suddenly, such things as affordable housing and health-care benefits loom much larger in the typical American's mind than does the defense budget. The fear of poverty is, in fact, a much more real fear for many Americans than any fear of the "Evil Empire" ever was. And with the ranks of those officially designated as impoverished reaching nearly 36 million Americans there is no mystery as to why this is so. Not since Lyndon Johnson declared the "War on Poverty" in 1964 have the poverty numbers been this high.

Increasingly both rank-and-file Americans and economists, though concerned about the enormous federal deficit, are turning away from the idea that government spending is categorically bad. There is a perceived need for judicious, phased deficit reduction *and* redirected government spending. "Neglect of our internal needs is undermining our future," asserts financial expert Felix Rohatyn, addressing graduates of the Wharton School, University of Pennsylvania. "The role of government and the behavior of a great, modern world power consists of more than just presiding over deficit reduction. It consists in investing for the future to be competitive and to provide opportunity for all its citizens."

Charlotte Saikowski, writing for *The Christian Science Monitor*, notes that "even corporate leaders who applaud the Reagan administration's assault on government intervention express concern about the 'benign neglect' of social needs" and national infrastructure. After documenting the scope of the neglect, Saikowski writes: "In the face of this and other pent-up social needs, pressures are mounting for government action." And because the federal government has been defaulting, she adds, increasingly, state and other local governments have been trying to fill the void:

> Led by innovative, dynamic governors, many states across the country are reforming education and health systems, experimenting with workfare programs [work and job-training for people on welfare], promoting industrial development, and building new roads and other public works. They are cutting deals with foreign governments to attract foreign investment and expanding regulation into areas untouched by Washington.
>
> . . . But the states cannot do everything. Many already feel overloaded . . . there appears to be a growing consensus that the federal government will have to play a more active role than it has. . . .

Even with respect to that most volatile of issues—welfare—there are signs that the public will move toward a new perspective in pursuit of a greater sense of national fairness, confidence and community. Stephanie Coontz, in her recent book *The Way We Never Were: American Families and the Nostalgia Trap*, an excerpt of which appeared in *Harper's*, provides a preview of that changing perspective, one that argues for thoughtful government assistance. Many of those who complain today of "freeloaders" and the like do so either in ignorance of their own government-subsidized heritage or in outright hypocrisy. "The myth of family self-reliance," Coontz relates, "is so compelling that our actual national and personal histories often buckle under its emotional weight." The pioneer family and the "traditional" nuclear family of the 1950s are often held up as exemplary symbols of self-reliance. But, in truth, Coontz asserts, "the ability of these families to establish and sustain themselves required massive underwriting by the government." The Homestead Act of 1862, for example, allowed pioneer families to purchase land at much less than it cost the government to acquire it.

She continues:

> The suburban family of the 1950s is another oft-cited example of familial self-reliance. According to legend, after World War II a new, family-oriented generation settled down, saved their pennies, worked hard, and found well-paying jobs that allowed them to purchase homes in the suburbs. In fact, however, the 1950s suburban family was far more dependent on government assistance than any so-called underclass family of today. Federal GI benefit payments, available to 40 percent of the male population between the ages of twenty and twenty-four, permitted a whole generation of men to expand their education and improve their job prospects without forgoing marriage and children.

Coontz goes on to detail a plethora of additional federal programs that subsidized the new suburbanites. She does not lament these programs. On the contrary, it's her point that all of this government largesse failed to produce any of the "demoralization usually presumed to afflict recipients of government handouts."

> Instead, federal subsidies to suburbia encouraged family formation, residential stability, upward occupational mobility, and rising educational aspirations among youth who could look forward to receiving such aid. Seen in this light, the idea that government subsidies intrinsically induce dependence, undermine self-esteem, or break down family ties is exposed as no more than a myth.

After the Los Angeles riots and the continued economic distress of 1992, some of the most successful election-year rhetoric assumed a tone quite different from what many had expected in hard times. Instead of a prevailing rhetoric of exclusion and scapegoating there emerged, in many circles, a more constructive and conciliatory tone in closer concert with the electorate's desire for a genuine rebirth and rebuilding of our national community.

Related to this are signs that the nation is more ready to confront racial and other social inequities than at any time since the 1970s. Some 60 percent of Americans now believe the country is spending "too little" "on problems of the big cities" and "on improving conditions of blacks," according to a *New York Times*/CBS News poll. "More police to reduce racial tension and prevent riots" is the prescription of only 24 percent of Americans as opposed to 78 percent who believe the best way to achieve these ends is through "more jobs and job training."

This is not to say that we will enjoy a golden era of racial and social harmony in the next two decades; indeed, the next round of "adjustments" may produce notable sparks in many communities, but both the people and their policymakers are more aware than they have been in years that we are still a sharply divided society and that these divisions, if not addressed, will eventually tear the nation apart.

Richard J. Cattani writes, in *The Christian Science Monitor*, of the "seismic urban disruptions" that have racked the nation at roughly quarter-century intervals, and concludes, "Despite the obvious, painful evidence of urban destruction and the need to understand the tensions that lead to [such disruptions], the larger trend continues toward the American democratic vision of political and social equality for all citizens." (That trend has been examined in a preceding chapter.) "Overall," he continues, "America is working out the tensions inherent in the human condition as regards race, religion and class. It is doing rather better than other parts of the world in all three."

What is needed to sustain real progress, Cattani observes, is "a clear vision at the top of . . . government and every institution of the need to expunge divisiveness based on race, ethnicity, and class." That view is gaining in currency and will have positive impact. Concurrently, some of the minorities themselves are recognizing the degree to which they have internalized social oppression and are taking active steps to overcome that.

Itabari Njeri, author of the recent book *The Last Plantation*, describes the mind itself as "the last plantation" for many African-Americans, whose oppression, it is argued, is partly self-imposed. "But," she asserts, "we have the power to resolve all these conflicts and change our social reality. We are not merely prisoners of history. We have changed our fates in the past—the civil rights movement is but one example—and we can again."

Alex Kotlowitz and Suzanne Alexander, writing in *The Wall Street Journal*, produce evidence that a "code of silence" among blacks helps perpetuate the divisions between the races:

> For a variety of reasons, blacks often don't share their experiences and feelings with whites. In some ways, the difficulty they face in talking is like that of war veterans who find it hard to share their combat experiences with civilians.
>
> . . . many African-Americans in this country live with a surging

river of indignities dammed up inside, a deep reservoir of what one psychologist calls "microinsults."

But many blacks suffer these everyday slights privately. They offer many reasons for their silence. Some simply assume that whites will be insensitive to their stories. In other cases, blacks feel that whites won't believe them or that simply bringing up issues of race is too explosive. And some are concerned about whites considering blacks hypersensitive.

And, of course, on many occasions, African-Americans are confirmed in their fears about speaking up. Some whites are nonresponsive or hostile but far more, the evidence suggests, are ignorant of the extent to which many minorities feel oppressed. But there appears to be a trend in the making, one that raises this vital communications issue in our collective consciousness. Some businesses are trying out seminars aimed at improving interracial communications, and following the 1992 Los Angeles riots, as *The Wall Street Journal* noted, "the wall of silence" seems to be cracking, however tentatively. The situation "has gotten some whites to listen and some blacks to talk. Already, on TV talk shows and in newspaper interviews, such prominent African-Americans as . . . Oprah Winfrey and Michael Jordan have revealed personal tales of humiliation and pain."

Njeri notes that even among themselves many African-Americans do not constructively communicate these hurts. But, she too now sees some opportunity for that to change—and she outlines the directions in which blacks need to move:

> We need to develop support groups in our community—block-by-block, church-by-church—in which we can take turns listening to each other—not just venting. We need to talk about our grief . . . over our daily hurts, over the fact that we have had no safe place to share our pain. And once we put some attention on the grief, we need to commit ourselves to developing specific plans of action for our neighborhoods. We have to make everyone in the African-American community a leader responsible for our mutual liberation.

A strong, productive government and harmony among diverse people are certainly among the most important factors that help produce a stable, satisfying sense of community. Many have expected increased immigration and cultural diversity to create greater dissatisfaction in this country and, in some circles, no doubt, they have. Overall, however, America seems to be strengthened by this diversity and to take cultural satisfaction in its nearly unique ability to assimilate and accommodate so many unlike peoples. Philosopher John Stuart Mill, more than one hundred years ago, wrote:

> It is hardly possible to overrate the value, in the present low state of human development, of placing human beings in contact with persons dissimilar to themselves, and with modes of thought and action unlike those with which they are familiar. Such communication has always been onc of the primary sources of progress.

As we rebuild our inner cities in the next two decades, a process that is already well underway in a few cities, urban planners are bringing people together, as Mill advocated. As Carl Abbott, professor of urban studies at Portland (Oregon) State University and the author of several texts on urban history and planning says, "downtown is everybody's neighborhood." He elaborates (quoted in the Portland *Oregonian*):

> Downtowns are the only truly common ground within the fragmented fabric of modern communities. There are at least three ways in which they serve as the modern equivalent of the village square of earlier centuries:
>
> - They are natural centers for our subdivided and segregated cities and towns.
> - They are common spaces.
> - They provide our only shared symbols for representing the entirety of our communities.

Whereas Portland and some other cities have already successfully helped to revitalize their economies and their communities through urban designs that focus first on central city renewal, several other cities are *creating* new central cities from scratch. As Abbott observes, "San Jose—the prototype of the suburbanized city . . . managed to get away without a downtown from the 1950s to the 1970s. In the 1980s residents of this suburb without a center decided to spend nearly $1.5 billion to *manufacture* a comprehensive downtown where none existed."

Relative levels of permanence and mobility are other factors that impinge on our sense of community and satisfaction therewith. Here, too, there is some good news for the next two decades. Some urban planners have worried that telecommuting will soon undermine communities by making them so mutable that no one will have a vested interest in their maintenance and identity. In fact, however, the telecommuting revolution, important though it is, has been vastly overestimated in terms of number of participants. A far more significant trend in this context is the overall reduction in nomadism that is already occurring as a result of economic slowdown. Even in a recovery phase many experts now predict that migration from region to region in pursuit of jobs will continue to slow. As Gary Blonston and Robert A. Rankin, reflecting the views of many economic experts, write (Knight-Ridder News Service): "Fewer people will be uprooting to seek their fortunes elsewhere." They add:

> On balance, the aftermath of the recession will find less economic differences from region to region than has existed for many years, as the boom industries on the coast struggle to cope, the hard-pressed heartland industries that downsized in the '80s now press their advantage and cost differentials shrink.
>
> . . . The growing sameness of regional economies will mean fewer starkly different opportunities from place to place for employers or employees.

And, because births were sharply down in the depressed 1930s, there won't be nearly as many people retiring in the 1990s. "So the flow of senior citizens carrying their nest eggs to Florida, Arizona, Texas and California likely will slow significantly," Blonston and Rankin point out.

On balance, then, communities should experience more population stability than they have in decades. And even the telecommuters, many believe, will add, rather than detract, from that stability. Rather than flit from one locale to another, most telecommuters appear to be choosing their home-away-from-the-traditional-workplace with great care. A number of communities, reluctant though some members of those communities are to admit it, have been substantially strengthened by the inflow of these electronic nomads. Several semirural areas, small towns and cities in various parts of the country have been revitalized by this in-migration of refugees from the big city. These newcomers often bring with them very valuable skills and keen insights into how to avoid the kind of problems that fractured the communities from which they are fleeing. And they are often highly motivated to devote long volunteer hours to help restore and preserve the communities into which they move. Many local economies have boomed due to what in the West is known as the "California invasion."

Satisfaction and Spiritual Values

Religious belief, as noted in the introduction to this chapter, has correlated weakly with levels of satisfaction in this country. *In general*, as the Russell Sage researchers observe, a strong religious faith, as a determinant of life satisfaction, "is described as being more important by women than men, by older people than by younger people, by those with less formal education than by those with more, and by those with low incomes than by those who are better off financially." But, as Christopher G. Ellison of Duke University and collaborators report (*Social Forces*), results of research, including their own, "indicate that both *devotional* (private) and *participatory* (public) aspects of religiosity have relatively small but persistent positive relationships with life satisfaction."

The trend is toward assigning even less importance to traditional religiosity in the future. Most mainstream churches have had steadily declining memberships since the mid-1960s. The Presbyterian Church, for example, has seen its faithful decline from more than 4 million to less than 3 million in that time frame. During the same period, membership in the United Methodist Church has declined from more than 11 million to about 9 million. The baby boomers in particular have turned away from established churches in droves.

But Americans in high numbers continue to account themselves interested in spiritual matters, though these are often widely defined to include not only such things as Eastern philosophies but various pursuits related to psychological self-help and anything that purports to explore "the meaning of life." Interest in "the unexplained" is on the rise and this, in itself, seems to substitute in some lives for other spiritual inquiries. Notable among "the unexplained" are UFOs. And many see "New Ageism" continuing to infiltrate mainstream society. There is some evidence that an aging society will, increasingly, turn to philosophical, if not traditionally religious, interests.

Fears that Americans will embrace harmful, perhaps "satanic," cults in large numbers as they abandon traditional religiosity appear to be entirely unfounded. Cult involvement is a fringe activity in our society and will continue to be. There have been predictions since the 1960s that the United States would be virtually overrun by cults, but there has been no notable growth in cult activity, and the media attention given cults would seem to far exceed their significance. The 800 followers of Baghwan Shree Rajneesh, for example, made international headlines for a long period of time suggestive of a much more formidable group. And the "Moonies," followers of the Rev. Sun Myung Moon, were once so prevalent in the media that one might have thought their number was closer to 600,000 than the actual 6,000.

Both the public and law-enforcement officials are responding to charges of "satanism" with growing skepticism, a trend that is likely to strengthen as these charges, made primarily by fundamentalist Christians, fail to be substantiated. Sociologist David G. Bromley explains (in *Society*) the origins of the hysteria over satanism:

> Subversion fears have recurred throughout American history; countersubversion ideologies have targeted witches, Indians, Catholics, Mormons, the Mafia, communists, and religious cultists. Each time the fears emerged in a period of significant conflict between contemporary and traditional social patterns. The current satanism scare is similarly rooted in an institutional crisis: incompatibility between family and economy, which confronts individuals with contradictory behavioral imperatives.

Satanism, in short, is the current "bogeyman," a scapegoat upon which blame can be placed for the disintegration of the traditional family, for child abuse, for rape, for teen pregnancies, pornography, drug use, abortion, rock music, suicide and on and on.

Like satanism, drugs appear to have little appeal for Americans in search of "a new high" or spiritual renewal. Illicit drugs are here to stay, but there is little reason to expect that usage will increase by any substantial margin, if at all, in the next decade. Americans' intensifying interest in health, among other things, will help stem that tide.

The most significant trend in this domain is a shift in values that de-emphasizes consumption and assigns greater importance to both outward and inward engagement. This engagement is expressed in self-exploration and self-improvement and, as noted earlier, in greater investment in family life and other interpersonal relationships, community involvement and volunteer activities. Alan Durning, senior researcher at the Worldwatch Institute in Washington, D.C., has written (*International Wildlife*), "It would be naive to believe that entire populations will suddenly experience a moral awakening, renouncing greed, envy and avarice. What can be hoped for is a gradual weakening of the consumerist ethos of affluent societies." This is a task, he predicts, "that will occupy several generations."

It seems likely that this "gradual weakening" has already begun. Numerous surveys, polls and studies sometimes hint at, sometimes openly declare a consumer revolt in the making. Some of the economic figures support this idea, suggesting that Americans will spend less and try to save more in the next decade, and probably beyond. This, again, is in keeping with findings that as the baby boomers age their values change. As Cindy Skrzycki of *The Washington Post*, sums it up, "Social responsibility is in again. After a decade of excessive consumerism and blind ambition, American workers between the ages of 25 and 49 are beginning to emphasize public service and family life as measures of success."

Among the surveys that back this notion is one conducted for Chivas Regal. It found that young urban professionals, the "yuppies" of yore, in particular, are de-emphasizing materialism. Frank Walton, president of Research and Forecasts, Inc., the firm that conducted the survey, in commenting on the findings, concluded: "It's not that money and materialism are out. It's that money and materialism aren't enough."

Business is recognizing this and is scrambling to create products and advertising that will address the new emphasis on "social responsibility." A number of major companies are now focusing on racism and other issues of cultural diversity, on environmental concerns and so on. And there are some early indications that these companies, rather than be viewed as cynical opportunists, are actually changing some of their policies to conform with their new advertising.

And so, contrary to what might have been expected, the country is not in for a gigantic collective midlife crisis, as the baby boom ages, but, instead, seems poised for something considerably more soothing. In the wake of a number of new studies and surveys, many psychologists are revising their views of middle age. As noted earlier in this book, baby boomers, by virtue of their sheer numbers, have a way of amplifying things that might otherwise get lost in the social and demographic "noise."

Daniel Goleman, writing in *The New York Times*, sums up the findings of a number of these new studies: "While there is a reordering of priorities for most people in their 40s and 50s, that reassessment often leads to a more compassionate attitude, a richer emotional life, and a deepening of personal relationships." One recent survey, conducted by New World Decisions in Princeton, N.J,. found Americans strongly agreeing with that summation. Numerous studies, including some that have followed the same groups of people over decades of development, tend to confirm these conclusions, as well.

The baby boomers' willingness—and ability—to contemplate their own deaths earlier than some previous generations have been able to do was analyzed in a previous chapter. This clearer collective vision of mortality is apparently inspiring this group to extend itself in middle age, more forcefully than has been the case in preceding generations, toward family, friends, community, environment. "You gain a kind of symbolic immortality by furthering a group you belong to or a cause you identify with," explains Robert Michels, chairman of psychiatry and dean at Cornell Medical School.

These changes apply to both men and women, though as Goleman reports, the experts see some differences in emphasis:

> The opening that middle age brings differs for men and women according to studies by David Holmes, a psychologist at the University of Kansas. "Women say the happiest period of their lives is when their children grow up and leave home," Dr. Holmes said. "It opens up all kinds of possibilities for them; they report being more mellow, and yet more assertive. For men in their 40s, though, the big change is that they discover relationships. They turn from a focus on their careers to one that includes the people in their lives; they want both.

The Satisfaction of Freedom

Finally, I must return to the idea that Americans are among the most satisfied people in the world because they are among the most free. The civil liberties we have guaranteed ourselves as "inalienable rights" continue to illuminate and liberate collective psychology. Our satisfaction, in this context, is particularly high right now. In recent years we have been witness to the power our embrace of liberty has had on the world around us, encouraging positive change under even the most negative and adverse circumstances, further demonstrating that "bad times" do not lead to inevitable and intractable states of tyranny and despair. Neither surfeit nor deprivation, it appears, can dampen the transformative power of an idea as potent as that of freedom. In a moving summation of this idea, foreign affairs columnist Leslie H. Gelb (*The New York Times*) recently observed that "humankind seems poised to survive the 20th century . . . humanity's survival from the beginning of World War I until now, and arriving at this point with glimmers of freedom in places familiar only with tyranny, is a monumental achievement."

Out of the Holocaust has come "the state of Israel, free and democratic, however troublesome." Out of the Soviet Union, where Lenin and Stalin murdered millions and they and their successors enslaved millions more, has emerged a new set of leaders who "somehow . . . kept alive . . . a concept—the idea of liberty—never experienced in Russian history . . . understood only from jail or dangerous conversations or banned books."

Gelb writes of the idea of freedom empowering such individuals as Nelson Mandela, "who ultimately wielded more power in chains than his captors did from their seemingly impregnable fortress of apartheid," and Corazon Aquino, "the woman who listened to her husband plot an impossible liberation and made it come to pass in a yellow dress." Gelb adds:

> These are all awesome historical facts. They give new life to the discarded theories of the 18th-century enlightenment historians who believed that history was the story of progress toward liberty. . . .
>
> When there was mostly oppression, who could convince us that liberty might be the natural order of things? When there were constant wars, who could persuade us that peace might be the norm?
>
> Freedom's survival against totalitarian odds allows us to believe again in higher values and to hold leaders and followers to a higher measure.

And that seems to be precisely what Americans are doing—shifting toward more satisfying values while holding their leaders to higher standards. And however disheartened they may be by economic woes, Americans cannot but find vast satisfaction in the ascendance of freedom through parts of the world so long deprived of it. Sense of "community," particularly a community at peace, is an integral part of psychological satisfaction. And today, inasmuch as "community" is increasingly a global concept, Americans, understandably, feel more connected than at any time in decades.

Solutions/Recommendations

Satisfaction, it appears, is taking care of itself. A number of trends described in this and preceding chapters bode well for this quality, as do several new programs and other innovations that we have discussed.

To summarize, the growing interest of Americans in physical health is an especially positive sign; we still need good-quality universal health care, but that, too, is coming. Even mental-health research, which has long lagged, is finally coming into its own, focusing on and finding solutions to some of the most pressing mental disturbances that afflict men and women, children and adolescents, in various stages of their lives.

Women's health, in particular, both mental and physical, is getting long-overdue attention. The next two decades should see remarkable advances in this context. And as health care for men and women equalizes (with the older male also getting more effective health care, both interventive and preventive), the two sexes can expect to live together longer and in greater harmony. There is a chance that relationships among the young, as well as the old, will be enhanced as the sexes become more adept at meaningful cross-gender communication.

The reformulation of "the family," the freedom to form nontraditional liaisons, the movement toward genuine supports for "family" in its diverse manifestations—all of this portends a more satisfying future for millions of Americans.

Also promising are more meaningful efforts to deal with crime, to rebuild our inner cities, reinvigorate our educational system and attend to a decaying infrastructure. The idea that government *can* be good will be reborn as dollars are redirected from the Cold War to the war to restore our national economy and sense of security and purpose. Our level of satisfaction in "community"—from the global village to the neighborhood—will gradually heighten in the next several years.

Work should also become more satisfying. Aging, slower population growth and other demographic variables will soon conspire to make the worker a much more valued component of our society. Business and industry are already recognizing the need to make work a more satisfying and integral part of a rapidly changing world, one in which environmental and psychological values take precedence over salaries and monetary perks.

Americans are living in truly revolutionary times. We are jettisoning social and psychological constraints that many predicted, not so long ago, would be with us for decades to come. During this process, we will move closer to the late philosopher Joseph Campbell's vision:

> People say that what we're all seeking is a meaning for life. I don't think that's what we're really seeking. I think that what we're seeking is an experience of being alive, so that our life experiences on the purely physical plane will have resonances within our own innermost being and reality, so that we actually feel the rapture of being alive.

SOURCES

1. FURY: More Violent / Less Violent?

Adams, David et al. "The Seville Statement on Violence." *American Psychologist*, vol. 45, October 1990, pp. 1167–68.

"Alcohol and Violence." *The Lancet*, vol. 336, 1990, pp. 1223–24.

Anderson, Wayne, and Barbara Bauer. "Law Enforcement Officers: The Consequences of Exposure to Violence." *Journal of Counseling and Development*, vol. 65, March 1987, pp. 381–84.

Armstrong, Scott. "Executions: Should We Be Able to Watch Them on TV?" *The Sunday Oregonian*, May 12, 1991, p. E1.

———. "Murder Rate Is Rising in the U.S." *The Christian Science Monitor*, December 18, 1990, p. 1.

"Atlanta's Curfew Experiment." *The Christian Science Monitor*, January 10, 1991, p. 20.

Baker, Dean. "Sounding Off vs. Acting Out." *The Oregonian*, November 5, 1991, p. D1.

Baker, Sherry. "A Plague Called Violence." *Omni*, August 5, 1986, p. 42.

Barrett, Paul M. "Epidemic, Killing of 15-Year-Old Is Part of Escalation of Murder by Juveniles." *The Wall Street Journal*, March 25, 1991, p. 1.

Baxter, Mike. "Flesh and blood." *New Scientist*, May 5, 1990, pp. 37–41.

Billard, Mary. "The Satisfying Silliness of the Paintball Wars." *The New York Times*, October 20, 1991, p. F27.

Billingham, Robert E., and Kathleen R. Gilbert. "Parental Divorce During Childhood and Use of Violence in Dating Relationships." *Psychological Reports*, vol. 66, 1990, pp. 1003–9.

SOURCES

Black, Chris. "Paying the High Price of Being the World's No. 1 Jailer." *The Boston Globe,* January 13, 1991, Focus Section, p. 67.

Blackwell, Angela Glover, and Joan Walsh. "Head Start, a Healthy '60s Survivor, Should Be Expanded to Serve Needs of the '90s." *Los Angeles Times,* May 8, 1989, p. 5.

Bowen, Ezra. "Trying to Jump-Start Toddlers." *Time,* April 7, 1986, p. 66.

Bronner, Ethan. "Crime Report Unveiled Amid Disagreement on Remedies." *The Boston Globe,* March 24, 1991, p. 1.

Brosin, Henry W., et al. *Perspectives on Violence,* edited by Gene Usdin. New York: Brunner/Mazel, 1972, pp. ix–161.

Brush, Lisa D. "Violent Acts and Injurious Outcomes in Married Couples: Methodological Issues in the National Survey of Families and Households." *Gender & Society,* vol. 4, March 1990, pp. 56–67.

Bushman, Brad J., and Russell G. Geen. "Role of Cognitive-Emotional Mediators and Individual Differences in the Effects of Media Violence on Aggression." *Journal of Personality and Social Psychology,* vol. 58, 1990, pp. 156–63.

Calvert, William E., and Roger L. Hutchinson. "Vietnam Veteran Levels of Combat: Related to Later Violence?" *Journal of Traumatic Stress,* vol. 3, 1990, pp. 103–13.

Campillo, Linda. "Helping At-Risk Youths Called Matter of Money." *The Oregonian,* June 6, 1991, p. F2.

Canby, Vincent. "Now at a Theater Near You: A Skyrocketing Body Count." *The New York Times,* July 16, 1990, p. C11.

———. "Violence? In the Beholder's Eye." *The New York Times,* May 13, 1990, p. H1.

Castelli, Jim. "Campus Crime 101." *The New York Times,* November 4, 1990, p. Ed 34.

Cauchon, Dennis. " 'Lock 'em up' policy under attack." *USA Today,* April 1, 1992, p. 4A.

Chira, Susan. "Preschool Aid for the Poor: How Big a Head Start?" *The New York Times,* February 14, 1990, p. A1.

Cohen, Alex. "A Cross-Cultural Study of the Effects of Environmental Unpredictability on Aggression in Folktales." *American Anthropologist,* vol. 92, 1990, pp. 474–79.

Colburn, Don. "Murder Epidemic Spreads in U.S. Cities." *The Washington Post,* January 1, 1991, p. WH 6.

Collison, Brooke B., et al. "After the Shooting Stops." *Journal of Counseling and Development,* vol. 65, March 1987, pp. 389–90.

Comstock, George, and Victor C. Strasburger. "Deceptive Appearances: Television Violence and Aggressive Behavior." *Journal of Adolescent Health Care,* vol. 11, 1990, pp. 31–44.

"Crime Rises in Europe." *The Wall Street Journal,* November 20, 1990, p. A17.

"Crimes Against Individuals Drop; Blacks, Hispanics Suffer Most." *The Boston Globe,* October 21, 1991, p. 98.

"Delusional (Paranoid) Disorder." In *American Psychiatric Association Diagnostic and Statistical Manual of Mental Disorders* (DSMIII-R), 3rd edition revised. Washington, D.C.: American Psychiatric Association, copyright 1987, pp. 199–203.

Dodge, Kenneth A., et al. "Mechanisms in the Cycle of Violence." *Science,* vol. 250, December 21, 1990, pp. 1678–83.

Enriquez, Sam. "Toughen Discipline Policy, Report Urges L.A. Schools." *The Los Angeles Times,* March 20, 1990, p. A1.

SOURCES

Escobar, Gabriel. "Rapes in the District Up 66 Percent." *The Washington Post,* October 22, 1990, p. A8.

Fagan, Jeffrey. "Social and Legal Policy Dimensions of Violent Juvenile Crime." *Criminal Justice and Behavior,* vol. 17, March 1990, pp. 93–133.

"F.B.I. Report Confirms Sharp Rise in Violent Crime." *The New York Times,* August 6, 1990, p. A10.

Feshbach, Seymour. "Psychology, Human Violence, and the Search for Peace: Issues in Science and Social Values." *Journal of Social Issues,* vol. 46, 1990, pp. 183–98.

Fitzgibbon, Joe. "Breaking the Cycle, One Child at a Time." *The Sunday Oregonian,* February 2, 1992, p. L3.

Flynn, Clifton P. "Sex Roles and Women's Response to Courtship Violence." *Journal of Family Violence,* vol. 5, 1990, pp. 83–94.

Foster, Catherine. "Celebrated Program for Children Adapts to Meet New Challenges." *The Christian Science Monitor,* March 28, 1990, p. 1.

———. "Head Start Confronts Challenges." *The Christian Science Monitor,* March 30, 1990, p. 7.

Frank, Charlotte, and Leslie Goldman. "Growing Healthy in New York City." *Phi Delta Kappan,* February 1988, pp. 454–55.

Frazier, Shervert H. Speech on Law and Psychiatry, American Association of Psychiatry and Law, Philadelphia, PA, 1986.

"Frontier Justice." *The Wall Street Journal,* June 16, 1988, p. 18.

Gardner, Marilyn. "Will Literary Mirror Reflect Ogre, or Ogreish Society?" *The Oregonian,* March 21, 1991, p. A18.

Garfinkel, Barry D. "School-Based Prevention Programs." Alcohol, Drug Abuse and Mental Health Administration, *Report of the Secretary's Task Force on Youth Suicide,* vol. 4, Strategies for Prevention of Youth Suicide, DHHS Publication No. (ADM) 89-1624, Washington D.C., 1989, pp. 3-294–3-304.

Gest, Ted, with Pamela Ellis-Simons. "Victims of Crime." *U.S. News & World Report,* July 31, 1989, pp. 16–19.

Gilliam, Dorothy. "Proceed With Caution." *The Washington Post,* April 25, 1988, p. D3.

Glick, Barry, and Arnold P. Goldstein. "Aggression Replacement Training." *Journal of Counseling and Development,* vol. 65, March 1987, pp. 356–61.

Goleman, Daniel. "Tough Call for Psychiatrists: Deciding Who Is Dangerous." *The New York Times,* July 13, 1986, p. 1.

———. "Treating Trauma." *The New York Times,* January 7, 1990, p. ED 39.

Gorney, Roderic. "Basic Humanity vs. Base Behavior." *The Los Angeles Times,* January 18, 1990, p. B7.

Greenberg, Harvey R. "Just How Powerful Are Those Turtles?" *The New York Times,* April 15, 1990, p. H1.

Gugliotta, Guy, and Michael Isikoff. "Violence in the '90s: Drugs' Deadly Residue." *The Washington Post,* October 14, 1990, p. A1.

Hansen, Christine Hall, and Ranald D. Hansen. "The Influence of Sex and Violence on the Appeal of Rock Music Videos." *Communication Research,* vol. 17, April 1990, pp. 212–34.

Hayman, Peter M., et al. "Aftermath of Violence: Posttraumatic Stress Disorder Among Vietnam Veterans." *Journal of Counseling and Development,* vol. 65, March 1987, pp. 363–65.

SOURCES

Hevesi, Dennis. "TV News: Children's Scary Window on New York." *The New York Times,* September 11, 1990, p. B1.

Hey, Robert P. "Rise in Crime Rate Shows Trends, Raises Questions." *The Christian Science Monitor,* August 7, 1990, p. 9.

Hill, Clare. "Protecting Employees from Attack." *Personnel Management,* February 1988, pp. 34–39.

Hill, Richard L. "Experts Urge More Study of Inner-City Crime Causes." *The Oregonian,* February 10, 1992, p. B1.

———. "Teen Violence Rampant in U.S." *The Oregonian,* February 17, 1991, p. E6.

Hinds, Michael de Courcy. "Feeling Prison's Costs, Governors Weigh Alternatives." *The New York Times,* August 7, 1992, p. B8.

Hoberman, Harry M. "Study Group Report on the Impact of Television Violence on Adolescents." *Journal of Adolescent Health Care,* vol. 11, 1990, pp. 45–49.

Hodge, Marie, and Jeff Blyskal. "Who Says College Campuses Are Safe?" *Reader's Digest,* October 1989, pp. 141–48.

Howe, Marvine. "Church Leaders Declare A 'Holy War' on Drugs." *The New York Times,* October 14, 1990, p. 30.

Hurley, D. J., and P. Jaffe. "Children's Observations of Violence: II. Clinical Implications for Children's Mental Health Professionals." *Canadian Journal of Psychiatry,* vol. 35, August 1990, pp. 471–76.

Isikoff, Michael. "Federal Poll Says Drug Use Declining." *The Oregonian,* December 20, 1990, p. C2.

Jaffe, Peter G., et al. "Children's Observations of Violence: I. Critical Issues in Child Development and Intervention Planning." *Canadian Journal of Psychiatry,* vol. 35, August 1990, pp. 446–70.

Jennings, Jerry L. "Preventing Relapse Versus 'Stopping' Domestic Violence: Do We Expect Too Much Too Soon from Battering Men?" *Journal of Family Violence,* vol. 5, 1990, pp. 43–60.

Kantrowitz, Barbara, and John McCormick. "Head Start's Success Fails Long-Term Test." *The Oregonian,* January 22, 1992, p. A3.

Kirn, Timothy F. "Prevention Starts in Kindergarten in New York City." *Journal of the American Medical Association,* vol. 259, May 6, 1988, pp. 2516–17.

Kiyomura, Cathy. "Family Violence Rises; More Money Sought." *The Oregonian,* December 5, 1991, p. C4.

Koretz, Gene. "Economic Trends." *Business Week,* March 18, 1991, p. 20.

Krakowski, Menachem, et al. "Psychopathology and Violence." *Comprehensive Psychiatry,* vol. 27, March/April 1986, pp. 131–48.

Kruttschnitt, Candace, et al. "Abuse-Resistant Youth: Some Factors That May Inhibit Violent Criminal Behavior." *Social Forces,* vol. 66, December 1987, pp. 501–15.

Laatz, Joan, and Holley Gilbert. "Offender Treatment: The Last Hope?" *The Oregonian,* October 27, 1991, p. 1.

Landers, Ann. "Male Violence Issue Spurs Deluge." *The Sunday Oregonian,* December 1, 1991, p. L9.

Lantos, Vera. "On the 'Organicity' of Paranoid Syndromes." *Psychiatric Journal of the University of Ottawa,* vol. 13, 1988, pp. 32–35.

Lawder, Dave. "There's No Escape at Paintball Dave's." *The Business Journal* (Milwaukee), October 3, 1988, p. 1.

Linz, Daniel, et al. "Mitigating the Negative Effects of Sexually Violent Mass Communications Through Preexposure Briefings." *Communication Research,* vol. 17, October, 1990, pp. 641–74.

Lorch, Donatella. "Record Year for Killings Jolts Officials in New York." *The New York Times,* December 31, 1990, p. 25.

Lundberg, Sherry G. "Domestic Violence: A Psychodynamic Approach and Implications for Treatment." *Psychotherapy,* vol. 27, Summer 1990, pp. 243–48.

McCartney, Scott. "Videotape of Police Beating May Show Way to Reforms." *The Sunday Oregonian,* March 24, 1991, p. A5.

McKeown, L. A. "Violence on Television May Affect Children's Values." *Medical Tribune,* November 14, 1991, p. 11.

Margasak, Larry. "System Fails to Aid Addict Prisoners." *The Oregonian,* October 31, 1991, p. A8.

Marohn, Richard C. "Violence and Unrestrained Behavior in Adolescents." *Adolescent Psychiatry,* vol. 17, 1990, pp. 419–32.

Matchan, Linda. "Violence Among Girls on Rise, Youth Workers Say." *The Boston Globe,* March 11, 1991, p. 13.

Merl, Jean. "Head Start Studied as Model for the Future." *Los Angeles Times,* March 15, 1990, p. A3.

"The Message of a Vigilante Killing." *The New York Times,* March 23, 1988, p. A26.

Methvin, Eugene H. "Lock Up More Criminals." *The Oregonian,* February 2, 1992, p. C7.

———. "Why Don't We Have the Prisons We Need?" *Reader's Digest,* November 1990, pp. 70–74.

Minow, Newton N. "Putting Vision into Television." *The Oregonian,* May 12, 1991, p. B1.

"More Prisons, But Still More Crime." Letters to the Editor, *The Wall Street Journal,* June 11, 1992, p. A15.

Mydans, Seth. "Homicide Rate Up for Young Blacks." *The New York Times,* December 7, 1990, p. A26.

———. "Schools Fight Gang Violence with 'Duck and Cover' Drills." *The Sunday Oregonian,* June 16, 1991, p. A19.

"Number of Criminals on Parole Soared 16.3% in 1990, to 531,407." *The Boston Globe,* November 25, 1991, p. 32.

O'Connor, John J. "Today TV Outshines the Movies." *The New York Times,* July 8, 1990, p. H1.

O'Connor, Rose Ellen. "School Violence Is Rising, Experts Warn." *Los Angeles Times,* February 22, 1990, p. A28.

Ota, Alan K. "Herndon Calls for Boost in Head Start Spending." *The Oregonian,* December 6, 1991, p. D6.

Pope, Alexander. *Poems of Alexander Pope, An Essay on Man,* Vol. III, i. Maynard Mack, Editor. London: Methuen & Co. Ltd.; New Haven: Yale University Press, 1950, pp. 81–82.

Raspberry, William. "Head Start: A Program That Works." *The Washington Post,* January 19, 1990, p. A21.

Recer, Paul. "Study Ties Child Abuse to Adult Aggression." *The Oregonian,* December 21, 1990, p. A24.

Refuerzo, Ben J., and Stephen Verderber. "Dimensions of Person-Environment Relationships in Shelters for Victims of Domestic Violence." *The Journal of Architectural and Planning Research*, vol. 7, Spring 1990, 33–52.

Ribadeneira, Diego. "Students Offer Adults Their Vision of Ways to Curb Teenage Violence." *The Boston Globe*, January 31, 1991, Metro Section, p. 18.

Roark, Mary L. "Preventing Violence on College Campuses." *Journal of Counseling and Development*, vol. 65, March 1987, pp. 367–70.

Robb, Christina. "Are We Hooked on Media Violence? Scientists Say Yes." *The Boston Globe*, July 8, 1991, p. 27.

Rosen, Ismond. "Self-esteem as a Factor in Social and Domestic Violence." *British Journal of Psychiatry*, vol. 158, 1991, pp. 18–23.

Rosenthal, Elisabeth. "U.S. Is by Far the Homicide Capital of the Industrialized Nations." *The New York Times*, June 27, 1990, p. A10.

Roth, Susan. "Book Reviews." *Signs*, Winter 1991, pp. 379–81.

Rowan, Carl T. "The New Lynch Mobs: Drug Vigilantes." *The Washington Post*, April 27, 1988, p. A21.

Rowley, James. "Conferees OK $3.1b Crime Bill." *The Boston Globe*, November 25, 1991, p. 1.

Sacco, Vincent F., and Meena Trotman. "Public Information Programming and Family Violence: Lessons from the Mass Media Crime Prevention Experience." *Canadian Journal of Criminology*, vol. 32, January 1990, pp. 91–105.

Santoli, Al. "What Can Be Done About Teen Gangs." *Parade*, March 24, 1991, pp. 16–19.

Shearer, Lloyd. "Intelligence Report: Family Violence." *Parade*, November 25, 1984, p. 8.

Shepherd, Jonathan. "Victims of Personal Violence: The Relevance of Symond's Model of Psychological Response and Loss-Theory." *British Journal of Social Work*, vol. 20, 1990, pp. 309–32.

Shipp, E. R. "Appeals Court Upholds Goetz's Gun Conviction." *The New York Times*, November 23, 1988, p. B3.

———. "The Perilous Right of Citizens to Make Their Own Arrests." *The New York Times*, June 19, 1988, p. E8.

Siemens, Cathy. "Portland's Involvement with Youth Gangs Visionary." *The Oregonian*, December 21, 1991, p. E13.

Sofaer, Abraham D. "Terrorism and the Law." *Foreign Affairs*, vol. 64, Summer 1986, pp. 901–22.

Sorenson, Susan B., and Vivian B. Brown. "Interpersonal Violence and Crisis Intervention on the College Campus." *New Directions for Student Services*, Spring 1990, pp. 57–66.

Stolberg, Sheryl. "Report on Child Abuse Finds Agencies Deluged." *Los Angeles Times*, November 14, 1990, p. A1.

"Study Finds Gun Control Law Cuts Firearm Homicide Rate." *The Oregonian*, December 5, 1991, p. B3.

"Suicide Prevention Goals Not Met by Current Programs." *Medical Tribune*, November 14, 1991, p. 11.

Tardiff, Kenneth J. "Violence." in *The American Psychiatric Press Textbook of Psychiatry*. Edited by J. Talbott, R. E. Hales, and S. C. Yudofsky. Washington, D.C.: American Psychiatric Press, 1988, pp. 1037–57.

Taylor, Paul. "Study Finds America's Children in Trouble." *The Oregonian*, January 3, 1992, p. A13.

SOURCES

"Television violence." *Nature,* vol. 346, July 26, 1990, p. 302.

"Terrorism in U.S. unusual in recent years." *The Oregonian,* March 5, 1993, p. A15.

Tooley, Jo Ann. "Jammed Jail Cells." *U.S. News & World Report,* July 24, 1989, p. 66.

Tooley, Jo Ann. "Murder, Mayhem and Other Offenses." *U.S. News & World Report,* October 29, 1990, p. 16.

"To Stem the Violence; Commitment and Coordination; The Winner's Circle Model; Stitching the Efforts Together." *The Boston Globe,* April 29, 1991, p. 10.

Toth, Jennifer. "Runaway Patterns Uncovered." *The Oregonian,* January 2, 1992, p. A9.

"25% of All US Slayings Recorded in Seven Cities, FBI Says." *The Boston Globe,* April 29, 1991, p. 3.

Tye, Larry. "Offscreen Violence Stirs Worry, Trouble Accompanies Opening of Film on Urban Drug Strife." *The Boston Globe,* March 12, 1991, p. 1.

U.S. Department of Justice. "Crime in the United States." *Uniform Crime Reports,* 1990, pp. i–51.

Vickers, Robert J. "Head Start Widely Hailed as Boost for Poor Children." *Los Angeles Times,* September 29, 1989, p. 13.

"Violence Among the Young." *The Washington Post,* December 29, 1990, p. A18.

"When Students Tote Guns, Not Books." *Los Angeles Times,* May 9, 1990, p. B6.

Witkin, Gordon. "Kids Who Kill." *U.S. News & World Report,* April 8, 1991, p. 26.

"Vigilante Planning." *Los Angeles Times,* March 7, 1989, p. 6.

Yoder, Edwin M. Jr. "America's Culture of Permissive Gunplay." *The Boston Globe,* October 21, 1991, p. 13.

Zimring, Franklin, E. "Firearms, Violence and Public Policy." *Scientific American,* November 1991, pp. 48–54.

2. THE SEXES: Better Relationships / Worse Relationships?

Allis, Sam. "What Do Men Really Want?" *Time* Special Issue: *Women: The Road Ahead,* Fall 1990, pp. 80–82.

Angier, Natalie. "Americans' Sex Knowledge Is Lacking, Poll Says." *The New York Times,* September 6, 1990, p. B14.

Barbour, John. "Landmark Studies Shed the Sex Taboo." *The Sunday Oregonian,* December 22, 1991, p. L14.

Barringer, Felicity. "Children as Sexual Prey, and Predators." *The New York Times,* May 30, 1989, p. A1.

———. "Ethical Questions Arise from Dual-Career Marriages." *The Oregonian,* March 24, 1992, p. A10.

Bennet, James. "The Data Game." *The New Republic,* February 13, 1989, pp. 20–22.

Betcher, William, Ph.D., M.D., and William Pollack, Ph.D. *In a Time of Fallen Heroes.* New York: Atheneum, 1993.

Betz, Michael, et al. "Gender Differences in Proclivity for Unethical Behavior." *Journal of Business Ethics,* vol. 8, 1989, pp. 321–24.

Bishop, Jerry E. "How Films Affect Views on Women and Violence." *The Wall Street Journal,* November 25, 1988, p. 9.

Blakeslee, Sandra. "Navigating Life's Maze: Styles Split the Sexes." *The New York Times,* May 26, 1992, p. B1.

SOURCES

Bock, Paul. "Religious Responses to AIDS." *USA Today,* May 1989, pp. 66–67.

Booth, William. "College Women Surveyed About Sex." *The Washington Post,* March 22, 1990, p. A15.

Bradsher, Keith. "For Every Five Young Women, Six Young Men." *The New York Times,* January 17, 1990, p. C1.

Brody, Jane E. "Personal Health." *The New York Times,* August 18, 1988, p. B12.

Byrd, Robert. "54% of High School Students Have Had Sex, Survey Says." *The Oregonian,* January 4, 1992, p. A1.

Celis, William, III. "Students Trying to Draw Line Between Sex and an Assault." *The New York Times,* January 2, 1991, p. A1.

Chance, Paul. "The Trouble With Love." *Psychology Today,* February 1988, pp. 22–23.

Clements, Mark. "Should Abortion Remain Legal?" *Parade,* May 17, 1992, pp. 4–5.

Deacon, James. "Exotic Daydreams." *Maclean's,* January 7, 1991, p. 42.

Diliberto, Gioia. "Invasion of the Gender Blenders." *People,* April 23, 1984, p. 96.

Donnerstein, Edward, and Daniel Linz. "Sexual Violence in the Media: A Warning." *Psychology Today,* January 1984, pp. 14–15.

Dowd, Maureen. "Taboo Issues of Sex and Race Explode in Glare of Hearing." *The New York Times,* October 13, 1991, p. A1.

Dumaine, Brian. "Racy Movies for Wrung-Out Travelers." *Fortune,* December 10, 1984, p. 92.

Eagly, Alice H., and Blair T. Johnson. "Gender and Leadership Style: A Meta-Analysis." *Psychological Bulletin,* vol. 108, 1990, pp. 233–56.

Elliott, Stuart. "Advertising." *The New York Times,* October 15, 1991, p. D20.

Emmrich, Stuart. " 'Himbo' Flexes His Pecs in U.K. Ads." *Adweek,* August 12, 1991, p. 16.

Epstein, Cynthia Fuchs. "Ways Men and Women Lead." *Harvard Business Review,* January–February 1991, pp. 150–60.

Faludi, Susan C. "Women Lost Ground in 1980s, and EEOC Didn't Help." *The Wall Street Journal,* October 18, 1991, p. B4.

Fausto-Sterling, Anne. "Why Do We Know So Little About Human Sex?" *Discover,* June 1992, pp. 28–30.

Ferm, Deane William. "Is Swedish Sex for Us?" *Commonweal,* June 19, 1981, pp. 363–66.

Fowles, Jib. "Coming Soon: More Men than Women." *The New York Times,* June 5, 1988, p. F3.

Gardner, Marilyn. "A Nation in Love with Love." *The Christian Science Monitor,* February 7, 1989, p. 14.

———. "Who Won the Sexual Revolution?" *The Christian Science Monitor,* October 8, 1991, p. 14.

Gibbons, Ann. "The Brain as 'Sexual Organ.' " *Science,* vol. 253, August 30, 1991, pp. 957–59.

Gibbs, Nancy. "Teens: The Rising Risk of Aids." *Time,* September 2, 1991, pp. 60–61.

Gilbert, Holley. "Date Rape: Changing Culture, Changing Rules." *The Oregonian,* January 5, 1992, p. A1.

Goldman, Debra. "Vid Kids Embody Sexual Stereotypes." *Adweek,* March 11, 1991, p. 6.

Goodman, Ellen. "Feminism Isn't Dead, Just Undergoing Change." *The Oregonian,* February 26, 1992, p. B9.

SOURCES

Goodrich, Lawrence J. "Mainline Churches Debate Role of Human Sexuality." *The Christian Science Monitor,* June 14, 1991, p. 4.

Gould, Robert E. "Why Can't a [Working] Woman Be More Like a Man?" *Working Woman,* April 1985, pp. 104–8.

Gould, Stephen Jay. "The Birth of the Two-Sex World." *The New York Review,* June 13, 1991, pp. 11–13.

Green, Charles. "GOP Officials Fear Pro-Choice Voters to Defect to Perot." *The Sunday Oregonian,* June 7, 1992, p. D2.

Grimm, Matthew. "Introducing Miller Daft." *Adweek's Marketing Week,* March 20, 1989, p. 4.

Gross, Jane. "Golden Opportunity in California as Women Seek Gains in Politics." *The New York Times,* May 29, 1992, p. A1.

Gross, Michael. "Sex Sells." *Saturday Review,* July/August 1985, pp. 50–55.

Halpern, Diane F. "The Disappearance of Cognitive Gender Differences: What You See Depends on Where You Look." *American Psychologist,* vol. 44, August 1989, pp. 1156–57.

Hancock, Gary. "Sex Typing." *Manage,* October 1990, p. 27.

Hayes, Arthur S., and Gabriella Stern. "Adult Video Firms in California Are Indicted on Obscenity Charges." *The Wall Street Journal,* August 16, 1991, p. B2.

Hilts, Philip J. "Dark Ages of Birth Control." *The Sunday Oregonian,* December 16, 1990, p. F1.

Himmelfarb, Gertrude. "Self-Defeating Feminism." *The New York Times,* May 8, 1989, p. A19.

Holden, Constance. "Is 'Gender Gap' Narrowing?" *Science,* vol. 253, August 30, 1991, pp. 959–60.

Holloway, Marguerite. "Profile: Vive La Différence." *Scientific American,* vol. 263, October 1990, p. 40.

Hunt, Morton. "Sex Never Ages." *Psychology Today,* January 1984, pp. 16–17.

Hunter, Eva. "Women Climb Ladder Only to Bump into Glass Ceiling." *The Sunday Oregonian,* February 2, 1992, p. 16.

Huston, Bo. "Crosstalk." *San Francisco Bay Times,* December 19, 1991, p. 11.

"Is TV Becoming More Risqué, or Is It Just 'Condom Sense'?" *Television/Radio Age,* September 19, 1988, p. 26.

Jacklin, Carol Nagy. "Female and Male: Issues of Gender." *American Psychologist,* vol. 44, February 1989, pp. 127–33.

Kahn, Alice. "What's to Become of Office Flirting?" *The Sunday Oregonian,* December 1, 1991, p. L15.

Kanfer, Stefan. "Sauce, Satire and Shtick." *Time* Special Issue: *Women: The Road Ahead,* Fall 1990, pp. 62–63.

Kelley, Katy. "In the Name of Domestic Glasnost, Deborah Tannen Tries to Bridge the Linguistic Gap Between the Sexes." *People,* September 10, 1990, p. 133.

Kenton, Sherron B. "Speaker Credibility in Persuasive Business Communication: A Model Which Explains Gender Differences." *The Journal of Business Communication,* vol. 26, Spring 1989, pp. 143–55.

Kimura, Doreen. "Male Brain, Female Brain: The Hidden Difference; Gender Does Affect How Our Brains Work—but in Surprising Ways." *Psychology Today,* November 1985, p. 50.

Klinger, Eric. "The Power of Daydreams." *Psychology Today,* October 1987, p. 37.

SOURCES

Kolata, Gina. "Drop in Casual Sex Tied to AIDS Peril." *The New York Times,* May 15, 1991, p. A22.

Kolbert, Elizabeth. "Sexual Harassment at Work Is Pervasive, Survey Suggests." *The New York Times,* October 11, 1991, p. A1.

Kristin, Jack. "The Many Faces of Eve." *American Film,* April 1989, p. 39.

Landers, Ann. "Revealing the Joy, Pain of Being Gay." *The Oregonian,* April 27, 1992, p. C4.

———. "Two-Faced Stigma Shafts Teen Girls." *The Sunday Oregonian,* February 23, 1992, p. L9.

Langer, Gary. "Men! The Louts! Who Needs 'Em? U.S. Women Ask." *The Oregonian,* April 26, 1990, p. 1.

Laporte, Suzanne B. "The Sting of the Subtle Snub." *Working Woman,* January 1991, p. 53.

Leerhsen, Charles, et al. "Ann Landers and 'the Act.' " *Newsweek,* January 28, 1985, p. 76.

Lemonick, Michael D. "Erotic Electronic Encounters." *Time,* September 23, 1991, p. 72.

Leo, John. "The Eleventh Megatrend." *Time,* July 23, 1984, p. 104.

Leonard, George. "An Erotic Society." *The Futurist,* April 1983, p. 24.

———. "The End of Sex." *The Futurist,* April 1983, p. 22.

Levine, Joshua. "Fantasy, Not Flesh." *Forbes,* January 22, 1990, pp. 118–20.

Lippert, Barbara. "With Ominous Sculpture, Calvin Again Breaks Sexual Mold." *Adweek's Marketing Week,* January 30, 1989, p. 55.

Lowry, Dennis T., and David E. Towles. "Soap Opera Portrayals of Sex, Contraception, and Sexually Transmitted Diseases." *Journal of Communication,* vol. 39, Spring 1989, pp. 76–82.

McDowell, Edwin. "Book Notes." *The New York Times,* July 24, 1991, p. C24.

Masters, Brooke A. "Madonna: Yuppie Goddess." *The Washington Post,* July 1, 1990, p. B5.

May, Elaine Tyler. "Women Stayed Home in the Cold War." *Los Angeles Times,* September 18, 1988, p. 3.

"Men Found to Outnumber Women in Only Five States." *The Wall Street Journal,* September 15, 1989, p. A14.

"The *Men's Health Newsletter* Survey of Male Sexuality." *Men's Health,* April 1992, pp. 6–13.

Miller, J. A. "Masculine/Feminine Behavior: New views." *Science News,* vol. 124, November 19, 1983, p. 326.

Mitchell, Jann. "Men Today Question Brutal Side to Masculine Image, Work to Redefine Role." *The Sunday Oregonian,* May 5, 1991, p. L15.

Moir, Anne, and David Jessel. "Sex and Cerebellum." *The Washington Post,* May 5, 1991, p. K3.

Moore, Cynthia. "Conservatives Keep Information on Sex and AIDS Out of Reach for Most Teenagers." *The Advocate,* April 21, 1992, pp. 54–55.

Morin, Richard. "Americans Want Schoolchildren Told About AIDS, Survey Finds." *The Washington Post,* June 26, 1991, p. A2.

Mulac, Anthony, et al. "Male/Female Language Differences and Effects in Same-Sex and Mixed-Sex Dyads: The Gender-Linked Language Effect." *Communication Monographs,* vol. 55, December 1988, pp. 315–33.

SOURCES

"The New Teens." *Newsweek* Special Issue, June 1990, pp. 10–72.

Nordheimer, Jon. "When a Fellow Needs a Friend, Not Just a Buddy." *The Sunday Oregonian,* August 25, 1991, p. L5.

Okie, Susan. "Drug to Boost Sex Drive Tested." *The Washington Post,* May 15, 1988, p. A16.

Older, Jules. "Mother Nature's Dirty Trick." *Los Angeles Times,* March 12, 1988, p. 8.

Palmer, Beverly B., and Joe M. Coffman. "The Deathly Side of Love: The End of the Sexual Smokescreen." *USA Today,* May 1989, pp. 62–63.

"Panel Tentatively Recommends U.S. Sales of Women's Condom." *The Oregonian,* February 1, 1992, p. A12.

Parker, Seymour. "Rituals of Gender: A Study of Etiquette, Public Symbols, and Cognition." *American Anthropologist,* vol. 90, June 1988, pp. 372–83.

Person, Ethel S. "The Passionate Quest (Some Differences Between Men and Women)." *The Atlantic,* March 1988, p. 71.

"Physicians Organize to Make Abortion Pill Available for Research." *The Oregonian,* March 27, 1992, p. A20.

Pintarich, Paul. "Love-Book Author's Message 'Right On.' " *The Oregonian,* November 18, 1984, p. 13.

Quinn, Sally. "Dispelling the Feminist Movement's Mystique." *The Sunday Oregonian,* March 15, 1992, p. L4.

Ragins, Belle Rose. "Power and Gender Congruency Effects in Evaluations of Male and Female Managers." *Journal of Management,* vol. 15, 1989, pp. 65–76.

Rapoport, Carla. "No Sexy Sales Ads, Please—We're Brits and Swedes." *Fortune,* October 21, 1991, p. 13.

Raspberry, William. "Stages of Racism and Sexism." *The Washington Post,* May 31, 1989, p. A23.

———. "What Values Can Fathers Pass Down to Their Sons?" *The Oregonian,* January 26, 1992, p. B10.

Rich, Spencer. "Critics Say Sullivan Lets Conservatives Guide Policy." *The Washington Post,* July 28, 1991, p. A4.

———. "HHS Cancels Teen Sex Survey After Conservatives Complain." *The Washington Post,* July 24, 1991, p. A2.

Richardson, John T. E. "The Menstrual Cycle and Student Learning." *Journal of Higher Education,* vol. 62, May/June 1991, pp. 317–34.

Robinson, Ira, et al. "Twenty Years of the Sexual Revolution, 1965–1985: An Update." *Journal of Marriage and the Family,* vol. 53, February 1991, pp. 216–20.

Rosenfield, Allan. "Sex Education Must Reach Teens." *Medical Tribune,* December 26, 1991, p. 13.

Ross, Art. "Sexual Advertising on TV in the Post Sexual Revolution Era." *Back Stage,* August 28, 1987, p. 39.

Rosser, Phyllis. "Girls, Boys, and the SAT: Can We Even the Score?" *NEA Today,* vol. 6, January 1988, p. 48.

Rossi, Alice S., "Sex and Gender in an Aging Society." *Daedalus,* vol. 115, Winter 1986, pp. 141–69.

Salovey, Peter, and Judith Rodin. "The Heart of Jealousy." *Psychology Today,* September 1985, p. 22.

Sanger, Carol. "Just Say 'No,' Just Hear 'No.' " *Los Angeles Times,* April 25, 1991, p. B7.

SOURCES

Scheider, Karen, and Angelia Herrin. "Activists Plot Strategy to Carry On After Roe." *The Oregonian,* January 23, 1992, p. A11.

Scher, Murray, and Glenn E. Good. "Gender and Counseling in the Twenty-First Century: What Does the Future Hold?" *Journal of Counseling and Development,* vol. 68, March/April 1990, p. 388.

Seligmann, Jean, et al. "Dial a Date—With No Hang-ups." *Newsweek,* May 30, 1988, p. 72.

Severn, Jessica, et al. "The Effects of Sexual and Non-sexual Advertising Appeals and Information Level on Cognitive Processing and Communication Effectiveness." *Journal of Advertising,* vol. 19, 1990, pp. 14–22.

Seymour, B. J., "Brains of Men and Women Differ; Either Brain Can Exist in Either Body." *The Oregonian,* January 16, 1992, p. E3.

Shafroth, Frank. "High Court Provides Guides on Sex-Oriented Businesses." *Nation's Cities Weekly,* January 22, 1990, p. 2.

Silberman, Rosalie Gaull. "A Glass Ceiling." *Restaurant Hospitality,* June 1991, p. 65.

Slade, Margot. "Father-Son Coolness Slowly Warming." *The Oregonian,* February 17, 1985, p. 4.

Sobel, Dava. "Sex Grows Up." *Health,* October 1989, p. 76.

Sojacy, Linda. "Power Play. Boys Want to Be the Strongest; Girls Want to Be the Center of Attention. The Power Games We Play Start Early." *Working Woman,* September 1985, p. 160.

Stanton, Doug. "Inward, Ho!" *Esquire,* A Special Issue: *Wild Men and Wimps,* October 1991, pp. 113–22.

Stein, Ruthe. "Billfold Dates a Measure of Desperation." *The Oregonian,* July 19, 1990, p. D1.

Steinfels, Peter. "What God Really Thinks About Who Sleeps With Whom." *The New York Times,* June 2, 1991, p. E4.

Steinhauer, Jennifer. "Prosecute Porn? It's on the Decline." *The Wall Street Journal,* December 28, 1989, p. A8.

Stewart, Al. "Smut Out of Rut, Defying Its Foes." *Variety,* January 17, 1990, p. 1.

Sullivan, Andrew. "Flogging Underwear." *The New Republic,* January 18, 1988, p. 20.

Suplee, Curt. "Psychology: Sexual Fantasies and Evolution." *The Washington Post,* December 10, 1990, p. A2.

———. "Sex in the '90s." *The Washington Post,* January 8, 1989, p. C1.

Tavris, Carol. "Jokes & Gender: Where's the Punch Line?" *Vogue,* January 1988, p. 28.

Thomas, Jack. "The New Man; Finding Another Way to Be Male." *The Boston Globe,* August 21, 1991, p. 43.

Tifft, Susan. "Better Safe Than Sorry? The Notion of Handing Out Condoms in the Nation's High Schools Is Gaining Adherents—and Attracting Vociferous Opposition." *Time,* January 21, 1991, p. 66.

Thompson, Keith. "Robert Bly on Fathers and Sons." *Esquire,* April 1984, p. 238.

Thompson, Larry. "Treating Sexual Disorders; Experts Examine a Wide Range of Behaviors." *The Washington Post,* May 1, 1990, p. WH7.

Tomlinson-Keasey, Carol. "Developing Our Intellectual Resources for the 21st Century: Educating the Gifted." *Journal of Educational Psychology,* vol. 82, 1990, pp. 399–403.

Toufexis, Anastasia. "Coming from a Different Place." *Time* Special Issue: *Women: The Road Ahead,* Fall 1990, p. 64.

———. "Sex Lives and Videotape." *Time,* October 29, 1990, p. 104.

Trueheart, Charles. "Women Jump onto Campaign Bandwagon." *The Oregonian,* April 14, 1992, p. A3.

Tsalikis, J., and M. Ortiz-Buonafina. "Ethical Beliefs' Differences of Males and Females." *Journal of Business Ethics,* vol. 9, 1990, pp. 509–17.

Van Buren, Abigail. "You'll Find Mr. Right—Just Look in the Right Place." *The Oregonian,* June 25, 1990, p. 78.

Verner, Gayle. "Too Tough to Cry." *People,* September 23, 1991, p. 111.

Williams, Lena. "Teen-Age Sex: New Codes Amid the Old Anxiety." *The New York Times,* February 27, 1989, p. A1.

3. FAMILY: More Traditional / Less Traditional?

Appleman, Rose. "Touching Up the Family Portrait: Mayor's Task Force Readies Report." *The San Francisco Bay Times,* May 1990, p. 16.

Belser, Ann. "Rights, Privileges, and Gay Lovers." *The Advocate,* February 25, 1992, pp. 56–58.

Berardo, Felix M. "Trends and Directions in Family Research in the 1980s." *Journal of Marriage and the Family,* vol. 52, November 1990, pp. 809–17.

Boynton, Barbara, and John Odom. "Five of Today's Families." *The New York Times,* August 31, 1989, p. C6.

Brazelton, T. Berry. "The Family Leave Act, From the Baby's Point of View." *The Wall Street Journal,* September 19, 1991, p. A15.

Brody, Jane E. "Children of Divorce: Steps to Help Can Hurt." *The New York Times,* July 23, 1991, p. C1.

Bull, Chris. "New York Judge Grants Adoption to Lesbian Couple." *The Advocate,* March 10, 1991, p. 17.

Carlson, Allan. "The GOP and the Family Issue: A Swedish Lesson." *The Wall Street Journal,* June 6, 1991, p. A16.

"Change in the American Family: Now Only One in Four Is 'Traditional.' " *The New York Times,* January 30, 1991, p. A19.

"Church to Bless Homosexual Union." *The New York Native,* March 16, 1992, pp. 16–17.

Coleman, Thomas F. "The Family Is Changing and We Should Admit It." *Los Angeles Times,* July 26, 1989, p. 7.

Collins, Karyn D. "Interracial Couples Cope with Hostility in Two Worlds." *Asbury Park Press,* October 13, 1991, B10.

Coontz, Stephanie. " 'The Family' Has Many Definitions." *The Christian Science Monitor,* February 27, 1989, p. 18.

———. "Pro-Family but Divorced from the Facts." *The Wall Street Journal,* August 9, 1989, p. A10.

Cornell, George W. "Jewish Group Blesses Same-Sex Unions." *The Oregonian,* March 14, 1992, p. C12.

Creighton, Linda L. "Silent Saviors." *U.S. News & World Report,* December 16, 1991, p. 80.

Dawson, Deborah A. "Family Structure and Children's Health and Well-Being: Data from the 1988 National Health Interview Survey on Child Health." *Journal of Marriage and the Family,* vol. 53, August 1991, pp. 573–84.

SOURCES

"D.C. Council Approves 'Domestic Partners' Bill." *New York Native,* March 16, 1992, p. 12.

Dean, Craig R. "Gay Marriage: A Civil Right." *The Lavender Network,* February 1992, p. 16.

Decker, Cathleen. "Clinton Attacks Bush on 'Family Values' stance." *The Oregonian,* May 11, 1992, p. A6.

"Despite Skepticism, the Predominant Feature of the Family Throughout This Century Has Been Its Resilience." *Marketing,* July 5, 1990, p. 3.

Deutsch, Claudia H. "Corporate Advocates for the Family." *The New York Times,* November 11, 1990, p. F27.

Exter, Thomas. "Faltering Families." *American Demographics,* November 1988, p. 13.

———. "Look Ma, No Spouse." *American Demographics,* March 1990, p. 63.

———. "Married With Kids." *American Demographics,* February 1990, p. 55.

"Families evolve with the times." *USA Today,* February 17, 1992, p. 5D.

Franklin, James L. "Back Traditional Family, Bishops Say." *The Boston Globe,* May 10, 1991, p. 1.

Gardner, Marilyn. "Pat Schroeder and Friends Take to the Road for the Family." *The Christian Science Monitor,* January 21, 1988, p. 6.

———. "The New Realities of Being a Parent." *The Christian Science Monitor,* May 2, 1991, p. 10.

Goldman, Debra. "A Death in the Family." *Adweek,* October 7, 1991, p. 20.

Gross, Jane. "More Young, Single Men Living at Home." *The Oregonian,* June 21, 1991, p. A4.

Gutis, Philip S. "What Is a Family? Traditional Limits Are Being Redrawn." *The New York Times,* August 31, 1989, p. C1.

Henry, William A., III. "The Lesbians Next Door." *Time* Special Issue: *Women: The Road Ahead,* Fall 1990, p. 78.

Hernandez, Peggy. "Grandparents Find Themselves Drafted for Child Care." *The Boston Globe,* February 5, 1991, p. 1.

Houlbrooke, Ralph. "The Pre-Industrial Family." *History Today,* April 1986, p. 49.

"Judge Overturns State Law Banning Gay People from Adoption." *The New York Native,* April 1, 1991, p. 7.

Kornhaber, Arthur. "The Vital Connection—1983: Grandparents Are Coming of Age in America." *Children Today,* July–August 1983, p. 31.

La Franchi, Howard. "Swedes face cuts in social benefits." *The Sunday Oregonian,* May 9, 1993, p. A10.

Lawson, Carol. "Taking Family Feuds to Court." *The New York Times,* May 24, 1990, p. C1.

Lipman, Joanne. "Mr. Mom May Be a Force to Reckon With." *The Wall Street Journal,* October 3, 1991, p. B6.

Longcope, Kay. "Gay Parenthood Comes of Age." *The Boston Globe,* December 17, 1990, p. 38.

———. "New View of 'Families' Sought for Insurance." *The Boston Globe,* March 27, 1991, p. 79.

———. "Religious Leaders, Gay Groups Back Bill to Redefine 'Family.' " *The Boston Globe,* May 16, 1991, p. 83.

Mann, Judy. "Making Time for the Families." *The Washington Post,* January 9, 1991, p. B3.

SOURCES

Margolick, David. "Lesbian Child-Custody Cases Test Frontiers of Family Law." *The New York Times,* July 4, 1990, p. 1.
Martellaro, John. "More and More, Couples Go Childless." *Bucks County Courier Times,* July 6, 1986, B11.
Miller, Julie Ann. "All Kinds of Families." *BioScience,* vol. 39, April 1989, p. 227.
Mitchell, Jann. "Childless by Choice." *The Sunday Oregonian,* January 26, 1992, p. L1.
Moynihan, Daniel Patrick. "The Family and the Nation—1986." *America,* March 22, 1986, p. 221.
"National briefs: California." *Just Out,* May 1991, p. 8.
Neuffer, Elizabeth. "Bishop's Family Stance Criticized as Outdated." *The Boston Globe,* May 11, 1991, p. 1.
"News in Brief: National." *The Advocate,* March 24, 1992, p. 32.
"News in Brief: Pennsylvania." *The Advocate,* March 24, 1992, p. 34.
Norton, Arthur J. "Families and Children in the Year 2000." *Children Today,* July–August 1987, p. 6.
Olson, David H., and Meredith Kilmer Hanson. "The Revolution in Family Life." *The Futurist,* October 1990, p. 53.
Otten, Alan L. "Non-Traditional Homes Can Hurt Kids' Health." *The Wall Street Journal,* July 5, 1990, p. B1.
———. "Religious Beliefs Tied to Views of Family Life." *The Wall Street Journal,* November 29, 1990, p. B1.
"Out-of-Wedlock Babies: 1 in 4." *U.S. News & World Report,* December 16, 1991, p. 38.
Pae, Peter. "Californians Get Infant-Care Credit if They Forgo Income and Stay Home." *The Wall Street Journal,* December 26, 1990, p. 1.
Phillips, Marshal Alan. "Does the Word Family Mean Anything Anymore?" *The Advocate,* January 14, 1992, p. 98.
Popenoe, David. "Beyond the Nuclear Family: A Statistical Portrait of the Changing Family in Sweden." *Journal of Marriage and the Family,* vol. 49, February 1987, pp. 173–83.
———. "Family decline in the Swedish welfare state." *The Public Interest,* vol. 102, Winter 1991, pp. 65–77.
———. "The Family Trend of Our Time." Adapted from *Disturbing the Nest: Family Change and Decline in Modern Societies.* New York: Aldine de Gruyter, 1988, ch. 13.
Quindlen, Anna. "In the Name of the Family, Society Must Allow Any Couple's Commitment." *The Oregonian,* February 7, 1992, p. D7.
Reese, Shelly. "Experts Study Ties Between More Babies, Fewer Women Workers." *The Sunday Oregonian,* February 16, 1992, p. R2.
Riche, Martha Farnsworth. "All Mixed Up." *American Demographics,* November 1989, p. 15.
———. "Spouses and Equivalents." *American Demographics,* November 1988, p. 8.
Russel, Cheryl. "Throw Out the Script." *American Demographics,* September 1990, p. 2.
Santi, Lawrence L. "Change in the Structure and Size of American Households: 1970 to 1985." *Journal of Marriage and the Family,* vol. 49, November 1987, pp. 833–37.
Sarasohn, David. "Bishops, Gay Voters Agree—on Kids." *The Oregonian,* February 7, 1992, p. D6.

SOURCES

Schwartz, Patricia Roth. "The State of the Gay Union." *The Advocate,* February 25, 1992, p. 52.

Seixas, Suzanne. "Come Together in Joyous Reunion." *Money,* December 1989, p. 13.

"Senate Panel Backs Family Leave Measure." *The Boston Globe,* April 25, 1991, p. 23.

Skrzycki, Cindy. "More fathers making time for parenting." *The Oregonian,* December 31, 1990, p. E1.

Smolowe, Jill. "Last Call for Motherhood." *Time* Special Issue: *Women: The Road Ahead,* Fall 1990, p. 76.

Sorrentino, Constance. "The Changing Family in International Perspective." *Monthly Labor Review,* vol. 113, March 1990, p. 41.

Spock, Dr. Benjamin. " 'It's All Up to Us.' " *Newsweek* Special Edition: *The 21st-Century Family,* Winter/Spring 1990, p. 106–7.

Taylor, Paul. "Tax Code Increasingly Unfriendly to Families, Hill Committee Told." *The Washington Post,* April 16, 1991, p. A17.

Trost, Cathy. "Work and Family." *The Wall Street Journal,* November 15, 1988, p. A1.

Vobejda, Barbara. "Most Unwed Pregnant Women Stay Single." *The Oregonian,* December 4, 1991, p. A15.

———. "Psychology: Family Size and Personality Traits." *The Washington Post,* April 8, 1991, p. A2.

Waldrop, Judith. "The Fashionable Family." *American Demographics,* March 1988, p. 22.

"We Now Pronounce You a Family." *The New York Times,* December 15, 1989, p. A42.

Wetzel, James R. "American Families: 75 Years of Change." *Monthly Labor Review,* vol. 113, March 1990, p. 4.

"What Is Family?" *The Washington Post,* July 13, 1989, p. A22.

"What Would the Beaver Think?" *The Oregonian,* January 6, 1992, p. D8.

White, Lynn K. "Determinants of Divorce: A Review of Research in the Eighties." *Journal of Marriage and the Family,* vol. 52, November 1990, p. 904–12.

Wilkerson, Isabel. "Interracial Marriage: Stares Linger." *The Oregonian,* December 10, 1991, p. A5.

Wingert, Pat, and Barbara Kantrowitz. "The Day-Care Generation." *Newsweek* Special Edition: *The 21st-Century Family,* Winter/Spring 1990, p. 86.

Wood, Daniel B. "Helping to Bring Up Baby." *The Christian Science Monitor,* January 31, 1989, p. 12.

4. HEART: Kinder and Gentler / Meaner and More Hateful?

Akst, Daniel. "The Crusader Against Executive Greed." *Business and Society Review,* Summer 1991, pp. 52–53.

"Assembly Committee Passes Bill to Ban Job Discrimination." *New York Native,* April 13, 1992, p. 21.

Baden, Tom. "Congress Attempts to Reform Itself." *The Sunday Oregonian,* July 5, 1992, p. A16.

Baldwin, Pat. "Mainstream Advertisers Increasingly Focus on Gay Community." *The Sunday Oregonian,* June 14, 1992, p. E9.

Barry, William A. "Should Religion Concern Itself With Political and Social Questions?" *America,* August 5, 1989, p. 61.

SOURCES

Batson, C. Daniel. "How Social an Animal?" *American Psychologist,* vol. 45, 1990, pp. 336–46.

Bayles, Fred, and David Foster. "LA after Watts: Hope Has Come and Gone." *The Sunday Oregonian,* May 10, 1992, p. 1.

Bellah, Robert, et al. " 'The Good Society.' " *Commonweal,* July 12, 1991, p. 425.

Bernstein, Nina. "Unhappy German Youths Turn to Nazism." *The Sunday Oregonian,* June 16, 1991, p. A16.

Beyer, Lisa. "Issues of Color and of Creed." *Time,* May 28, 1990, p. 35.

Bivins, Larry. "Investment Group Cultivates Roots in Inner-City Area." *The Oregonian,* June 11, 1992, p. A14.

Black, Chris. "Politicians Recognizing AIDS Issue." *The Oregonian,* June 2, 1992, p. A8.

"Breaking the Codes." *The New Republic,* July 8, 1991, pp. 7–8.

Brookhiser, Richard. "Taming the Tribes of America." *National Review,* November 5, 1990, pp. 63–65.

Bruce, Neil, and Michael Waldman. "The Rotten-Kid Theorem Meets the Samaritan's Dilemma." *The Quarterly Journal of Economics,* vol. 105, February 1990, p. 155.

Bull, Chris. "Rights Issues Get Attention from Baptists." *The Advocate,* April 7, 1992, p. 20.

Burt, Martha R., and Barbara E. Cohen. "Differences Among Homeless Single Women, Women with Children, and Single Men." *Social Problems,* vol. 36, December 1989, pp. 508–22.

"Bush Shrugs Off Inquiry into Perks at White House." *The Oregonian,* April 3, 1992, p. A11.

Butterfield, Fox. "Asian-American Population Explodes All Around U.S." *The Sunday Oregonian,* February 24, 1991, p. A28.

"Capitalism Versus Altruism." *Management Today,* June 1990, p. 3.

Catano, James V. "The Rhetoric of Masculinity: Origins, Institutions, and the Myth of the Self-made Man." *College English,* vol. 52, April 1990, pp. 421–35.

Chargot, Patricia. "Group of Successful Black Men Alters Outlook of At-risk Children." *The Oregonian,* June 9, 1992, p. A9.

"C.S. Thoughts." *Christopher Street,* Issue 158, April 1991, p. 48.

Clark, Alfred W., et al. "Social Darwinism: A Determinant of Nuclear Arms Policy and Action." *Human Relations,* vol. 42, 1989, pp. 289–303.

Cornell, George W. "Methodists Plan to Study Homosexuality." *The Oregonian,* May 12, 1992, p. A8.

Costello, Nancy. "In Disaster, the Woman May Have the Edge." *The Oregonian,* November 27, 1991, p. B7.

Cowley, Geoffrey. "A Disaster Brings Out the Best in People. Why?" *Newsweek,* November 6, 1989, p. 40.

Delgado, Richard. "Regulation of Hate Speech May Be Necessary to Guarantee Equal Protection to All Citizens." *The Chronicle of Higher Education,* September 18, 1991, p. B1.

DeParle, Jason. "When Giving Up Welfare for a Job Just Doesn't Pay." *The New York Times,* July 8, 1992, p. 1.

De Vries, Paul. "The Taming of the Shrewd." *Christianity Today,* March 19, 1990, p. 14.

Dewar, Helen. "Senator Finds He Can't Cut Deficit, Honors Vow to Quit." *The Oregonian,* April 3, 1992, p. A11.

SOURCES

Dugger, Celia W. "On the Edge of Survival: Single Mothers on Welfare." *The New York Times,* July 6, 1992, p. A1.

Edmundson, Mark. "Freudian Mythmaking: The Case of Narcissus." *The Kenyon Review,* vol. 10, Spring 1988, p. 17.

Ellerbee, Linda. "Hope Necessity as U.S. Struggles to End Racism." *The Oregonian,* May 12, 1992, p. A12.

Etzioni, Amitai. "The 'Me First' Model in the Social Sciences Is Too Narrow." *The Chronicle of Higher Education,* February 1, 1989, p. A44.

Farnham, Alan. "What Comes After Greed?" *Fortune,* January 14, 1991, pp. 43–44.

Fellman, Bruce. "Looking Out for Number One." *National Wildlife,* December–January 1992, pp. 46–49.

Fisher, Anne B. "Who's Hurt by Salomon's Greed?" *Fortune,* September 23, 1991, pp. 71–72.

"Flight of Middle Class Shadows Future of New York City." *The Oregonian,* October 26, 1990, p. A2.

Focer, Ada. "Bank Insiders Who Bend to Greed." *Bankers Monthly,* September 1988, p. 14.

Foley, Denise. "The Hero in All of Us." *Prevention,* August 1985, pp. 72–79.

Freeman, Carol. "Difficult Times, Growing Anger May Lie Ahead." Excerpted from: *Race: How Blacks and Whites Think and Feel About the American Obsession,* by Studs Terkel, in *The Oregonian,* May 5, 1992, p. A3.

Gabler, Neal. "Morality Molds Us into One." *The Oregonian,* June 16, 1992, p. C7.

"Gay Publications Attracting Mainstream Advertising." *New York Native,* April 13, 1992, p. 15.

"Gay Rights Bill Wins Senate Backing." *New York Native,* April 13, 1992, p. 16.

"Gay Rights Coalition Releases Eagleton Poll on State Attitudes." *New York Native,* June 24, 1991, p. 12.

Gelman, David. "Why We All Love to Hate." *Newsweek,* August 28, 1989, p. 62.

Gibbs, Nancy. "Bigots in the Ivory Tower." *Time,* May 7, 1990, p. 104.

———. "For Goodness' Sake." *Time,* January 9, 1989, p. 20.

Goleman, Daniel. "As Bias Crime Seems to Rise, Scientists Study Roots of Racism." *The New York Times,* May 29, 1990, p. C1.

———. "Homophobia: Scientists Find Clues to Its Roots." *The New York Times,* July 10, 1990, p. C1.

Goodman, Ellen. "File This Story Under Willie Horton." *Los Angeles Times,* January 7, 1990, p. M7.

Grady, Robert C. "Workplace Democracy and Possessive Individualism." *Journal of Politics,* vol. 52, February 1990, pp. 146–66.

Graves. Bill. "Hate Crime Against Jews Rises in U.S." *The Oregonian,* February 17, 1992, p. B1.

Green, Charles, and David Hess. "Bush, Congress Ready to Work Together on Urban Agenda." *The Oregonian,* May 12, 1992, p. A10.

Greenhouse, Linda. "Two Visions of Free Speech." *The New York Times,* June 24, 1992, p. 1.

Growald, Eileen Rockefeller, and Allan Luks. "Beyond Self." *American Health,* March 1988, pp. 51–53.

Harvey, F. Barton. "A New Enterprise." *The Humanist,* May–June 1989, p. 14.

Heidkamp, Maria. "Looking Out for Number One." *Publishers Weekly,* February 3, 1992, p. 52.

SOURCES

"Help from Your Friends May Be Best Medicine." *The Oregonian,* November 27, 1991, p. B6.

Henry, Tamara. "Status Quo in U.S. Dissatisfies Students." *The Oregonian,* January 28, 1991, p. A7.

Herek, Gregory. "Why Are Hate Crimes Against Lesbians and Gays on the Rise?" *The Advocate,* November 5, 1991, p. 106.

Himes, Michael J., and Kenneth R. Himes. "The Myth of Self-Interest." *Commonweal,* September 23, 1988, p. 493.

Holmes, Thomas P. "Self-interest, Altruism, and Health-Risk Reduction: An Economic Analysis of Voting Behavior." *Land Economics,* vol. 66, May 1990, pp. 140–48.

"Homelessness, A Humanist Response." *The Humanist,* May/June 1989, p. 7.

Horgan, John. "A Modest Proposal on Altruism." *Scientific American,* March 1991, p. 20.

Hughes, Claire D. "Human Impact." *Sky,* February 1991, pp. 28–35.

Jones, Timothy K. "Klansmen Wise Up." *Christianity Today,* July 16, 1990, p. 13.

Jordan, Mary. "Unrest Spawns Search for Cure to Inner-City Ills." *The Oregonian,* May 9, 1992, p. A5.

Kelly, Katy. "Fewer Aim for Career in Business." *USA Today,* January 13, 1992, p. 1.

Kessler-Harris, Alice. "Trade Unions Mirror Society in Conflict Between Collectivism and Individualism." *Monthly Labor Review,* August 1987, p. 32.

Kilborn, Peter T. "Lives of Unexpected Poverty in Center of a Land of Plenty." *The New York Times,* July 7, 1992, p. 1.

King, Charles E. "Homelessness in America." *The Humanist,* May/June 1989, p. 8.

Kleiman, Carol. "Anti-Greed Views Boost Social Work." *The Oregonian,* May 23, 1990, p. D1.

Kohn, Alfie. "Do Religious People Help More? Not So You'd Notice." *Psychology Today,* December 1989, p. 66.

Ladd, Everett Carll. "Individualism in America." *The Christian Science Monitor,* January 3, 1989, p. 19.

Lalli, Frank. "Family Values That Bring Us Together and Tear Us Apart." *Money,* December 1989, p. 4.

"Landers Gives Bush Advice." *The Oregonian,* June 2, 1992, p. D2.

Lane, Vincent. "A Plan to Help the Inner City." *Newsweek,* August 13, 1990, p. 8.

Lee, Felicia R. "Intolerance Will Be Topic for Students." *The New York Times,* September 18, 1989, p. B1.

Lens, Sidney. "Blaming the Victims, 'Social Darwinism' Is Still the Name of the Game." *The Progressive,* August 1980, pp. 27–28.

Leo, John. "The Politics of Hate." *U.S. News & World Report,* October 9, 1989, p. 24.

Levine, Art. "America's Youthful Bigots." *U.S. News & World Report,* May 7, 1990, pp. 59–60.

Lewis, Anthony. "Unconcerned Government Abandoned Inner Cities." *The Oregonian,* May 5, 1992, p. C5.

Lewis, Paul. "Earth Summit Offers Portents of World's New Politics." *The Oregonian,* June 15, 1992, p. A8.

———. "Nations Agree on Plan for Cleaning Up World's Environment." *The Sunday Oregonian,* April 5, 1992, p. A18.

Locke, Edwin A. "The Virtue of Selfishness." *American Psychologist,* vol. 43, June 1988, p. 481.

SOURCES

"Loosing Hateful Speech." *The New York Times,* June 24, 1992, p. A16.
Luciano, Lani. "A Cure Your M.D. Won't Like." *Money,* Fall 1990, p. 54.
McAnally, Gene. "I Was Homeless." *The Humanist,* May/June 1989, p. 12.
McCabe, Bruce. "New Housing Puts Single Parents First." *The Boston Globe,* May 9, 1991, p. 77.
McCallum, John S. "Of Self-Interest, Economic Policy and Influencing the Government." *Business Quarterly,* Spring 1990, pp. 54–57.
McCarthy, Terrence. "YIMBY: Yes, in My Back Yard." *The Wall Street Journal,* January 31, 1992, p. A14.
McDermott, Judy. "Skinflints." *The Sunday Oregonian,* November 24, 1991, p. L1.
Mahar, Ted. "Study: 22% Back Green Politics." *The Oregonian,* June 19, 1992, p. C6.
Makihara, Kumiko, "No Longer Will to Be Invisible." *Time,* May 28, 1990, p. 36.
Marmillion, Valsin A. "Are We on the Verge of a Lesbian and Gay Revolution?" *The Advocate,* November 19, 1991, p. 114.
Martz, John M. "Giving Batson's Strawman a Brain . . . and a Heart." *American Psychologist,* vol. 46, February 1991, pp. 162–63.
Mathews, Tom. "Picking Up the Pieces." *Newsweek,* July 23, 1990, p. 19.
Mills, Kim I. "Gay-Bashing Highest in North Carolina." *The Oregonian,* June 8, 1990, p. A17.
Monje, Kathleen. "Gay Congressman Believes Prejudice on Decline." *The Oregonian,* April 20, 1991, p. C11.
Moore, Thomas, with Marianna I. Knight. "Idealism's Rebirth." *U.S. News & World Report,* October 24, 1988, pp. 37–40.
Murphy, Ryan. " 'Dynasty' Returns More Queer Than Ever." *The Advocate,* October 22, 1991, p. 66.
Nalley, Richard. "The Littlest Blackmailer." *Science Digest,* July 1982, p. 66.
"The New Activism." *Amnesty Action,* September/October 1991, p. 1.
Nickel, Jeffrey. "When Justice Prevails." *Christopher Street,* Issue 170, January 20, 1992, pp. 13–15.
"The NIMBY Syndrome." *Commonweal,* May 22, 1987, p. 310.
Oliver, Gordon. "Oregon's Child Poverty on Increase." *The Oregonian,* July 8, 1992, p. B1.
"An Outbreak of Bigotry." *Time,* May 28, 1990, p. 35.
Page, Clarence. "For War, Military Bends Its Gay Rule." *The Oregonian,* February 14, 1991, p. B11.
Peirce, Neil R. "National Youth Service the Ticket to Civic Health." *The Oregonian,* June 15, 1992, p. B7.
Perloff, Robert. "Self-Interest and Personal Responsibility Redux." *American Psychologist,* vol. 42, January 1987, pp. 3–10.
Platt, Polly. "Unease in Utopia." *International Management,* October 1990, p. 77.
Prowse, Michael. "Blazing Paths for New Options in U.S. Schools." *The Oregonian,* June 16, 1992, p. A3.
Quindlen, Anna. "Fitness, Not Sex, Gauge for Service." *The Oregonian,* June 25, 1992, p. D9.
———. "Only 'Authentic' Americans Desired." *The Sunday Oregonian,* November 24, 1991, p. C10.
Quintero, Fernando. "School Helps Young, Unwed Mothers." *The Oregonian,* June 8, 1992, p. A8.

SOURCES

Rankin, Robert A. "Island of Hope in Baltimore May Show Way." *The Oregonian,* June 12, 1992, p. A5.

———. "Self-Help Inner-City Remedy?" *The Oregonian,* June 7, 1992, p. A4.

Rauch, Jonathan. "Thought Crimes." *The New Republic,* October 7, 1991, p. 17.

Ridley-Thomas, Mark, and Rita Walters. "A Chance to Put NIMBYism Behind Us." *Los Angeles Times,* November 29, 1991, p. B5.

Rodgers, William H., Jr. "Intuition, Altruism, and Spite." *American Behavioral Scientist,* vol. 34, January/February 1991, pp. 386–406.

"Romer, Webb Support Special Legal Protections for Gays, Lesbians." *New York Native,* April 13, 1992, p. 21.

Rossi, Alice S. "Sex and Gender in an Aging Society." *Daedalus,* vol. 115, Winter 1986, pp. 141–69.

Schneider, Keith. "Environmental Groups Run into Time of Trouble." *The Oregonian,* April 3, 1992, p. A5.

"Seattle Begins Anti-Bigotry Campaign with TV Commercial." *The Oregonian,* July 4, 1992, p. D1.

Seixas, Suzanne. "Running from Racists." *Money,* July 1991, p. 81.

Settle, Mel. "Must We Tear Them Down?" *The Humanist,* May/June 1989, p. 9.

Shogan, Robert. "Poll Shows Growing Antipathy to Politics." *The Oregonian,* September 19, 1990, p. A12.

Simon, Herbert A. "A Mechanism for Social Selection and Successful Altruism." *Science,* vol. 250, December 21, 1990, pp. 1665–68.

Skerry, Peter. "Individualist America and Today's Immigrants." *The Public Interest,* Winter 1991, p. 104.

Smolla, Rodney A. "The Price of Free Speech." *The Sunday Oregonian,* June 28, 1992, p. D1.

Solomon, Nancy, and Richard Nalley. "Selfish Genes, Unselfish Acts." *Science Digest,* July 1982, p. 66.

Stark, Oded. "Altruism and the Quality of Life." *American Economic Review,* vol. 79, May 1989, p. 86.

Stevens, William K. "Earth Summit Pacts Hide Teeth That Someday Will Have Bite." *The Sunday Oregonian,* June 14, 1992, p. A10.

Taylor, Paul. "Welfare Mess: Intractable and Untamable." *The Sunday Oregonian,* March 22, 1992, p. P1.

"Teaching Tolerance." Edited by Sara Bullard, vol. 1, Spring 1992, pp. 1–65.

" 'Teaching Tolerance' Launched." *Law Report,* January 1992, p. 1.

Thomas, Lewis. "Are Altruism and Cooperation Natural?" *Harper's,* July 1984, p. 26.

Thrasher, Penelope. "On Altruism: Comment on Batson." *American Psychologist,* vol. 46, February 1991, p. 163.

Tims, Dana. "Bell Sounds Alarm on Civil Rights Threat." *The Oregonian,* October 19, 1990, p. B7.

Toolan, David. "The Me Decade Fallacy." *Commonweal,* May 20, 1983, pp. 292–93.

Tranquada, Jim. "Welfare-slashing measure being defeated in California." *The Oregonian,* November 4, 1992, p. B8.

Ulrich, Roberta. "Public Resentment of Homeless Rises." *The Oregonian,* December 20, 1990, p. C2.

Updegrave, Walter L. "Race and Money." *Money,* December 1989, pp. 152–72.

Vobejda, Barbara. "Ethnic Profile of U.S. Changes Markedly." *The Oregonian,* March 11, 1991, p. C12.

———. "Immigrants Transformed Los Angeles' Racial Profile." *The Oregonian,* May 11, 1992, p. A7.

Vuyst, Alex. "Self-Help for the Homeless." *The Humanist,* May/June 1989, p. 13.

Walters, Nolan, and Carl Cannon. "Racial Politics Becoming Current and Perilous Issue." *The Oregonian,* December 11, 1990, p. A12.

Weiss, Stefanie. "No Place Called Home." *NEA Today,* September 1988, p. 10.

Weld, Elizabeth New. "Area Shelters Cope with New Homeless." *The Boston Globe,* December 16, 1990, p. 1.

Willard, Timothy, and Daniel M. Fields. "The Community in an Age of Individualism." *The Futurist,* May–June 1991, pp. 35–39.

Williams, Lena. "Blacks Debating a Greater Stress on Self-Reliance Instead of Aid." *The New York Times,* June 15, 1986, p. 1.

Williamson, Don. "Vicious Racial Bias Stains Fabric of Nation's Culture." *The Oregonian,* December 20, 1990, p. A20.

Yim, Miko. "Portland-Area Teen-agers Volunteer Time, Talents." *The Oregonian,* February 2, 1992, p. C1.

Young, Thomas J. "Violent Hate Groups in Rural America." *International Journal of Offender Therapy and Comparative Criminology,* vol. 34, April 1990, pp. 15–20.

5. LIFE: More Respect / Less Respect?

Addelson, Kathryn Pyne. "Some Moral Issues in Public Problems of Reproduction." *Social Problems,* vol. 37, February 1990, pp. 1–15.

Allegretti, Joseph. "Reproductive Technology Invades the Divorce Court." *America,* October 27, 1990, pp. 304–5.

Alper, Joe. "Environmentalists: Ban the (Population) Bomb." *Science,* vol. 252, May 31, 1991, p. 1247.

"American Survey: The politics of death." *The Economist,* March 24, 1990, pp. 25–26.

". . . And Health Care for All." *American Health,* July/August 1992, p. 20.

Ames, Katrine, et al. "Last Rights." *Newsweek,* August 26, 1991, p. 40.

Anderson, Howard J. "Hospitals Get Help in Running Hospices." *Hospitals,* August 5, 1990, p. 73.

Aronowitz, Stanley. "Backdoor to Eugenics." *American Journal of Sociology,* vol. 96, May 1991, p. 1575.

Bacard, Andre. "The Second Genesis." *The Humanist,* September/October 1989, p. 9.

Bailey, William C., and Ruth D. Peterson. "Murder and Capital Punishment: A Monthly Time-Series Analysis of Execution Publicity." *American Sociological Review,* vol. 54, October 1989, pp. 722–43.

Balzar, John. "Right-to-Die Measure Trails in Washington." *Los Angeles Times,* November 6, 1991, p. A1.

Beaty, Jonathan, and Jay Carney. "Bad News for Death Row." *Time,* July 10, 1989, p. 48.

Beck, Melinda, et al. "The Geezer Boom." *Newsweek,* Special Edition: *The 21st-Century Family,* Winter/Spring 1990, p. 62.

Berlfein, Judy. "The Earliest Warning." *Discover,* February 1992, p. 14.

SOURCES

Bernhoft, Robin. "But No Safeguards Against Overdoing It." *Medical Tribune,* November 14, 1991, p. 28.

Blakeslee, Sandra. "Ethicists See Omens of an Era of Genetic Bias." *The New York Times,* December 27, 1990, p. B9.

———. "A Road Map for Genes." *The New York Times,* October 10, 1989, p. C7.

Booth, William. "Fast Population Growth, Social Problems Linked." *The Washington Post,* June 26, 1989, p. A2.

———. "Judge Orders Birth Control Implant in Defendant." *The Washington Post,* January 15, 1991, p. A1.

Bouvier, Leon F. "How to Get There from Here: Achieving Optimal Population Size." *USA Today,* January 1991, p. 17.

Boyce, James K. "The Bomb Is a Dud." *The Progressive,* September 1990, p. 24.

Brower, Vicki. "The Right Way to Die." *Health,* June 1991, p. 39.

Bulger, Roger J. "How the Genome Project Could Destroy Health Insurance." *The Washington Post,* August 4, 1991, p. C4.

Burleigh, Michael. "Euthanasia and the Third Reich." *History Today,* February 1990, p. 11.

Butler, Robert N. "Planning for Death." *The Washington Post,* June 25, 1991, p. WH6.

Bynum, W. F. "The Politics of Our Genes." *Nature,* vol. 356, April 16, 1992, p. 641.

Cameron, Nigel M. de S. "Living Wills and the Will to Live." *Christianity Today,* April 6, 1992, p. 22.

Cantor, Charles R. "Orchestrating the Human Genome Project." *Science,* vol. 248, April 6, 1990, p. 49.

Carr, William F. "Lead Me Safely Through Death." *America,* March 25, 1989, p. 264.

Cassel, Christine K., and Diane E. Meier. "Morals and Moralism in the Debate Over Euthanasia and Assisted Suicide." *The New England Journal of Medicine,* vol. 323, September 13, 1990, p. 750.

Cato, Phillip C. "The Management of the Biosphere." *Vital Speeches,* vol. 56, November 1, 1989, p. 53.

Cavalieri, Liebe F. "Genetic Research: A Scientific Dilemma." *The Christian Science Monitor,* January 10, 1990, p. 18.

Chandler, Russell. "Religion Confronts Euthanasia." *Los Angeles Times,* November 2, 1991, p. A1.

"Changing Your Genes." *The Economist,* April 25, 1992, p. 11.

Chase, Marilyn. "Scientists Splice Genes into HIV to Derail It." *The Wall Street Journal,* May 15, 1992, p. B1.

———. "Scientists Work to Slow Human Aging." *The Wall Street Journal,* March 12, 1992, p. B1.

Cohn, Jeffrey P. "Reproductive Biotechnology." *BioScience,* vol. 41, October 1991, p. 595.

Colasanto, Diane. "The Right-to-Die Controversy." *USA Today,* May 1991, pp. 62–63.

Cosco, Joseph. "Zift, Gift, IVF." *Adweek's Marketing Week,* October 16, 1989, p. 38.

Courteau, Jacqueline. "Genome Databases." *Science,* vol. 254, October 11, 1991, p. 201.

Cowley, Geoffrey, et al. "Made to Order Babies." *Newsweek* Special Edition: *The 21st-Century Family,* Winter/Spring 1990, p. 94.

SOURCES

"Death Penalty Protocol Adopted, World Conference on Human Rights Considered." *UN Chronicle,* March 1990, p. 85.

DeParle, Jason. "Beyond the Legal Right." *The Washington Monthly,* April 1989, p. 28.

Dumanoski, Dianne. "Coming to Grips with the Mess We're In." *The Boston Globe,* February 10, 1992, p. 29.

Edmondson, Brad. "Demanding Death with Dignity." *American Demographics,* November 1991, p. 14.

Edwards, Rem B. "Abortions Rights: Why Conservatives Are Wrong." *Phi Kappa Phi Journal,* Fall 1989, p. 19.

Elshtain, Jean Bethke. "Technology as Destiny." *The Progressive,* June 1989, p. 19.

Epstein, Debbie. "Pharmacists Needed to Play Vital Role on Hospice Teams." *Drug Topics,* September 18, 1989, p. 24.

"Ethical Problems to Merit the Name." *Nature,* vol. 352, August 1, 1991, p. 359.

"Euthanasia: What Is the 'Good Death'?" *The Economist,* July 20, 1991, p. 21.

"Executions Don't Deter Murderers." *USA Today,* May 1992, p. 12.

Feifel, Herman. "Psychology and Death, Meaningful Rediscovery." *American Psychologist,* vol. 45, April 1990, pp. 537–42.

"*Final Exit:* Euthanasia Guide Sells Out." *Nature,* vol. 352, August 15, 1991, p. 553.

Finkelstein, Joanne L. "Biomedicine and Technocratic Power." *Hastings Center Report,* July/August 1990, p. 13.

"Forecasters Predict Radical Changes." *USA Today,* May 1992, pp. 12–13.

Fornos, Werner. "Gaining People, Losing Ground." *The Humanist,* May/June 1990, p. 5.

Fox, Sidney W. "Synthesis of Life in the Lab? Defining a Protoliving System." *The Quarterly Review of Biology,* vol. 66, June 1991, p. 181.

Friedrich, Otto. "A Limited Right to Die." *Time,* July 9, 1990, p. 59.

Gallo, Robert. "An AIDS Vaccine Will Excite the World." *Fortune,* March 26, 1990, p. 96.

Gelbspan, Ross. "Racing to an Environmental Precipice." *The Boston Globe,* May 31, 1992, p. 1.

———. "Remaking Society to Save the Planet." *The Boston Globe,* February 10, 1992, p. 29.

Geller, E. Scott. "Behavior Analysis and Environmental Protection: Where Have All the Flowers Gone?" *Journal of Applied Behavior Analysis,* vol. 23, Fall 1990, p. 269.

"Gene Experts Tell of Possible Abuse." *The New York Times,* October 18, 1991, p. A18.

Gershon, Diane. "New Panel for Ethical Issues." *Nature,* vol. 349, January 17, 1991, p. 184.

Givens, Ron, with Ted Kenney. "Death-Row Murderers Could Be Lifesavers." *Newsweek,* January 9, 1989, p. 49.

Gould, Stephen Jay. "The Smoking Gun of Eugenics." *Natural History,* December 1991, p. 8.

Grad, Frank P., George W. Rathjens, and Albert J. Rosenthal. *Environmental Control: Priorities, Policies, and the Law.* New York: Columbia University Press, 1971, pp. 48–65.

Green, Charles. "Bush Gives Low Priority to Issue of Health Care Reform." *The Sunday Oregonian,* July 5, 1992, p. A12.

Green, Rochelle. "Tinkering with the Secrets of Life." *Health,* January 1990, p. 46.

Greil, Arthur L. "The Religious Response to Reproductive Technology." *The Christian Century*, January 4–11, 1989, p. 11.
Grogger, Jeffrey. "The Deterrent Effect of Capital Punishment: An Analysis of Daily Homicide Counts." *Journal of the American Statistical Association*, vol. 85, June 1990, pp. 295–302.
Haines, Herb. "Primum Non Nocere: Chemical Execution and the Limits of Medical Social Control." *Social Problems*, vol. 36, December 1989, pp. 442–51.
Haub, Carl. "2050: Standing Room Only?" *The Washington Post*, July 8, 1990, p. C3.
Henderson, Martha. "Beyond the Living Will." *The Gerontologist*, vol. 30, 1990, pp. 480–85.
Henig, Robin Maranta. "High-Tech Fortunetelling." *The New York Times Magazine*, December 24, 1989, p. 20.
Hentoff, Nat. ". . . And the Specter of Pro-Choice Eugenics." *The Washington Post*, May 25, 1991, p. A31.
———. "Execution in Your Living Room." *The Progressive*, November 1991, p. 16.
Hirschman, Elizabeth C. "Babies for Sale: Market Ethics and the New Reproductive Technologies." *The Journal of Consumer Affairs*, vol. 25, Winter 1991, pp. 358–89.
Hood, Leroy. "An Incredible Impact on Medicine." *Fortune*, March 26, 1990, pp. 92–93.
Horgan, John. "The Death Penalty." *Scientific American*, July 1990, pp. 17–20.
"How Low Can We Go." *The Progressive*, May 1992, p. 9.
Humphry, Derek. "For Whom Do Ethicists Speak?" *Los Angeles Times*, August 16, 1991, p. B7.
Huxley, Aldous. *Brave New World*. New York: Harper & Row, 1960.
Imber, Jonathan B. "The Future of Abortion Politics." *Contemporary Sociology: An International Journal of Reviews*, vol. 19, March 1990, pp. 176–81.
"Into the Unknown." *The Economist*, September 2, 1989, pp. 17–18.
Johnson, Martin. "Did I Begin?" *New Scientist*, December 9, 1989, p. 39.
"Judge Says Suicide Doctor Does a 'Service.' " *The New York Times*, October 27, 1991, p. 21.
Kaplan, David A. "The Fryers Club Convention." *Newsweek*, August 27, 1990, pp. 54–55.
Kase, Lori Miller. "Mixed Blessings." *Health*, November 1990, p. 64.
Kass, Leon R. "Death With Dignity and the Sanctity of Life." *Commentary*, March 1990, pp. 33–43.
Kissinger, David. "Can TV Deal with a Healthy Dose of Death?" *Variety*, April 18, 1990, p. 3.
Kitzmiller, Michael. "Environment and the Law." In *Ecocide . . . and Thoughts Toward Survival*. Edited by Clifton Fadiman and Jean White. New York: Interbook, 1971, pp. 140–59.
Knickerbocker, Brad. "Society Divided on Assisted Suicide." *The Christian Science Monitor*, November 8, 1991, p. 3.
Lacayo, Richard. "The Politics of Life and Death." *Time*, April 2, 1990, p. 18.
Lawton, Kim A. "The Doctor as Executioner." *Christianity Today*, December 16, 1991, pp. 50–52.
Le Draoulec, Pascale. "The Children of the Nobel Sperm Bank." *Medical Economics*, February 17, 1992, pp. 106–23.
Levine, Joshua. "Dr. Pangloss, Meet Ingmar Bergman." *Forbes*, March 30, 1992, p. 96.

SOURCES

Lipman, Larry. "Medicare for All Could Save $26.3 Billion, Study Says." *The Oregonian,* January 8, 1992, p. A7.

Locke, Michelle. " 'Granny Dumping' Increases at Nation's Hospitals." *The Sunday Oklahoman,* December 8, 1991, p. 35.

Lovelock, James E. "Hands Up for the Gaia Hypothesis." *Nature,* vol. 344, March 8, 1990, pp. 100–102.

McCleary, Elliot H. "A Medical Breakthrough That Will Change Our Lives." *Consumer's Digest,* May/June 1992, p. 29.

MacKenzie, Debora. "Europe Debates the Ownership of Life." *New Scientist,* January 4, 1992, p. 9.

Martin, G. M., et al. "Dominant Susceptibility Genes." *Nature,* vol. 347, September 13, 1990, p. 124.

Marx, Jean. "Dissecting the Complex Diseases." *Science,* vol. 247, March 30, 1990, p. 1540.

Maugh, Thomas H., II. "Drawing the Human Blueprint." *Los Angeles Times,* October 8, 1989, p. 3.

Maurice, John. "Improvements Seen for Ru-486 Abortions." *Science,* vol. 254, October 11, 1991, p. 198.

Merriam, J., et al. "Toward Cloning and Mapping the Genome of Drosophila." *Science,* vol. 254, October 11, 1991, pp. 221–55.

Myers, Jane E., and Barbara Shelton. "Abuse and Older Persons: Issues and Implications for Counselors." *Journal of Counseling and Development,* vol. 65, March 1987, pp. 376–79.

National Council on Family Relations. "2001: Preparing Families for the Future." Minneapolis, Minn.: Bolger Publications/Creative Printing, 1990, pp. 1–40.

Neuhaus, Richard John. "All Too Human." *National Review,* December 2, 1991, p. 45.

"No law against death . . ." *The Missoulan,* July 22, 1992, p. A-5.

Orr, Robert D. "Get It In Writing." *Christianity Today,* April 6, 1992, p. 24.

Page, Talbot. "More Cooperation on the Environment?" *Fortune,* March 26, 1990, p. 92.

"Passive Euthanasia in L.A." *Los Angeles Times,* December 17, 1991, p. B6.

Pearson, P. L., et al. "The Human Genome Initiative—Do Databases Reflect Current Progress?" *Science,* vol. 254, October 11, 1991, pp. 214–15.

"People in Most Countries Rank Environment as Major Concern." *National Wildlife,* August–September 1992, p. 25.

Perrin, Noel. "Paying Kids Not to Get Pregnant." *The Washington Post,* July 8, 1990, p. C3.

Perry, Kent W. "Cops: We're Losing the War." *Newsweek,* March 13, 1989, p. 6.

Pfeffer, Naomi. "The Uninformed Conception." *New Scientist,* July 20, 1991, p. 40.

Pope, Lisa. "California voters give message: no." *The Oregonian,* November 5, 1992, p. 3M.

Popoff, Frank. "How to Recycle 70% of a Barrel of Oil." *Fortune,* March 26, 1990, p. 92.

Rechsteiner, Martin. "The Folly of the Human Genome Project." *New Scientist,* September 15, 1990, p. 20.

Relman, Arnold. "We Are Solving the Problem of Cancer." *Fortune,* March 26, 1990, p. 92.

Rheingold, Howard. *Virtual Reality,* New York: Summit Books, 1991, p. 364.

SOURCES

Roberts, Leslie. "A Genetic Survey of Vanishing Peoples." *Science,* vol. 252, June 21, 1991, pp. 1614–17.

———. "Genome Patent Fight Erupts." *Science,* vol. 254, October 11, 1991, pp. 184–86.

———. "Tough Times Ahead for the Genome Project." *Science,* vol. 248, June 29, 1990, pp. 1600–1601.

Rosendahl, Iris, and Tracey Maxwell. "Pharmacists Speak Out: Abortion and Euthanasia." *Drug Topics,* March 9, 1992, p. 38.

Rorvik, David. "Predestinations." *Omni,* October 1980, p. 68.

Rosenthal, Elisabeth. "In Matters of Life and Death, The Dying Take Control." *The New York Times,* August 18, 1991, p. D1.

Ryan, Maura A. "The Argument for Unlimited Procreative Liberty: A Feminist Critique." *Hasting Center Report,* July/August 1990, pp. 6–12.

Salholz, Eloise, et al. "The Right-to Lifers' New Tactics." *Newsweek,* July 9, 1990, p. 23.

Saltus, Richard. "Human Gene Therapy Begins Under Ethicists' Close Watch." *The Boston Sunday Globe,* September 22, 1991, p. 19.

Schneiderman, Lawrence J. "Euthanasia. Can We Keep It a Special Case?" *The Humanist,* May–June 1990, p. 15.

Schrage, Michael. "Genetic Maps Leading Us into Unknown Psychological Territory." *Los Angeles Times,* September 7, 1989, p. 1.

Snyder, Solomon. "Effective Treatment of Addiction by 2000." *Fortune,* March 26, 1990, p. 93.

Stegner, Wallace. "It All Began with Conservation." *Smithsonian,* vol. 21, April 1990, p. 35.

Steinbacher, Roberta, and Faith Gilroy. "Sex Selection Technology; A Prediction of Its Use and Effect." *The Journal of Psychology,* vol. 124, May 1990, pp. 283–88.

Steinbrook, Roberta. "Support Grows for Euthanasia." *Los Angeles Times,* April 19, 1991, p. A1.

Steinfels, Peter. "Dutch Study Is Issue in Euthanasia Vote." *The New York Times,* November 2, 1991, p. 11.

———. "Euthanasia: A Radical Issue that Demands Careful Consideration, Rather Than Drifting Judgment." *The New York Times,* May 11, 1991, p. 9.

———. "In Cold Print, the Euthanasia Issue Can Take On Many Shades of Color." *The New York Times,* November 9, 1991, p. 11.

"Steps Urged to 'Sustain Life' on Earth." *The Boston Globe,* February 27, 1992, p. 6.

Stout, Hilary. "Watson Resigns as Head of U.S. Gene-Mapping Project." *The Wall Street Journal,* April 13, 1991, p. B6.

Thomas, Cal. "It's a Short Step to the Next Horror of Eugenics." *Los Angeles Times,* December 30, 1990, p. M7.

Thorlakson, Neil. "Doctor Aid-in-Dying Offers Peace of Mind." *Medical Tribune,* November 14, 1991, p. 28.

Tierney, John. "Betting the Planet." *The New York Times Magazine,* December 2, 1990, p. 52.

"The Tiniest Transplants." *The Economist,* April 25, 1992, p. 95.

Truog, Robert D., et al. "The Problem with Futility." *The New England Journal of Medicine,* vol. 326, June 4, 1992, pp. 1560–63.

Turner, Graham. "The Lost Art of Dying." *World Press Review,* June 1989, p. 37.

Udall, Stewart L., and W. Kent Olson. "Me First, God and Nature Second." *Los Angeles Times,* July 27, 1992, p. B5.
"US Population Tops 253 Million." *The Boston Globe,* January 1, 1992, p. 57.
Waldholz, Michael, and Hilary Stout. "Rights to Life. A New Debate Rages Over the Patenting of Gene Discoveries." *The Wall Street Journal,* April 17, 1992, p. 1.
Watson, James D. "The Human Genome Project: Past, Present, and Future." *Science,* vol. 248, April 6, 1990, pp. 44–48.
"Watershed Decision on Euthanasia." *Medical Tribune,* November 14, 1991, p. 28.
Watts, Susan. "Surprise Success for Genetic Jabs." *New Scientist,* April 21, 1990, p. 31.
Weinberg, Robert A. "The Dark Side of the Genome." *Technology Review,* April 1991, p. 44.
Worsnop, Richard L. "Death Penalty Debate Centers on Retribution." *Editorial Research Reports,* July 13, 1990, p. 398.
Wright, Robert. "Achilles' Helix." *The New Republic,* July 9 and 16, 1990, pp. 21–31.
———. "The End of Insurance." *The New Republic,* July 9 and 16, 1990, p. 26.
Yancey, Philip. "Angel to the Dying." *Christianity Today,* December 17, 1990, p. 22.

6. SATISFACTION: More Content / Less Content?

Abbott, Carl. "Downtown: Where the Lights Are Bright." *The Sunday Oregonian,* October 4, 1992, p. B1.
"American Living Standards: Running to Stand Still." *The Economist,* November 10, 1990, p. 19.
Angier, Natalie. "Busy as a Bee? Then Who's Doing the Work?" *The New York Times,* July 30, 1991, p. C1.
Applegate, Jane. "Some Find Business Fulfillment by Taking on the Mother Load." *The Washington Post,* October 7, 1991, p. WB11.
Barber, Benjamin R. "Jihad vs. McWorld." *The Atlantic Monthly,* March 1992, p. 53.
Bearon, Lucille B. "No Great Expectations: The Underpinnings of Life Satisfaction for Older Women." *The Gerontologist,* vol. 29, 1989, pp. 772–78.
Beck, Melinda, et al. "Biosphere II: Science or Showmanship?" *Newsweek,* October 7, 1991, p. 58.
———. "The Geezer Boom." *Newsweek* Special Edition: *The 21st-Century Family,* Winter/Spring 1990, p. 62.
Bell, Daniel. "The World and the United States in 2013." *Daedalus,* Summer 1987, vol. 16, pp. 1–31.
Benedetto, Richard. "Economy Shakes American Dream." *USA Today,* January 16, 1992, p. 5A.
Bjornstad, James. "America's Spiritual, Sometimes Satanic, Smorgasbord." *Christianity Today,* October 23, 1981, p. 28.
Blonston, Gary, and Robert A. Rankin. "Economy of '90s to Affect All Aspects of Life." *The Oregonian,* December 23, 1991, p. C12.
Breathnach, Sarah Ban. "Living in a Lower Gear." *The Washington Post,* December 31, 1991, p. C5.
Briggs, David. "Baby Boomers Lose Interest in Church." *The Oregonian,* June 6, 1992, p. P12.
Brody, Jane E. "Suicide Myths Cloud Efforts to Save Children." *The New York Times,* June 16, 1992, p. C1.

SOURCES

Bromley, David G. "The Satanic Cult Scare." *Society,* May/June 1991, pp. 55.

Calonius, Erik. "Blood and Money." *Newsweek* Special Edition: *The 21st-Century Family,* Winter/Spring 1990, p. 82.

Campbell, Angus, et al. *The Quality of American Life.* New York: Russell Sage Foundation, 1976.

Campbell, Joseph, with Bill Moyers. *The Power of Myth.* Edited by Betty Sue Flowers. New York: Doubleday, 1988, pp. 3–35.

Cardullo, Bert. "Lonely People, Living in the World." *The Hudson Review,* vol. 44, 1991, p. 292.

Casey, Maura. "Myth of the Welfare Queen." *The Christian Science Monitor,* December 3, 1991, p. 19.

Cattani, Richard J. "Race, Class, and Acceptance." *The Christian Science Monitor,* May 6, 1992, p. 18.

Chapman, Stephen. "Media's Newest Myth: Those Poor, Overworked Americans." *The Oregonian,* February 25, 1992, p. B5.

Chusmir, Leonard H., and Barbara Parker. "Effects of Generation and Sex on Dimensions of Life Success." *Psychological Reports,* vol. 68, 1991, pp. 335–38.

Colburn, Don. "Early Retirement by Men Linked to Job Stress." *The Washington Post,* August 29, 1989, p. WH5.

Collins, Ronald K. L., and Michael F. Jacobson. "Commercialism Versus Culture." *The Christian Science Monitor,* September 19, 1990, p. 19.

Coontz, Stephanie. "A Nation of Welfare Families." *Harper's Magazine,* October 1992, pp. 13–16.

Cowen, Emory L. "In Pursuit of Wellness." *American Psychologist,* vol. 46, April 1991, pp. 404–8.

Creagh, Ronald. "The American Laboratory." *UNESCO Courier,* February 1991, p. 26.

Davidson, Andrew. "The Yuppie Boom Is Finally Over." *Marketing,* January 19, 1989, p. 1.

Dervin, Daniel. "Splitting and Fragmentation of Group-Fantasy During the Reagan Years." *The Journal of Psychohistory,* vol. 18, Winter 1991, pp. 283–92.

DeWitt, Paula Mergenhagen. "Mental Health Therapy Grows in Popularity." *The Sunday Oregonian,* October 4, 1992, p. L15.

Durning, Alan. "The Grim Payback of Greed." *International Wildlife,* May–June 1991, p. 36.

Ellison, Christopher G., et al. "Does Religious Commitment Contribute to Individual Life Satisfaction?" *Social Forces,* vol. 68, September 1989, pp. 100–123.

"Living Digest: Empty Nest." *The Oregonian,* April 18, 1987, p. C1.

Evans, Gary W., et al. "Residential Density and Psychological Health: The Mediating Effects of Social Support." *Journal of Personality and Social Psychology,* vol. 57, 1989, pp. 994–99.

Galbraith, John Kenneth. "The Price of Comfort." *Los Angeles Times,* January 6, 1991, p. M1.

Gardner, Marilyn. "Real-life Parents, Not Toys, Determine Child's Outlook." *The Oregonian,* December 19, 1991, p. A23.

Gladstone, Rick. "Consumer Faith Worst Since '74 Recession." *The Oregonian,* February 26, 1992, p. D1.

Goldman, Debra. "In My Time of Dying." *Adweek,* March 2, 1992, p. 18.

Goldstein, Laurence. "UFOs Are Real—in Our National Psyche." *Los Angeles Times,* May 27, 1992, p. B7.

SOURCES

Goleman, Daniel. "Compassion and Comfort in Middle Age." *The New York Times,* February 6, 1990, p. C1.

———. "Feeling Unreal? Many Others Feel the Same." *The New York Times,* January 8, 1991, p. C1.

———. "Hope Emerges as Key to Success in Life." *The New York Times,* December 24, 1991, p. C1.

———. "Men at 65: New Findings on Well-Being." *The New York Times,* January 16, 1990, p. C1.

Gordon, Suzanne. "Men, Women and Work." *The Boston Globe,* July 28, 1991, p. 68.

Hampton, David R., Charles E. Summer, and Ross A. Webber, *Organizational Behavior and the Practice of Management.* Glenview, Ill.: Scott, Foresman and Company, 1987, pp. 3–31.

Harwood, Richard. "Gallup Study Defines American Essence." *The Oregonian,* September 18, 1992, p. D7.

Hilderbrand, Larry. "The Electronic Commute." *The Sunday Oregonian,* March 29, 1992, p. C1.

Hopkins, Joseph M. "Cult Specialists Assess Nontraditional Religions in the Mid-eighties." *Christianity Today,* August 9, 1985, p. 54.

Horovitz, Bruce. "Can Ads Help Cure Social Ills?" *Los Angeles Times,* June 2, 1992, p. D1.

Howe, Neil. "As Boomers get power, USA should worry." *USA Today,* July 30, 1992, p. 11A.

Huyck, Margaret Hellie. "Predicates of Personal Control Among Middle-Aged and Young-Old Men and Women in Middle America." *International Journal of Aging and Human Development,* vol. 32, 1991, pp. 261–75.

Insel, Paul M., and Henry Clay Lindgren. *Too Close for Comfort: The Psychology of Crowding.* Englewood Cliffs, N.J.: Prentice-Hall, 1978, pp. 1–37, 110–31, 143–56.

Iso-Ahola, Seppo E., and Edward D. Crowley. "Adolescent Substance Abuse and Leisure Boredom." *Journal of Leisure Research,* vol. 23, 1991, pp. 260–71.

Jackson, Judy, and Susan D. Cochran. "Loneliness and Psychological Distress." *The Journal of Psychology,* vol. 125, 1991, pp. 257–62.

Jackson, Richard. "What to Expect as America Begins to Gray." *The Wall Street Journal,* July 18, 1991, p. A10.

Johnson, George. "Back in 1979, The Word Was Malaise." *The New York Times,* December 24, 1989, p. E6.

Johnson, John, and Steve Padilla. "Satanism: Skeptics Abound." *Los Angeles Times,* April 23, 1991, p. 1.

Judd, Lewis L. "What Must Be Done to Ensure the Nation's Mental Health." *USA Today,* November 1990, p. 73.

Kaplan, Robert M., et al. "Gender Differences in Health-Related Quality of Life." *Health Psychology,* vol. 10, 1991, pp. 86–93.

Knutson, Lawrence L. "Answers to Census Questions Paint Revealing Portrait of America." *The Oregonian,* May 31, 1992, p. C17.

Kotlowitz, Alex, and Suzanne Alexander. "The Gulf: Tacit Code of Silence on Matters of Race Perpetuates Divisions." *The Wall Street Journal,* May 28, 1991, p. 1.

Kozol, Jonathan. "The New Untouchables." *Newsweek* Special Edition: *The 21st-Century Family,* Winter/Spring 1990, p. 48.

Kreitler, Shulamith, and Hans Kreitler. "The Psychological Profile of the Health-oriented Individual." *European Journal of Personality,* vol. 5, 1991, pp. 35–60.

SOURCES

Larson, Erik. "Watching Americans Watch TV." *The Atlantic Monthly,* March 1992, p. 66.

Lee, Gary R., et al. "Marital Status and Personal Happiness: An Analysis of Trend Data." *Journal of Marriage and the Family,* vol. 53, November 1991, pp. 839–44.

Leonard, George. "Sex and Other Pleasures; The Case for Pleasure." *Esquire,* May 1989, p. 153.

Lepore, Stephen J., et al. "Dynamic Role of Social Support in the Link Between Chronic Stress and Psychological Distress." *Journal of Personality and Social Psychology,* vol. 61, 1991, pp. 899–909.

Lin, Nan, and Walter M. Ensel. "Life Stress and Health: Stressors and Resources." *American Sociological Review,* vol. 54, June 1989, pp. 382–99.

Lipman, Larry. "Children in Danger, Report Says." *The Oregonian,* June 8, 1990, p. A18.

McCarroll, Thomas. "What New Age?" *Time,* August 12, 1991, p. 44.

McWhirter, Benedict T. "Loneliness: A Review of Current Literature, With Implications for Counseling and Research." *Journal of Counseling and Development,* vol. 68, March/April 1990, pp. 417–21.

"Many Seek Faith Along Other Paths." *U.S. News & World Report,* April 4, 1983, pp. 42–43.

Manz, Charles C., and Roger Grothe. "Is the Work Force Vanguard to the 21st Century a Quality of Work Life Deficient-Prone Generation?" *Journal of Business Research,* vol. 23, 1991, pp. 67–82.

Marlowe, Dick. "Rush to Early Retirement Puzzles Many." *The Oregonian,* July 19, 1990, p. F1.

Marsh, Barbara. "Tolerance Rises for Businesses Run in Homes." *The Wall Street Journal,* July 8, 1991, p. B1.

Menaghan, Elizabeth G. "Role Changes and Psychological Well-Being: Variations in Effects by Gender and Role Repertoire." *Social Forces,* vol. 67, March 1989, pp. 693–712.

Nadelson, Theodore. "On Purpose, Successful Aging, and the Myth of Innocence." *Journal of Geriatric Psychiatry,* vol. 24, 1991, pp. 3–12.

Njeri, Itabari. "People of Color Must Embrace Their Own Diversity." *Los Angeles Times,* May 15, 1992, p. T3.

Oldenburg, Don. "Touch of Evil." *The Washington Post,* March 3, 1992, p. B5.

"Panel's Report on U.S. Youths Grim." *The Oregonian,* June 9, 1990, p. A12.

Pear, Robert. "Ranks of U.S. Poor Reach 35.7 Million, The Most Since '64." *The New York Times,* September 4, 1992, p. 1.

Pickett, Melanie. "Is Consumerism a Rebel Cause?" *Los Angeles Times,* May 14, 1989, p. 3.

Pollan, Stephen M., and Mark Levine. "The Graying Yuppie: Reality Zaps the Baby-Boomers." *New York,* March 9, 1992, p. 28.

Rain, Jeffrey S., et al. "A Current Look at the Job Satisfaction/Life Satisfaction Relationship: Review and Future Considerations." *Human Relations,* vol. 44, 1991, pp. 287–304.

Reinharz, Shulamit. "Creating Utopia for the Elderly." *Society,* January/February 1988, pp. 52–58.

Roark, Anne C. "The Times Poll: Most Older Persons Say They're Happy With Lives." *Los Angeles Times,* May 4, 1989, p. A1.

Rodin, Judith, and Jeannette R. Ickovics. "Women's Health: Review and Research

Agenda as We Approach the 21st Century." *American Psychologist,* vol. 45, September 1990, pp. 1018–34.

Rossi, Alice S. "Sex and Gender in an Aging Society." *Daedalus,* vol. 115, Winter 1986, pp. 141–69.

Rovner, Sandy. "Affectionate Parents Foster Adult Happiness, Study Says." *The Washington Post,* May 28, 1991, p. WH5.

Rovner, Sandy. "Massive Study Finds Earlier Onset of Mental Illness." *The Washington Post,* October 9, 1990, p. WH5.

Rowe, Jonathan. "American Needs Perestroika for Ads." *The Christian Science Monitor,* April 25, 1990, p. 13.

Russell, James A., et al. "Affect Grid: A Single-Item Scale of Pleasure and Arousal." *Journal of Personality and Social Psychology,* vol. 57, 1989, pp. 493–502.

Ryff, Carol D. "Happiness Is Everything, or Is It? Explorations on the Meaning of Psychological Well-Being." *Journal of Personality and Social Psychology,* vol. 57, 1989, pp. 1069–81.

Saikowski, Charlotte. "Strengthening the Social Fabric." *The Christian Science Monitor,* November 15, 1988, p. 16.

Sanoff, Alvin P. "The Origins of Pleasure." *U.S. News & World Report,* February 3, 1992, p. 54.

Schor, Juliet B. "Americans Work Too Hard." *The New York Times,* July 25, 1991, p. A21.

———. "Work, Spend, Work, Spend: Is This Any Way to Live?" *The Washington Post,* January 19, 1992, p. C3.

Shields, Mark. "Mood Swings, '91." *The Washington Post,* January 31, 1991, p. A17.

Sirgy, M. Joseph. "Can Business and Government Help Enhance the Quality of Life of Workers and Consumers?" *Journal of Business Research,* vol. 23, 1991, pp. 1–7.

Skrzycki, Cindy. "Poll Finds Less Worker Emphasis on Materialism." *The Washington Post,* January 10, 1989, p. C1.

"Social Science and the Citizen." *Society,* March/April 1989, pp. 2–3.

Stassen, Marjorie A., and Sara R. Staats. "Hope and Happiness: A Comparison of Some Discrepancies." *Social Indicators Research,* vol. 20, 1988, pp. 45–58.

Swoboda, Frank. "Incomes of Workers Lose Ground in '80s." *The Oregonian,* September 8, 1992, p. A14.

Thomas, L. Eugene. "Correlates of Sexual Interest Among Elderly Men." *Psychological Reports,* vol. 68, 1991, pp. 620–22.

Thorne, Paul. "In Quest of Happiness." *International Management,* July 1990, p. 64.

Tolchin, Martin. "Suicide Rate Among Elderly Increases 25% from 1981 to '86." *The Sunday Oregonian,* July 23, 1989, p. A17.

"Traditional Values Play Well on Campaign." *USA Today,* January 16, 1992, p. 5A.

Treaster, Joseph B. "Infatuation with Mary Jane Is Fading." *The Sunday Oregonian,* November 3, 1991, p. A21.

"Unhappiness Might Be Inherited." *USA Today,* January 1990, p. 8.

Updegrave, Walter L. "How Are We Doing?" *Money Extra 1990,* Fall 1990, p. 18.

Usdansky, Margaret L. "As People Live Longer, Choices Get Tougher." *USA Today,* July 23, 1992, p. 7A.

Veysey, Laurence. "Ideological Sources of American Movements." *Society,* January/February 1988, p. 58.

SOURCES

Waldrop, Judith. "You'll Know It's the 21st Century When . . ." *The Saturday Evening Post,* April 1991, p. 68.

Warsh, David. "Adapting to Changing Times Is a Mark of Personal and Economic Maturity." *The Washington Post,* March 18, 1992, p. F3.

Wartik, Nancy. "Why Are Our Children Killing Themselves?" *American Health,* October 1991, p. 73.

Winefield, Anthony H., and Marika Tiggermann. "Employment Status and Psychological Well-Being: A Longitudinal Study." *Journal of Applied Psychology,* vol. 75, 1990, pp. 455–59.

Wood, David. "Wall of National Defense Crumbles as '92 Campaign Issue." *The Sunday Oregonian,* January 26, 1992, p. A13.

Woodward, Kenneth L., et al. "Young Beyond Their Years." *Newsweek* Special Edition: *The 21st-Century Family,* Winter/Spring 1990, p. 54.

Wynne, Edward A. "Preventing Youth Suicide Through Education." Alcohol, Drug Abuse and Mental Health Administration, *Report of the Secretary's Task Force on Youth Suicide,* vol. 4, DHHS Publication No. (ADM) 89-1624, Washington D.C., 1989, pp. 4-171–4-185.

Yenkin, Jonathan. "Study Finds 50% Rise in Hunger." *The Oregonian,* September 10, 1992, p. A13.

"Zestful Outlook Starts to Get on in Years." *The Wall Street Journal,* January 4, 1991, p. B1.

INDEX

INDEX

INDEX

INDEX

INDEX

INDEX

INDEX

INDEX

INDEX

INDEX

INDEX

(continued from page 4)

Age" by Daniel Goleman, February 6, 1990; and "Despite Worries, Future Looks Hopeful" by Leslie H. Gelb, January 4, 1992, copyright © 1990/92 by The New York Times Company. W. W. Norton & Company, Inc., for material from "Sex and Gender in the Aging Society," by Alice S. Rossi, from Our Aging Society: Paradox and Promise, *edited by Alan Pifer and Lydia Bronte, copyright © 1986 by Carnegie Corporation of New York.* People *for material from* People *magazine, September 10, 1990, © 1990, Time Inc. The Russell Sage Foundation for material reprinted from* The Quality of American Life: Perceptions, Evaluations, and Satisfactions *by Angus Campbell, Philip E. Converse, and Willard L. Rodgers, copyright © 1976 by Russell Sage Foundation, New York.* U.S. News & World Report *for material from "Idealism's Rebirth," Oct. 24, 1988, copyright, 1988, U.S. News & World Report.* The Wall Street Journal *for material from "The GOP and the Family Issue: a Swedish Lesson," by Allan Carlson, June 6, 1991; and "Pro-Family but Divorced from the Facts," by Stephanie Coontz,* The Wall Street Journal, *August 8, 1989; © 1991 and 1989 by Dow Jones & Company, Inc. Washington Post Writers Group for material from "National Youth Service the Ticket to Civic Health," by Neil R. Peirce,* The Oregonian, *June 15, 1992, p. B7, © 1993 Washington Post Writers Group.* Working Woman *for material from "Why Can't a Woman Be More Like a Man?" by Robert E. Gould, M.D., that first appeared in* Working Woman *in April 1985, copyright © 1985 by* Working Woman *magazine.*